D1160026

Men of Vision

Men of Vision

Anglo-Jewry's Aid to Victims of the Nazi regime
1933–1945

Amy Zahl Gottlieb

Weidenfeld & Nicolson
London

First published in Great Britain in 1998
by Weidenfeld & Nicolson

A CIP catalogue record for this book is available from the British Library.

ISBN 0 297 84230 7

Typeset by Selwood Systems, Midsomer Norton
Printed in Great Britain by Butler & Tanner Ltd
Frome and London

Weidenfeld & Nicolson
The Orion Publishing Group Ltd
Orion House
5 Upper Saint Martin's Lane
London, WC2H 9EA

Thou shalt leave all things that most tenderly
Are loved by thee; and this is from the bow
Of exile the first arrow that doth fly

How salt the bread doth taste thou then shalt know
That others give thee, and how hard the way
Or up or down another's stairs to go.

Dante, *Paradiso* (canto XV.58)

To the memory of David

Contents

Preface

The Central British Fund for German Jewry (CBF) – synonymously referred to by refugees as Woburn House – was almost unknown outside of the coterie of families and friends involved in its efforts to raise funds and aid refugees from persecution in Nazi Germany. From its inception in 1933, publicity outside of the Jewish parochial press was not sought.

Even after the war with Germany ended, the life-saving endeavours of the CBF and its auxiliary agencies were not broadcast. It is not surprising, therefore, that people often ask 'So what did they do?' An indisputable answer would have remained obscure, were it not for the fact that in the late 1980s a garage in the Heinrich Stahl Home for Aged Refugees, located in The Bishop's Avenue in London, was found to contain a number of cabinets filled with files which Eva Mitchell, then director of the CBF, herself a former refugee, identified as the records of the CBF and its auxiliary agencies dating from 1933 through the immediate post-war period. She was determined that they should be preserved.

I was invited to review the material, and then to compile an archive, a task in which I was ably assisted by Rachel Kalman and Heather Salmon. We were pleased to find that a large number of files relating to individual adults and unaccompanied children, and all the registration slips of the many thousands of refugees who had registered with the Jewish Refugees Committee, had survived intact. The latter have proved of tremendous help to former refugees, now scattered in countries around the world, who have sought to claim reparations and restitution as well as pensions from the German and Austrian governments. The registration slips have also served as aids in tracing and reuniting families.

On completion the archive was microfilmed and the administrative records were made available for distribution to university and national libraries. Individual case records are closed to the public. I was then asked to record the story of Anglo-Jewry's effort, through the CBF, to aid victims of Nazi oppression. The Elaine Blond Trust made a generous grant towards the research.

I decided that I would limit my research to documentary evidence, and refrain from using anecdotal sources, which experience has taught are all too selective. I knew that I had set myself a difficult task, in view of the fact that very little of the correspondence – the meat on the bone, so to speak – between the CBF and other voluntary organizations, as well as governmental agencies, was available in the CBF archive.

Bearing the foregoing in mind, compiling the narrative has not been an easy task. While minutes of meetings of the Executive and the Council of the CBF – sometimes cryptic and always very concise – have for the most part been preserved, those of the Allocations Committee and the Jewish Refugees Committee, the Refugee Children's Movement, regional committees and related correspondence have almost all been destroyed. In addition, the paucity of copies of correspondence made it difficult to trace reasoning behind decisions prior to committee actions. It has been altogether impossible to define precisely the organization's income and expenditures. Figures that I have cited are taken from minutes and annual reports. Decisions and policies were often confirmed through agencies with which the CBF co-operated, or archives of individuals who were involved in the CBF's activities.

Documents relevant to the activities of the CBF were located in the excellent archive of the American Jewish Joint Distribution Committee, New York; the Central Zionist Archives, Jerusalem; the papers of Felix Warburg at the American Jewish Archives, Hebrew Union College, Cincinnati; the Rothschild Archive, London; and the Louis L. Strauss Archive at the American Jewish Historical Society at Brandeis University, Boston. The Public Records Office at Kew houses a wealth of information, while the Wiener Library in London and the columns of the weekly *Jewish Chronicle* contributed grist to the CBF story. Their librarians and archivists were always helpful and I wish here to express my thanks for their courteous attention and assistance. I am also deeply indebted to Charles Tucker, director of the research unit and archivist to the London Beth Din, who found yet another cabinet filled with CBF archival material when emptying the basement strongroom at Woburn House. Although this discovery necessitated a lengthy revision of some of my earlier findings, it was most helpful in explaining some of the decisions taken by the Executive of the CBF.

I have deliberately omitted the names of the many individuals who gave untold hours over a period of years in a lay or professional capacity, in various areas of the British Isles, to assist in the work of the Jewish Refugees Committee, the Refugee Children's Movement and the numerous other committees that were created for the benefit of refugees, more especially since records of several committees are no longer extant. I trust, none the less, that those who served will recognize that their contribution to the work of the CBF and its auxiliary agencies has been acknowledged.

I wish here to thank Dame Simone Prendagast, who was chairman of the Jewish Refugees Committee, and David Cope-Thompson, chairman of the CBF, both of whom believed that the organization's story should be recorded, and encouraged me to undertake the assignment. Janet Cohen and members of the present-day Jewish Refugees Committee, which continues its concern for victims of persecution, have helped make this venture a compelling task.

I acknowledge with gratitude Jill Leuw's reading of the manuscript as it progressed and the late Mona Tait's support and encouragement. Joan Stiebel, who served the CBF from its inception, provided anecdotal accounts that helped to bring some of the players in the story to life.

I also record my appreciation to Dr Thomas Eckman, associate vice-president at the University of Illinois, and his staff for their never-failing courtesy and help; to Raymond Kalman for providing me with rare books from his library; and to Christopher Davis, who 'found' text inexplicably lost and who spent many an hour keeping my PC functioning.

The CBF was a unique agency, led by a group of remarkable men and women. I wonder whether we shall see their like again. I hope that I have been able to convey something of their courage and determination to succour refugees from Nazi Germany, in which task, in large measure, they succeeded.

Abbreviations

AAC	Academic Assistance Council
AJA	American Jewish Archives
AJHS	American Jewish Historical Society
BD	Board of Deputies of British Jews
CBF	Central British Fund for German Jewry. The CBF changed its name at different times during the years from 1936 to 1945. To avoid confusion to the reader it has been referred to as the CBF (1933–5) throughout the text, or as the Council (1936–45), after which it is known as the Central British Fund for Jewish Relief and Rehabilitation.
CCJR	Central Council for Jewish Refugees, September 1939–45
CGJ	Council for German Jewry, March 1936–September 1939
DORSA	Dominican Republic Settlement Association
FO	Foreign Office
HO	Home Office
ICA	Jewish Colonization Association
JC	*Jewish Chronicle*
JCRA	Jewish Committee for Relief Abroad
JDC	American Jewish Joint Distribution Committee
JRC	Jewish Refugees Committee
JRU	Jewish Relief Unit
Movement	Movement for the Care of Children from Germany. Renamed the Refugee Children's Movement in 1940.
ORT	Organization for Rehabilitation and Training
RAL	Rothschild Archive, London
RCM	Refugee Children's Movement
SCF	Save the Children Fund
SPSL	Society for the Protection of Science and Learning

1

Introduction

BRITAIN WAS IN sombre mood when news was broadcast of President Paul von Hindenburg's appointment of Adolf Hitler as Chancellor of Germany, on 30 January 1933. Less than fifteen years had passed since the carnage of the Great War of 1914–18, and Britain was still lauding its heroes and mourning its dead. A generation of its young men had been decimated on the battlefields of Europe, and maimed survivors were still much in evidence. Anti-German sentiment had not diminished. The country was in a deep economic depression, and the unemployed in the labour force had peaked at three million. Germany's internal affairs were of little concern to the man in the street.

Jews with relatives in Germany were aware of the escalation of antisemitic activity there, and they heard of Hitler's appointment with some misgivings. The news also caused a stir among leaders in the Anglo-Jewish community, estimated at some 300,000 persons. For many Jews in Britain, however, Germany was a far country. The largest number in Britain were of eastern European origin, with no familial ties to Germany. Many of them had been participants in the exodus of millions who left countries in Europe in the latter part of the nineteenth century, all of them bound for the United States.[1]

Most of the Jews among the immigrants who travelled via British ports paused there only briefly before continuing their outbound journey, but an estimated 120,000 of them remained in Britain and made that country their permanent home. Many of these Jews had planned to journey on to the United States, but were unable to do so because they lacked funds, or had been cheated by unscrupulous shipping touts. Others had lost contact with family members who had preceded them.[2]

A majority of the Jews who remained in Britain crowded into the existing Jewish quarter of Whitechapel, in the borough of Stepney, on the north bank of the River Thames. There, in London's East End, they were in close proximity to each other and near to relatives and friends from home towns and villages, some of whom had made the move earlier. They provided social contact and Yiddish cultural activity, and helped the new arrivals to adjust to life in a strange land. The East End of London was also identified with their primary occupations of tailoring, boot and shoe making, cigarette and cigar making, and the furniture industry. Small numbers of the newcomers migrated to the Leylands area of Leeds, or to the Redbank district of Manchester, or to other towns in the Midlands and the north of England. Still others settled in towns in Scotland and in Wales, many following pathways already cleared by relatives and friends. Within the immigrant Jewish community, friendly societies, synagogues and other self-help groups provided sustenance and clothing, medical care and access to employment.

The established Anglo-Jewish community that the immigrants joined was at the orthodox end of the liturgical spectrum, and of broad political mien. British Jews, some of whom could trace forebears in Britain to the seventeenth century, regarded themselves as culturally and socially emancipated in comparison with the more recent emigrant Jews from eastern Europe. They were without doubt economically more viable, but stronger and more enduring than this was their shared messianic religion, which bound them together across their national, social and economic differences. Although religious observance among them varied, they worshipped the same deity and followed similar rituals and teachings. In religious practice there was mutual respect and a universally accepted code for a way of life.

The leadership of the Anglo-Jewish community paralleled the wider British community in its discernible stratification. It was held within an extended cousinhood of the well-established and financially successful Beddington, Cohen, Franklin, Goldsmid, Lucas, Montagu, Montefiore, de Rothschild, Samuel and Sassoon families, whose progeny also married within this cousinhood, or with members of other Jewish families who had achieved status in the community and had accumulated wealth.[3] All of them had benefited from Britain's liberalism of the late nineteenth century, which had granted political emancipation to its Jews. Members of the cousinhood were soon elected to Parliament. Some were elevated to the peerage, a result of their service to the government of their day.

In Jewish religious doctrine and practice, charity holds a high place. Thus, in 1859 members of the cousinhood created the London Jewish Board of Guardians which, with attendant institutions, provided a measure of relief from destitution for the needy in their midst.[4] They also built Jewish day schools in London's East End and in other districts, and made formal religious and secular education available to large numbers of the immigrants' children, thus helping to speed their anglicization. In addition, they established orphanages and public housing in an effort to alleviate slum dwelling among the immigrant families. As the community grew, they organized the United Synagogue (1870), which was granted statutory authority to define the function and relationship of the principal London orthodox synagogues.[5]

As a consequence of the highly visible and large-scale settlement of Jews from eastern Europe in the East End of London, in Manchester and in Leeds, xenophobes and anti-semites successfully challenged Britain's long-held policy of asylum. Their demand for immigration restriction resulted in the Aliens Act of Parliament of 1905, which empowered immigration officers to refuse entry to undesirables and to restrict admission and length of stay to refugees and to immigrants. None the less, Jews continued to gain entry, albeit on a limited scale, until the advent of the First World War.

Intense anti-German feeling in Britain at that time resulted in the introduction, on 4 August 1914, of an Aliens Restriction Bill. It was enacted a day later.[6] The statute required that all aliens register with the police, and the Home Secretary was empowered to exclude or deport without appeal. Of an estimated 50,000 German nationals resident in England in 1914, some 40,000 of them were interned or deported at the outbreak of war.[7] A later generation of Jewish refugees from Germany included British-born individuals whose German parents had been deported under the provisions of the 1914 statute.[8] Although compulsory war-time military conscription in Britain came into force only in 1916, 10,000 Jews had already volunteered, and some 41,500 of them served in the armed forces before the war ended in 1918.[9]

Jewish emigration from Russia was again stimulated by the revolution there in October 1917. As in former years, Britain provided sanctuary for some of these refugees, who brought with them their own Jewish communal activities and philanthropies, the most important among the latter being the Organization for Rehabilitation and Training (ORT), which was to influence British educational policy when 'training' was an issue in the 1980s, and which today still serves communities around the world.[10]

A result of continued anti-German and anti-alien sentiment in Britain, and the government's cautious post-war immigration policy, was the Aliens Restriction Act of 1919 and the Aliens Order that followed in 1920. In addition to the restrictions imposed in 1914, these provided that aliens might enter the country only temporarily unless they had visible means of support, or Ministry of Labour permits to accept employment.[11] Such permits were issued sparingly, and only after the ministry was satisfied that no British labour was available to take up the positions sought by the aliens. Immigration officers were empowered to refuse entry and, as in earlier legislation affecting aliens, there was no right of appeal from the Home Secretary's decision. This legislation remained on the statute book until 1973 when, following Britain's entry into the European Economic Community (1972), it was superseded by the Treaty of Rome, which provided for the free movement of labour among member countries.[12]

Across the North Sea in Germany, a Jewish presence had been known for more than a thousand years. In 1933 Jews in the German population numbered some 500,000. A majority of them were native born, secularly educated and middle class. They were probably the most culturally assimilated among their co-religionists in all of Europe. German Jews were well established in business and in commerce, and were members of the professions, particularly medicine and law, out of all proportion to their number in the German population. They were also very well represented in the fields of music and the other arts. More than two-thirds of them were concentrated in cities; almost one-third of them lived in Berlin alone. A further 20 per cent lived in Breslau, Cologne, Dresden, Dortmund, Essen, Frankfurt, Hamburg, Leipzig and Munich, while almost 100,000 lived in rural communities whose populations were fewer than 20,000.[13]

Hitler's opponents and observers of the German scene optimistically perceived the Nazi phenomenon as a temporary political aberration.

Few German Jews thought of leaving the Fatherland. They viewed the anti-semitic focus of Hitler's book *Mein Kampf* as beyond credulity, his ideology outrageous and too preposterous to merit serious concern.

In March 1933 the German legislature vested the Chancellor with dictatorial authority. As a result, Hitler and the National Socialist Democratic Workers' (Nazi) party were able to assume full political reign. Although only a small number of German Jews felt compelled to leave Germany at this time, several thousand of eastern European origin now believed themselves to be in jeopardy, and they and their German-born children left the country. Many of them were turn-of-the-century Polish immigrants; others had fled to Germany from Poland before the Russian onslaught during the war of 1914–18.[14] Only a few thousand of them had become German citizens. In July 1933 a newly enacted German statute abrogated the citizenship of most of them, and they were rendered stateless.[15] Some Jews returned to Poland. Several thousand others sought refuge in France, whose liberal refugee policy enabled them to enter the country without restriction. The Netherlands and other countries on Germany's borders, which were similarly liberal, also provided Jewish refugees with sanctuary.[16] Britain did not accept eastern European passport holders as refugees, since they were not barred from their countries of origin. They were, however, permitted entry to Britain as visitors if they were able to produce evidence of financial means.

Early in April 1933, newly enacted German anti-Jewish legislation began to deprive Jews and non-Aryans (persons whose progenitors included a Jewish grandparent) of the right to participate in the economic, professional and civil life of Germany.[17] Persecution of Jews in Germany differed from the anti-semitism manifest in Poland and Romania. The Germans appeared intent on excluding Jews from the political, economic and social life of the country, and systematically undertook statutory measures to achieve their goal. Refugees arriving in London told of violent anti-semitic outrages perpetrated among Jews in rural communities. It was at this time that Jews, and Christians who were known political opponents of the Nazi regime, were being taken into 'protective custody' and interned in concentration camps, where torture, beating and killing took place. But none could have envisaged the extent of the tyranny that the Germans would perpetrate, or the degree to which fundamental moral principles would be corrupted. It is well for us to remember Professor William Rubenstein's admonition that 'hind-sight is not historical evidence'.[18]

Leaders in the Anglo-Jewish community viewed developments in Germany with foreboding, and as though with prescience, agreed that Jews there must be helped to leave the country. The British government would not welcome German Jews as immigrants, but would permit them transient stay while countries of permanent settlement were found. The effort to achieve these goals through the Central British Fund for German Jewry, which leaders in the Anglo-Jewish community created in 1933, is an epic tale of Jewish political alliances, of transatlantic co-operation and dissension between British and American Jewish leaders, and of noble actions. It produced the greatest communal endeavour in the history of Anglo-Jewry, and resulted in the saving of thousands of lives. The testimony that follows will enlighten the reader on an extraordinary period in British and Anglo-Jewish history, and the role in shaping it played by the Central British Fund for German Jewry.

2

Otto Schiff and the Jewish Refugees Committee

MONDAY, 30 JANUARY 1933, was a normal working day at the Jews' temporary shelter located in Mansell Street, a thoroughfare of commercial properties on the western edge of the borough of Stepney. Tenants in buildings along the street were accustomed to seeing individuals and groups of people come and go from number 63. Otto Moritz Schiff, the Shelter's long-time president, took a personal interest in those who sought its services, and after a day at his office in the City he would appear at the Shelter and interview those who were of special concern. It was his habit to visit the Home Office every Friday afternoon, to discuss the status of those whose stay in Britain required clarification. He was said to have been held in such high esteem by officials there that his word was accepted as the Jewish community's bond.[1]

Adolf Hitler's appointment as Chancellor of Germany was probably of little concern to those engrossed in ministering to the transients at the Jews' Temporary Shelter. Otto Schiff, in his City office, doubtless heard with dismay the news broadcast by the BBC, and then switched to a German radio station that was blasting out the ominous tidings. He was well informed on political developments in Germany, and was concerned for their portent for Jews living there.

Otto Schiff, a stockbroker, was a member of a well-known rabbinical, banking and philanthropic family with origins in Frankfurt am Main. He had immigrated to England in 1896, when he was 25. His brother Ernst, six years his senior, had joined him at the turn of the century.[2] Other family members – most notably their uncle, Jacob Schiff, America's pre-eminent Jewish philanthropist – had established themselves in New York.[3] During and following the First World War, Otto and Ernst had aided thousands of refugees who had fled from Belgium to Britain, and Otto had been awarded the Order of the British Empire (OBE) for his efforts on their behalf.[4] He had served with the British troops in France during the war and had been wounded. Even after years in England he had not lost his guttural German accent, and he knew from personal experience the British public's xenophobia and its hatred of Germans.[5] Schiff was aware that, if Jews decided to leave Germany for England, the British public would still regard them as Germans. Indeed, that was how they viewed themselves.

Otto Schiff contacted Rabbi Dr Leo Baeck, the internationally known and respected spiritual leader of the German Jewish community in Berlin, to tell him of his concern at the turn of events in Germany, and to assure him that he would do all he could to aid those who decided to emigrate. Rabbi Baeck, too, was apprehensive about developments on the political scene. He said, sadly, that the thousand-year history of Jews in Germany had ended ('das Ende des deutschen Judentums ist gekommen'), but the Jews in Germany failed to hear him.[6] Few, if any, gave thought to the possibility that the Nazis would survive a brief period of dominance in the legislature. Fewer still gave thought to leaving the Fatherland.

Jewish communal organizations, staffed by trained social workers and administrators, were well established in Germany. It was as an extension of this network that soon after Hitler's appointment Rabbi Baeck, Dr W. Alexander, Carl Melchior, a banker and lawyer, Dr Ludwig Tietz, a medical specialist and leader of the German Jewish Youth Movement, and Dr Werner Senator, an economist, set about organizing the Zentral Ausschuss der deutschen Juden für Hilfe und Aufbau (Central Committee for Relief and Rehabilitation of German Jews), to support the economic position of Jews in Germany and those intending to emigrate, and to assist non-German citizens to return to their countries of origin. The Zentral Ausschuss was superseded a few months later by the Reichsvertretung der deutschen Juden (National Board of German Jews), also headed by Rabbi Baeck, and it operated until the end of the 1930s.[7] Dr Otto Hirsch of Württemberg served as its chairman.

Throughout the pre-war years, Otto Schiff maintained close contact with Rabbi Baeck and members of the Reichsvertretung. Another frequent contact in Berlin was Wilfred Israel, a grandson of Hermann Adler,

Britain's first Chief Rabbi. So was Dr Bernhard Kahn, who began his career with the American Jewish Joint Distribution Committee (JDC) in 1921, and was the director of its European operations, with offices in Berlin. Dr Kahn was another important link with the Reichsvertretung.

Otto Schiff was keenly aware that, if German Jewish refugees were to arrive in London, no appropriate body existed to which they might be referred for counsel and possible financial assistance. Established Jewish philanthropic organizations, among which the Jewish Board of Guardians was the most prominent, had been created for the benefit of impoverished emigrant Jews from eastern Europe. Neither the Jewish Board of Guardians nor any of the other communal organizations was equipped to treat the Jews from Germany, who were generally acculturated, well educated and not in poverty. Otto Schiff concluded that a new and discrete organization, one that would cater to their specific concerns, was badly needed. This was, perhaps, also a political stratagem. Schiff was cognizant of the fact that most of the Jews in Britain were of eastern European origin, and that there was little rapport between them and German Jews, who were known to be condescending and seen as arrogant in their attitudes toward 'Ostjuden', whose Yiddish language and Yiddish culture they disdained. If Schiff organized a committee at the Jews' Temporary Shelter, and called on members of the established German-Jewish fraternity to join him in ministering to the newcomers' needs, potential friction in the community might be averted. Schiff discussed his proposal with the Board of Deputies of British Jews and with the trustees of the Nathan and Adolphe Haendler Charity, and both agreed to support his proposal to create a special committee for this purpose.[8]

It was without ceremony, therefore, that early in March 1933 Otto Schiff asked several friends 'representing the various sections of the community', including members of an independent Jewish fraternal order, the B'nai Brith (Sons of the Covenant), most of whom were of German origin, to join him at the Jews' Temporary Shelter to discuss how aid could be provided to German Jews who sought counsel, temporary housing or financial assistance.[9]

The response to Schiff's invitation was immediate and positive. Ernest Mainz and Eric Turk, who were both members of the Board of the Jews' Temporary Shelter, Bernard Davidson, Frank Lazarus, E. L. Rawson and 'three outstanding women workers' – Cissie Laski (wife of Neville Laski),

Alice Model, a pioneer in infant and mother welfare, and Anna Schwab, of the Ellern banking family of Frankfurt, and a founder of a B'nai Brith sponsored girls' club in Stepney, who was to become an indefatigable worker in the refugee cause – joined Schiff as the first members of the Jewish Refugees Committee (JRC), by which title that committee is still known.[10]

Like so many of their contemporaries, Otto Schiff and his colleagues doubtless speculated that Hitler's dominance of Germany would be of a temporary nature, and that he and the Nazi Party would be ousted at the next general election. While they were in power, however, Schiff postulated that, at most, three or four thousand Jews might travel to England, some to try to establish businesses there, others to seek visas to other countries, and in its early years, he tailored the policies and activities of the JRC accordingly.[11]

One of the first tasks assigned to members of the JRC, who were assisted by the staff at the Jews' Temporary Shelter, was to meet trains from the continent at London railway stations, or planes landing at the Croydon or Heston airports, which served London, and escort Jews from Germany, who were without friends or relatives, to the Shelter. Few German Jews had relatives in Britain, since almost all emigration from Germany in the nineteenth and early twentieth centuries had been focused on the United States. At the Shelter, refugees with limited funds were provided with short-term accommodation and help in planning their future. Schiff decided that the JRC would also assist non-Aryan Christian German refugees, since the only other major voluntary agency aiding refugees from the Nazis at this time was the German Emergency Committee of the Friends Service Committee (later known as the Friends Committee for Refugees and Aliens), founded by the Quakers, with which organization he had established a sound working relationship. The Christian Council for Refugees from Germany and Central Europe, sponsored by the Church of England, was not instituted until 1938.[12]

Despite Otto Schiff's initial assumptions, the JRC was soon obliged to broaden its activities to include housing those whose stay in Britain would be extended while they awaited Home Office consideration of their applications for permanent residence, or Ministry of Labour permission to accept employment, or consular decisions on the issuance of visas or shipping to overseas destinations. Anna Schwab, Olga Epstein,

Selma Heinemann, Sophie Taubkin and other members of the Women's Lodge of the B'nai Brith sought out families who would provide accommodation and friendship for these refugees. They also organized a Hospitality Committee, which arranged social contacts within the German Jewish community, and the B'nai Brith furnished a club room for their use.[13]

Early in April, trustees of the Nathan and Adolphe Haendler Charity donated £5,000 to the JRC.[14] The timing of this grant was propitious, for a few days later, on 7 April, the German government promulgated an Act for the Reconstruction of the Civil Service and a Law on Admission to the Bar.[15] These statutes aimed at ousting Jews and political opponents of the Nazi regime from employment by the state. Since most universities and research institutes in Germany were state bodies, their professors, lecturers, researchers, technicians and other workers were state employees, all of whom were subject to the terms of the Civil Service Code.

The effect of the revised legislation on Jews employed by the state was devastating. It resulted in the summary dismissal from their positions of more than 1,200 academicians, jurists, physicians and professionals, many of whom were of international renown. Jews had filled one-eighth of the professorial chairs in German universities and research institutes. They had been awarded six (25 per cent) of the Nobel prizes bestowed on German citizens.[16]

Additional anti-Jewish statutes, directed at municipal government employees, were enacted in the weeks that followed. Some exceptions were made in favour of those employed before August 1914; those who had fought for Germany in the First World War; and those who had lost fathers or sons in that war. These exceptions were revoked following enactment of the Nuremberg Laws in September 1935.[17]

Numbers of academicians affected by the revised Civil Service Code travelled to England in the hope of securing appointments to British institutions of higher learning, or approaching colleagues in the many universities and research facilities in the United States and other countries.[18] This upsurge in the number of Jews arriving in England did not go unnoticed by government officials at ports of entry, and it was not long before the Home Office alerted Otto Schiff to the fact that German-Jewish passport-holders were arriving in England in greater numbers than was customary.[19] Schiff was also told of the volume of applications being received from 'aliens of Jewish origin' who wished to extend their stay in Britain.[20]

German, as well as Austrian, Czechoslovak and other European citizens were permitted to enter Britain as visitors, businessmen or students without the need to secure British visas. This was the result of an international agreement that remained in effect until 1938. None was permitted to accept employment, however, or take up permanent residence unless their presence served the interest of British science or industry, or they possessed substantial financial resources. Those not meeting these criteria would be expected to depart for third country destinations within a reasonable period.[21] In addition to the Home Office concern, the British Passport Control Office in Berlin reported to London that it was overwhelmed by the number of applications being received from 'Jews... desirous of proceeding to Palestine, to England, to anywhere in the British Empire'.[22]

Otto Schiff immediately discussed with Neville Laski, president of the Board of Deputies of British Jews, and with others, the interest expressed by Home Office officials in the arrival of Jews from Germany, and they agreed that a delegation representing the Anglo-Jewish community should ask to meet Sir Ernest Holderness, head of the Aliens Department, to review Home Office concerns.[23] Even at this early date anti-refugee and anti-semitic statements were being published in the national press, while similar sentiments were expressed in the House of Commons in the guise of seeking protection for the multitude of unemployed in Britain.[24] The Home Office had constantly to respond to those who questioned the ease of entry of refugees, informing them that their stay was limited by a time condition affixed to their passports.[25] Disquiet voiced within the government regarding the number of German Jews entering the country would have to be assuaged without delay.

Anglo-Jewry's delegation to the Home Office

Neville Laski and Leonard Montefiore were co-chairmen of the Joint Foreign Committee which linked the Board of Deputies and the Anglo-Jewish Association. Leonard Montefiore was the Anglo-Jewish

Association's president. Together with Lionel Cohen, King's Counsel (KC), who was chairman of the Law and Parliamentary Committee of the Board of Deputies, and Otto Schiff, they were designated to represent the Anglo-Jewish community at the meeting at the Home Office.

The date on which the four men met Sir Ernest Holderness is not recorded, but it may be assumed that it took place after 1 April, when the German government officially launched its national boycott of Jewish shops and other Jewish enterprises. The stated intent of the boycott was to destroy the economic influence of Jews in Germany, even though Jews represented less than 1 per cent of the German population. In reality it gave official rein to an orgy of vicious assaults by mobs on Jews in public life, and on Jewish stores and businesses, particularly those in small towns and villages. As a result, hundreds of Jewish lawyers, judges, professors, musicians and journalists were forced from their positions, both by the violence and by administrative action. Lord Reading, president of the Anglo-German Association since its inception in 1929, resigned from the organization in protest. Even Field Marshal von Hindenburg voiced dismay at these events.[26] Another consequence of the boycott was the arrival in Britain of an increased number of German passport-holders: 150 of them landed within three days.[27]

The pledge to support refugees

When Neville Laski and his colleagues met Sir Ernest Holderness, they proposed that the government permit all Jewish refugees from Germany to enter Britain without discrimination, and that those already admitted as visitors, or others who might be granted permission to land in future, be authorized, while the emergency situation in Germany lasted, to prolong their stay indefinitely. In support of their proposal they pledged that 'all expense, whether in respect of temporary or permanent accommodation or maintenance, will be borne by the Jewish community without ultimate charge to the state'.[28] This undertaking, which had not been demanded, but which the government accepted, was without precedent. Never before had representatives of the Anglo-Jewish community felt obliged to undertake a blanket financial commitment to support Jews whose numbers, financial means or length of stay could not be predicted with any degree of accuracy. While this pledge was in the Jewish tradition of maintaining the needy in the community's midst, the gesture was in great contrast to the posture adopted by Anglo-Jewish organizations at the turn of the century, when they returned thousands of impoverished eastern European Jews to Europe.[29] The pledge was all the more surprising since there is no evidence to suggest that prior sanction had been sought from the Board of Deputies to make the commitment. The community was apprized of it in a report in the *Jewish Chronicle* on the recently formed Jewish Refugees Committee, which, it was noted, had advised the government that the Jewish community would be responsible for refugees regardless of their financial situation.[30]

The reason for the pledge in the name of the Anglo-Jewish community is open to speculation. Believing the Nazi regime to be of a temporary nature, Laski and his colleagues were probably of the opinion that the total number of refugees who would seek entry to Britain would not exceed Otto Schiff's estimate of 3,000–4,000, while contacts in Germany had presumably assured them that most would be able to finance their own stay, and that others would be maintained by relatives or friends, thus limiting any obligation on the part of the Anglo-Jewish community to sustain them. At this early date it was still possible for Germans of independent means to transfer their capital abroad after payment of the obligatory Flight Tax, first imposed by the German government in December 1931 in an effort to halt the export of foreign currency.[31] The pledge would cover the requirement in the British Aliens Order (1920) that immigrants demonstrate their ability to support themselves and their dependants. The path of German Jews would be smoothed at ports of entry, since immigration officers would be advised of the Anglo-Jewish community's undertaking in support of German-Jewish passport-holders.

The pledge may also have been given in response to the overt anti-refugee pronouncements being broadcast nationwide by several high-profile fascist organizations. Anti-semitism was an active component of these sentiments.[32] The pledge also suggests, perhaps, that despite the fact that they had achieved status and wealth, and a seemingly sound foothold in Britain, leaders of the Anglo-Jewish community had a tenuous sense of security and were afraid, in an atmosphere of rising political tension, of provoking generalized outbursts of anti-semitism that would affect the entire community.

Evidence has not been found to suggest that the possible long-term implications of the pledge had been discussed by the Jewish delegates, although Professor Geoffrey Alderman claims that it 'really meant that the community prevented itself from being able to call upon the government to admit more Jewish refugees than Anglo-Jewry itself could support', an approach that he found both cowardly and unimaginative, and one which 'played into the hands of anti-Jewish elements' in Britain.[33] In 1933 no one could imagine developments in Germany. The long-term implications of the pledge had surely been given little or no thought.

Throughout the years leading to the Second World War, the fear of inciting anti-semitism was a repeated theme at meetings with British government officials and at Jewish community gatherings. In accepting the delegation's bond, the government could assure friend and foe alike that the refugees were admitted at no cost to the British taxpayer.

Mindful of the possibility, however unthinkable, of further outbreaks of violence against Jews in Germany and the need to provide sanctuary for those who might travel to London, Otto Schiff assured Sir Ernest Holderness that if it were necessary, at short notice, to provide temporary accommodation for a larger number of visitors than usual, 500 individuals could be housed at the Jews' Temporary Shelter and at lodging houses of the London County Council, Salvation Army and other charitable institutions in London's East End.[34] Hopefully, such a commitment to contain the refugees in a limited geographical area would forestall restrictive action by the Home Office if in the future larger numbers of refugees were to arrive. Otto Schiff also advised Holderness that a Hospitality Committee, mainly for the benefit of members of the professions and students, was already in place. This, and a request by Schiff that the police be asked to telephone the Jews' Temporary Shelter to announce the arrival of refugees, and that refugees be asked by them to register with the JRC at the Shelter, was further assurance to the Home Office that the Anglo-Jewish community would care for those in need.[35] A large-scale exodus of Jews from Germany, or the enduring persecution of Jews there, was not envisaged by even the most astute observers of the political scene.

A few days after the meeting with Sir Ernest Holderness, the Home

Secretary, Sir John Gilmour, reported to his Cabinet colleagues that an abnormally high number of visitors had arrived and that most of them were found to be German passport-holders, 'mainly of the professional classes and probably Jews'. Gilmour noted that, while these visitors had satisfied immigration officers of their ability to maintain themselves during their stay in Britain, on investigation many had admitted that they were, in fact, refugees.[36] The Home Secretary further reported that, as a result of this influx, all German passport-holders allowed to land as visitors now had 'time conditions' attached to their stay. He added that this practice would be continued, even though generally speaking 'persons coming to this country on business, for visits to friends, for purposes of study, etc. ... are given leave to land freely, and no condition is attached to their stay'. He acknowledged that the Home Office would have power to regulate the length of stay of Jews coming from Germany by refusing to grant them further extensions, 'but that in practice it might prove difficult to insist on their return to Germany ... while present conditions there prevailed.' The Home Secretary also noted that 'Mr Schiff, of the Jews' Temporary Shelter, considers that the bulk of the refugees from Germany will be of the professional class and estimates that the total number should not exceed some three to four thousand', thus allaying fear of a mass movement of Jews into Britain.[37]

Otto Schiff's evaluation of the occupations of German Jews was reasonable, for he had already met with a number of them and had learned of the nature of their past employment. Schiff's assessment of the numbers who might seek refuge in Britain, however, was pure conjecture, and he might have believed that he was being unduly pessimistic. However, there were concerns regarding possible future action by the Nazi regime. At a meeting of the Joint Foreign Committee, held in February, Leonard Montefiore had expressed misgivings about the future of Jews in Germany. There was little doubt, he said prophetically, that 'every effort would be made to make the position of Jews untenable and the process which had begun before the accession of Herr Hitler to power, to exclude Jews from the Civil Service, the schools and universities, the theatre, the press and so on would be continued and intensified'.[38] The Home Secretary, however, accepted Otto Schiff's analysis of their position, and no further restrictions regarding the entry of refugees were added.

The London Jewish Board of Guardians agreed to assist British nationals, some of whom spoke little or no English, who returned following years of residence in Germany. Their number included the progeny of German Jews deported by Britain at the start of the First World War. The Board noted that a 'large proportion of them are highly intelligent and experienced people of a superior grade ... but they are penniless'.[39] The Board was not prepared to extend any of its services to Jews of German birth, even to those who might need only advisory aid.

The Cabinet Committee on Aliens' Restrictions agreed to appoint a sub-committee to examine the proposals advanced by the Anglo-Jewish delegation and report back to the full Cabinet. When the sub-committee responded, it suggested that, while it was not possible to estimate how many of the 500,000 Jews in Germany might attempt to leave, the number might be 'substantial', implying that a large number of Jews might be expected to seek sanctuary in Britain. The Cabinet Committee considered and then rejected two possible solutions: making restrictions on entry more severe, or relaxing those presently in force. The latter, it was noted, would extend to German Jews without means, or to those seeking employment, the same privileges of entry enjoyed by those with financial resources.[40] It was obvious that refugees with capital would be favoured. At a time of high unemployment, refugees who could not maintain themselves or contribute to the economy would not find sanctuary in Britain, despite the assurance that the Anglo-Jewish community would support those in need.

The Cabinet Committee concluded that it would be best to maintain, for the time being, the existing provisions for admission of German-Jewish refugees. However, it recommended adding the condition that they register with the police immediately upon reaching their destinations in Britain, instead of doing so following the customary three months' wait. This would, of course, enable government authorities to locate them in case of need, a reminder of the ease with which German citizens were rounded up and interned or deported at the time of the First World War. The Anglo-Jewish community was to be apprized of this decision, and advised that, in cases where refugees desired to obtain permission to extend their temporary stay, 'the government would be prepared to consider a further extension provided that the Jewish community were prepared to guarantee, so far as it might be necessary, adequate means of maintenance for the refugees concerned'.[41]

In these few words the government relegated the entire German-Jewish refugee problem to the Anglo-Jewish community, and it was to be held to its pledge and made to bear the financial cost. In an obviously political move, the government had decided to absolve itself of any moral or financial responsibility for the refugees. The government could honestly advise both its supporters and opponents that the Anglo-Jewish community was caring for the refugees; that they were not being encouraged to seek sanctuary in Britain; and that those allowed to enter the country did so at no cost to the state. Since the government was concerned to appease the Germans, it could not be seen to be conceding that there was indeed a refugee problem.

The Cabinet Committee met again on 12 April, when discussion hinged on whether the government should 'try and secure for this country prominent Jews who were being expelled from Germany and who had achieved distinction whether in pure science, applied science, such as medicine or technical industry, or in music or in art'. Not only would the country benefit from their knowledge and experience, it was noted, but a favourable impression of Britain would be created around the world, 'particularly if our hospitality were offered with some warmth'.[42]

Government officials had undoubtedly been made aware that the United States was luring numbers of world-renowned refugee scholars and artists to its shores, and that Britain's arts and sciences would benefit from an infusion of intellectual stimulus. But the government equivocated. Perhaps the Foreign Office was afraid of evoking censure by the Germans if the government acted to attract these refugees, particularly since an international disarmament conference involving the Germans was in session in Geneva. The Cabinet finally agreed to approve the proposals of its Committee on Aliens' Restrictions, and asked that offers of hospitality to refugees from Germany who were 'eminent in science, technology, art, music, etc.' be considered.[43] Notwithstanding, there is no evidence to suggest that the Cabinet Committee on Aliens' Restrictions furthered the idea, or that subsequent meetings were held to discuss this or any other aspect of the refugee question. It would appear that the government preferred to maintain the status quo rather than attempt to attract refugees of distinction. Britain's lack of initiative was to redound to the benefit of the United States, which welcomed them.

The delegation to the Home Office could not possibly have envisaged the extent of the financial burden it had undertaken in the name of the Anglo-Jewish community. The irony was that until the end of 1939 more than 40 per cent of the refugees permitted to enter Britain, many of whom were sponsored by government departments, were admitted without consultation with the JRC or any other organization concerned for the welfare of refugees. None the less, those so admitted were advised to register with the JRC in the knowledge that the Jewish community would carry the onus of their maintenance when this was sought.[44]

3

The Central British Fund for German Jewry is organized

NO ACCOUNT HAS BEEN found of consultations that Neville Laski, Leonard Montefiore, Lionel Cohen or Otto Schiff may have held with community leaders in London or in other cities following their visit to the Home Office in April 1933. Nor is there a record of discussions regarding the financial commitment made to the government on behalf of the Anglo-Jewish community. Neville Laski and Leonard Montefiore did arrange a meeting with Anthony Eden, secretary to the British Foreign Office, which Major Harry Nathan, MP, Lord Reading and Sir Herbert Samuel also attended, in the hope that a diplomatic protest by the government might have a positive effect on the treatment of Jews in Germany.[1] Harry Nathan had a further meeting with Anthony Eden to ask his opinion on the advisability of a delegation, composed of two members of the House of Commons (himself and Lionel de Rothschild) and two of the Upper Chamber (Lord Melchett and one other to be named), travelling to Berlin to meet with Adolf Hitler to discuss the status of the Jews in Germany. Anthony Eden made the British government's position quite clear. While declining to advise on the proposed deputation to visit Hitler, he said that the government would make no representation to a foreign power on behalf of that country's citizens.[2]

Jews in a number of cities in Britain attempted to show their solidarity with Jews in Germany and held meetings protesting their abuse by the Nazis. Jews in the East End of London and in communities throughout the country raised a boycott of German goods, but these efforts were not supported by the Board of Deputies, which preferred to maintain a low profile lest an anti-semitic response be evoked from the general public.[3]

Lacking political influence in the wider community, established Jews saw a practical need as the most pressing: the raising of funds to aid those who sought refuge. The JRC was providing assistance on an ad hoc basis to a small but steady number of refugees. Its budget, however, was limited and Otto Schiff was in no position to undertake a fund-raising campaign on their behalf. It was obvious that a nationwide effort was needed, one in which all sections of the Jewish community could be asked to participate. In a disparate community, this would not be easy.

The men who had met with Sir Ernest Holderness were also aware of the need to establish a nationwide fund-raising organization, and they held discussions with individuals of wealth and position whose co-operation was essential if a national body for the benefit of German Jews was to be created. Dr Chaim Weizmann, the Zionist leader, who had made his home in Manchester after leaving Russia in 1904, was also consulted. Competing fund raising by Zionists for projects in Palestine had to be avoided if the various segments of the community were to be drawn together in a united effort to aid German Jews.

The Keren Hayesod (Foundation Fund) of Palestine was a major Zionist fund-raising organization in Britain. While political Zionism had not taken a broad hold on Anglo-Jewry, the Keren Hayesod was well known, especially among Jews of eastern European origin. It had been established on a worldwide basis in 1920 to provide the funds for projects benefiting the infrastructure of Palestine.[4] Dr Weizmann's co-operation and that of the leadership of the Keren Hayesod would have to be secured if Anglo-Jewry was to be united in a campaign unrelated to the building of a Jewish homeland in Palestine. Sponsors of the Keren Hayesod in Britain would have to agree to set aside their own fund raising and join Anglo-Jewry's efforts to aid German Jews. Since Jews in Germany were not in the vanguard of membership of Zionist organizations in Europe, the promotion of efforts to ensure their welfare would not be an easy task.

Simon Marks, chairman and managing director of Marks and Spencer, a highly successful nationwide chain of retail clothing stores, was the chairman of the Keren Hayesod and vice-president of the British Zionist Federation. His extended family included Norman Laski, Harry Sacher and Israel Sieff (Simon was married to Israel Sieff's sister), each of whom was married to one of Simon's sisters: Elaine, Miriam and Rebecca respectively. The men were not only scions of the Manchester Jewish community, Britain's second largest, but also leading Zionists who provided substantial financial aid for projects in Palestine. Simon Marks, a persuasive man who had made known his concern for the refugees and Jews in Germany, was the obvious person to lead the Anglo-Jewish community's negotiations with Chaim Weizmann and other Keren Hayesod supporters.[5]

Norman Bentwich noted that it would be difficult and no mean achievement to obtain a unified approach and avoid duplication of effort, but Simon Marks was a skilled negotiator and he was able to secure an agreement with which Zionists and non-Zionists in the Anglo-Jewish community were able to live.[6] The agreement provided that the Keren Hayesod would receive a mutually agreed annual allocation of funds, equal to its average income in each of the preceding three years (£23,000), on condition that it did not exceed 25 per cent of the money raised for German Jews in any one year.[7] The Keren Hayesod would also be kept in the eye of its supporters because its fund-raising staff would organize the new campaign.

Non-Zionists, among whom Sir Robert Waley Cohen was perhaps the most vociferous, were vehement in their opposition to the agreement. Waley Cohen had known of the Keren Hayesod since its formation. He had, in fact, been invited to serve as one of its sponsors, but he had differed with Chaim Weizmann on its financial accountability and that conflict had never been resolved to Waley Cohen's satisfaction.[8] He now objected to joining with the Keren Hayesod in raising funds for German Jews. He believed that this would be of ultimate benefit to the Zionists, and aid them in achieving their goal: a national homeland in Palestine. It was difficult to placate Waley Cohen and numerous others who opposed the agreement with the Keren Hayesod, particularly since no mention of it was to be broadcast.[9] They showed their disapproval by withholding or limiting their contributions to the new organization, a price that was paid in order that a united front might be presented to the community. Anthony de Rothschild was later to tell Simon Marks that he had 'constantly encountered the view that our combining of these two appeals has been one of the causes which has led to large numbers of Jews in this country to refrain from responding' to the appeal.[10] Notwithstanding, in 1933 expediency had won the day, and the marriage of convenience with the Keren Hayesod was honoured until the agreement was revised in 1940.

Perhaps it was because negotiations between various factions in the community were protracted that more than three weeks were to pass, subsequent to the meeting at the Home Office, before Neville Laski and Leonard Montefiore agreed to contact Lionel de Rothschild at New Court in the City of London, the banking headquarters of N.M. Rothschild and Sons, concerning the role that Anglo-Jewry would be urged to play in relation to refugees and the Jews in Germany.

Lionel de Rothschild and his younger brother Anthony, both pillars of the community, were unreservedly the best qualified of their peers to call Anglo-Jewry to action. Their family name commanded respect; its munificence was legendary. An appeal to the community inaugurated by the Rothschilds would be heeded by all sectors. Laski and Montefiore jointly addressed Lionel de Rothschild: 'We feel that the time has come when a Special Committee should be established to deal with the problems which have arisen, and will arise, in relation to the economic and social welfare of our German co-religionists' their letter began. 'Having regard to the exceptional nature of the problems involved ... the personnel of this committee should not ... be limited to members of the Board of Deputies or the Anglo-Jewish Association.' Instead, they recommended that they be drawn from a broad spectrum of the Jewish community. Thus it was that a benign oligarchy of ten men (by coincidence the minimum required for a 'minyan', a quorum according to Jewish law) banded together to contribute time and effort and substantial financial support for the creation of the Central British Fund for German Jewry, an ad hoc organization that they would dismantle as soon as the expectedly short-lived German-Jewish crisis came to an end.

Montefiore and Laski recommended that Lionel Cohen, Neville Laski, Otto Schiff, Sir Robert Waley Cohen, Sir Osmond Elim d'Avigdor Goldsmid, Simon Marks and Major Harry Nathan be invited to participate, as well as the Chief Rabbi the Very Rev. Dr Joseph Herman Herz, and Chaim Weizmann. Furthermore, Montefiore and Laski added, 'We hope that you and your brother [Anthony] will consent to act as joint chairmen.' Although Laski and Montefiore indicated that they could not exactly define the scope and functions of the committee, they foresaw that it would 'deal with questions of constructive work for the assistance of our German co-religionists and the raising of any necessary funds'.[11]

Anthony and Lionel de Rothschild were aware of the negotiations concluded with the Zionists and, despite their known antipathy towards political Zionism, they were ready to co-operate for the benefit of the task before them. Lionel de Rothschild's response to the letter was immediate and positive. He and his brother agreed that a meeting of the gentlemen named should be called at New Court at an early date, when they would discuss means by which the suggestions embodied in the letter might be executed. In conclusion Lionel de Rothschild declared, 'All efforts to ameliorate the condition of our co-religionists in Germany must have the sympathy of the community.'[12] An organization to raise funds and distribute them, which would be led by the Rothschilds and supported by other members of the cousinhood and Simon Marks' extended family, was thus assured of success.

The *dramatis personae*

With the exception of the Hungarian-born, American-educated Chief Rabbi Dr Herz, a Zionist, leader of the established Orthodox Ashkenazi community and spiritual head of the United Synagogue, and the Swiss-educated Dr Chaim Weizmann, a brilliant chemist who was a lecturer in organic chemistry at the University of Manchester, all the men named in the Laski–Montefiore letter were sons of wealthy patrician families. With the exception also of Neville Laski and Simon Marks, they were members of the cousinhood by which all their families were embraced.[13] Most of them, including Laski, had attended the same Jewish private boarding school – Clifton – or had been students together at the same university. All of them were Victorians, born in the years during which Disraeli bestowed the title 'Empress of India' upon the Queen. They had been inculcated with a sense of responsibility towards less fortunate Jews, whom they aided financially through support of the philanthropic institutions created by their forebears, and on whose Boards of Governors they served. They represented the lay and religious leadership of the assimilated Anglo-Jewish 'Establishment' and were the embodiment of prestige, wealth and philanthropy.[14] Within the wider Anglo-Jewish community their family names were mentioned with deference.

Almost all of the men named had served as officers in the British Expeditionary Forces in the First World War and undoubtedly retained military ties through their regimental associations. Lionel Nathan and Anthony Gustav de Rothschild had both seen active service. Lionel had served in the Royal Artillery with the rank of major and had been awarded the OBE. He was a bon vivant and devoted much of his energy to motoring and botanical and horticultural interests at his Exbury estate in Hampshire. He was said to be 'a gardener by profession, a banker by hobby'.[15] Anthony, five years Lionel's junior, had held the rank of major in the army and was injured in the Gallipoli campaign. Anthony was both a scholar (he took a double first at Trinity College, Cambridge) and a practical man. He was also of diplomatic mien, and helped smooth relations between Sir Robert Waley Cohen and other members of the community.[16]

Lionel Leonard Cohen, KC, injured during service in the London Regiment during the war, was a member of a family long distinguished in service to the Jewish community. It had established the Jewish Board of Guardians, in which he too was deeply involved. Lionel Cohen was regarded as having a brilliant intellect by his peers in the judiciary and was a respected jurist. As noted earlier, he was chairman of the Law and Parliamentary Committee of the Board of Deputies of British Jews.[17]

Sir Robert Waley Cohen, a huge man, well over six feet in height, was an eminently successful industrialist and a managing director of the Shell Oil Company. During the First World War he held a commission in the Royal Navy.[18] Waley Cohen was a communal leader of long standing and vice-president of the United Synagogue, with whose spiritual leader, Chief Rabbi Herz, friction was legendary. Waley Cohen did not agree on the extent of the Chief Rabbi's authority, and he disapproved the Chief Rabbi's denunciation of the Reform and Liberal Jewish congregations, more especially since his mother had been a life-long member of the former. Those who knew Waley Cohen said that he could be gentle and helpful, but that he had a choleric temper which he frequently vented; that 'even a blessing in his mouth often sounded like a threat'.[19]

Sir Osmond Elim d'Avigdor Goldsmid, who had inherited the Somerhill estate and a considerable fortune while still a student, was of pleasant disposition, a merchant banker and a vice-president of the Council of the Jewish Colonization Association. He and Sir Robert Waley

Cohen met while students at Cambridge University, and together they embarked on a grand world tour.[20] Neville Jonas Laski, the president of the Board of Deputies, was a man of dynamic energy. He had served as an officer in the Lancashire Fusiliers in the First World War. He was also a jurist who had built a distinguished reputation at the Bar. His father, an emigrant from eastern Europe, was a successful textile merchant, a prominent member of the Jewish community in Manchester and the recognized leader of Jewry in the provinces. Neville, a son-in-law of Dr Moses Gaster, rabbinical leader of the Sephardi community, was an active member of that congregation.[21]

Simon Marks, a brusque man of great nervous energy, was regarded as a workaholic with a dynamic and direct approach to problems. As noted earlier, he was chairman and managing director of Marks and Spencer, the firm founded by his immigrant father, which he had built into a highly successful nationwide chain of retail stores. During the First World War, Simon had been released from army service to work on a number of government projects. He and Chaim Weizmann had met in Manchester in 1913 and they had become life-long friends. Under Weizmann's influence, Simon Marks had also become an ardent Zionist. In 1919 he served as secretary of the Zionist delegation to the Versailles Peace Conference. Simon Marks was munificent and ever ready to contribute handsomely to institutions and causes he favoured.[22]

Leonard Nathaniel Goldsmid Montefiore, known for his gentle puckish humour and kindness, was a generous man of independent means. He was the only son of Claude Joseph Goldsmid Montefiore, scholar, theologian and founder of the Liberal Jewish synagogal movement in Britain. Leonard Montefiore, also a scholar, wrote on German Jewish history, theology and literature. He was awarded the OBE for his service in the armed forces during the war of 1914–18. Leonard did not seek a leadership position in the CBF, but devoted his energies to aiding refugees.[23]

Harry L. Nathan, who had served in the army with the rank of major, was a senior partner in the law firm of Oppenheimer, Nathan and van Dyke. He was a Liberal Member of Parliament for Bethnal Green in the East End of London in 1929–34 and a Labour member for Central Wandsworth in 1937–40. He was also a member of the Law and Parliamentary Committee of the Board of Deputies. His daughter Joyce was married to Bernard, son of Sir Robert Waley Cohen.[24]

As might have been expected of a member of an old-established and well-known German rabbinical family, Otto Schiff, in addition to serving as chairman of the Jewish Refugees Committee, was treasurer of Jews College which trained men for the rabbinate. He was also an Overseer of the Poor of the United Synagogue and chairman of the Jewish Ecclesiastical Advisory Committee on the Admission of Rabbis and Ministers from Abroad. At 58, he was the oldest member of the group.[25]

The men nominated by Laski and Montefiore were widely travelled and closely connected through their family, community, banking and business interests. These ties help explain how established channels of communication within community organizations and between families were activated during times of political tension, and decisions made in response to crises affecting refugees and the Anglo-Jewish community.

Only Simon Marks among those named was an affirmed Zionist. Such a stance might appear incongruous in view of the substantial financial investments in the economic and industrial development of Palestine made by several of them.[26] None the less, while they viewed that country as an area of settlement for Jews, they did not envisage it as a Jewish political entity, and they were outspoken in their opposition to such a concept. They regarded themselves as emancipated British subjects professing the Jewish religion, and their political allegiance was to Britain alone. Nowhere was this more clearly stated than in the manifesto circulated in 1917 by the League of British Jews, which Lionel de Rothschild had founded following Britain's Balfour Declaration, or in the statement to the Secretary of State for the Colonies in 1923.[27] These men were not swayed by the fact that Anglo-Jewry, more than any other diaspora community, was involved in the development of Palestine as a Jewish national homeland, or by the British government's acceptance from the League of Nations, in 1922, of the Mandate for Palestine.

None the less, these men agreed to regard Palestine as the principal country of immigration and therefore the recipient of major funding by the CBF. The decision was a pragmatic one. Most importantly, immigration certificates were readily available, since Zionists in eastern European countries were not clambering to enter Palestine. Although it was not spelt out by the CBF, refugees who left for Palestine would infuse the sparse Jewish population there with a new element of young, educated, middle-class men and women, many of whom would be trained or retrained as agricultural or industrial workers. They would enhance the country's economic growth potential through their utilization of opportunities provided by Jewish investors. In addition, German Jews with substantial funds, and business and industrial experience, would provide employment to both indigenous and immigrant Jews. As far as the Zionists were concerned, the immigrants from Germany would add human grist to their quest for a national home for the Jewish people, promised them by the British government in the Balfour Declaration of 1917.

Rabbi Leo Baeck, Dr Ludwig Tietz and other German-Jewish community leaders were early advocates of sponsored immigration to Palestine and they made their views known in London when they attended meetings of the CBF Allocations Committee.[28] While there can be little doubt that German Jews might have preferred to join relatives in the United States, American Consuls were often deliberately slow in issuing visas, and the full quota available to German-born citizens was not reached before Britain declared war on Germany in 1939.[29] The British Dominions of Australia, Canada, New Zealand and South Africa admitted only limited numbers of Jewish immigrants, who were required to provide evidence of financial independence.[30] Only Palestine welcomed Jewish immigrants from across the economic spectrum.

Anthony and Lionel de Rothschild followed their response to the Laski–Montefiore letter by inviting those named to a meeting at New Court.[31] While Chief Rabbi Herz was to have no decision-making authority, his ecclesiastical weight might be wielded to advantage. The Reform and Liberal Jewish congregations, both of which were attracting constituents among more affluent members of the Anglo-Jewish community, were not recognized by the Chief Rabbi; and they did not acknowledge him as their spokesman.

A brief had already been prepared by Lionel Cohen, Neville Laski and Leonard Stein, the latter also a jurist, a keen Zionist and a friend of Leonard Montefiore since their university days.[32] Their submission, which was approved, set out the principles that would guide the solicitation of funds and subsequent allocation of moneys raised. It stated, 'it is believed that the best field for reconstruction and development will be in Palestine, and the Committee intend to allocate substantial sums for this purpose'.[33] There can be little doubt that this was the assurance that Simon Marks, Chaim Weizmann and other Zionists had demanded in return for their co-operation. A final version of a fund-raising appeal to the 'British Empire' and to the Anglo-Jewish community, also prepared in advance, was similarly accepted.[34] It was agreed that minutes of deliberations would be taken, although on that occasion the names of those present were not recorded. However, a note was made that Simon Marks, Edward S. Baron, chairman of the Carreras Tobacco Company, founded by his great-uncle Bernhard Baron, and Philip S. Waley would serve as directors of the appeal. Anthony de Rothschild would officiate as its chairman.[35] The long list of members of the Appeals Council reads like a Who's Who in Anglo-Jewry.[36]

The Central British Fund for German Jewry

At Marks and Spencer headquarters in Baker Street, Simon Marks accepted the invitation to serve as chairman of the committee that would establish the Central British Fund for German Jewry.[37] Meyer Stephany and Lavi Bakstansky, who were present at that meeting, were appointed its joint secretaries. Meyer Stephany, an accountant, had spent his professional life with organizations within the Anglo-Jewish community. For the remainder of his career he served the CBF in the manner of a high-ranking civil servant: overseeing income and expenditures, visiting countries of German-Jewish refuge in Europe and Palestine, co-ordinating activities and providing competent guidance to the CBF's honorary officers. Lavy Bakstansky, whose service as secretary of the English Zionist Federation and general secretary of the Jewish Agency for Palestine was longstanding, was assigned the task of co-ordinating the CBF's fund-raising efforts.[38] Offices of the CBF were to be located in the newly constructed Jewish Communal Centre, at Woburn House, in Bloomsbury. In June, Otto Schiff moved the JRC from the Jews' Temporary Shelter to more adequate office space in the same building, so that both operations were housed under the one roof.[39]

Lionel de Rothschild now hosted a formal meeting at New Court, at which his brother Anthony, Lord Erleigh (son of Lord Reading), Simon

Marks, Dr Claude Montefiore, Otto Schiff, Leonard Stein, Dr Chaim Weizmann and the Chief Rabbi were present. They agreed that an Executive would serve as the policy-making body of the CBF, and as an expression of deference to the Chief Rabbi, he was invited to join.[40] Sir Louis Baron and Lt.-Col. Frederick D. Samuel, the CBF's treasurers, were co-opted on to the organizing committee, and the Rothschild Bank was selected as the CBF's banker. On 14 May the Keren Hayesod ceased to function as a separate body and, as formally agreed, its entire organizational machinery was placed at the disposal of the CBF.[41] All formalities were now completed and the sponsors of the CBF were ready to commence their fund-raising activities.

The CBF fund-raising campaign

Anthony and Lionel de Rothschild hosted a series of luncheons at New Court to which they invited businessmen, merchant bankers and other men of wealth, who were persuaded to provide generous financial support for the CBF. Their guests were advised that each contributor's name and gift would be published in the *Jewish Chronicle* and in other Jewish journals on Friday, 26 May, the date on which the appeal to the Anglo-Jewish community would be officially launched. An Emergency Conference on the appeal, to which some 600 representatives of synagogues and other Jewish institutions throughout the British Isles were invited, helped build momentum for the fund-raising effort.[42]

Zionists and non-Zionists sublimated their ideological differences in public, and the CBF's five presidents of the appeal – Lord Reading and Lionel de Rothschild, nominated by the New Court Committee; Dr Chaim Weizmann and Dr Nachum Sokolow (the latter had succeeded Weizmann as president of the World Zionist Organization), designated by the Jewish Agency; and the Chief Rabbi – appended their signatures to the appeal in the *Jewish Chronicle*.[43] Sir Osmond d'Avigdor Goldsmid was pleased to note that 'the names of the signatories to this Appeal ... evidence ... the fact that Jews of every shade of belief and political thought have united in their efforts to assist German Jewry'.[44]

Jews throughout Britain responded generously. The first advertisement in the *Jewish Chronicle* listed 42 individuals who had collectively contributed £61,900.[45] The appeal in the Jewish press was repeated in the weeks that followed. Lists of donors were published, comprising individuals, Jewish communities and a profusion of synagogue associations, clubs, friendly societies and other organizations, representing Jews across the political and religious spectrum throughout the British Isles. Contributions of less than 20 shillings were acknowledged together with those of thousands of pounds. Such public recognition served not only to broadcast the generosity or parsimony of members of the community, but to coerce those who had not yet responded. While the appeal was directed at the Jewish community, it was carried in *The Times* and contributions were also received from the general public.[46] The Jewish Board of Guardians observed that the CBF appeal had 'been a severe drain on the purse of the community', although it conceded that support of the Board had not suffered unduly.[47]

Before the end of 1933, an impressive sum of almost £250,000[48] had been donated to the CBF, an amount which proved to be proportionately more than the total donations to the American Jewish Joint Distribution Committee and the United Palestine Appeal in the United States in the same period.[49]

Despite the generous response to the CBF appeal, not all the moneys contributed were available for immediate distribution. This anomaly was a result of government encouragement of covenanted donations to recognized charities. In each of the seven years' legal lifetime of a covenant, the charity named was the beneficiary of the income tax paid by the donor (upon application to the Treasury) on the moneys pledged. Thus, over a period of seven years, wealthy donors in high tax brackets greatly increased the aggregate of their gifts.[50] Of greater significance in 1933, however, was the fact that the CBF was in place and ready to commence operations, and the JRC was assured of funding for the year ahead.

The success of the appeal had been due in no small measure to the agreement, even if tenuous, of the non-Zionists and Zionists to submerge their ideological difference in the interest of aid to the Jews in Germany. That agreement would be put to the test as the CBF Allocations Committee set about its task.

4

CBF Operations Begin

SIR OSMOND D'AVIGDOR GOLDSMID agreed to serve as chairman of the CBF's Allocations Committee, to which the Jewish Agency appointed Simon Marks, Professor Selig Brodetsky, a mathematician at Leeds University who was respected in both Zionist circles and the Jewish community at large, and Dr Chaim Weizmann.[1] The CBF's appointees were Walter S. Cohen, Lionel L. Montagu and Otto Schiff.[2] Chaim Weizmann withdrew from the committee less than three months after it began to operate, citing Sir Robert Waley Cohen's 'objectionable behaviour' towards him as his reason. Waley Cohen was delighted at the resignation. However, d'Avigdor Goldsmid was able to mollify Weizmann, and he attended meetings whenever he was in London.[3]

With the Keren Hayesod agreement in mind, d'Avigdor Goldsmid together with Lord Erleigh and Simon Marks attempted to conclude a similar fund-raising arrangement with Robert B. Solomon, head of the Jewish National Fund, the income of which was used to purchase land in Palestine. But that organization had financial obligations that it was legally bound to meet from its current income, so these early negotiations failed. However, a compromise was reached later, when it was agreed that the Jewish National Fund would apply contributions in excess of normal income, to the purchase of land in Palestine for the settlement of German Jews.[4]

Jewish women's organizations of differing political hues had no difficulty in working together for the benefit of refugees. The Women's Zionist Federation (founded by Rebecca Sieff) and the Union of Jewish Women (a conservative non-Zionist philanthropic organization) both responded favourably to the request that they launch an appeal in aid of refugees in Britain, specifically women and children, and Elaine Laski undertook to organize this effort.[5] Rebecca Sieff chaired the Women's Appeal and Yvonne de Rothschild (wife of Anthony de Rothschild) served as its president. The Viscountess Erleigh (later Lady Reading), a life-long practising Christian who had converted to the Judaism of her father following Hitler's rise to power, also played a leading role in the Women's Appeal. In the three years from 1933 to 1935 alone, the Women's Appeal Committee sponsored the training of more than 150 young women as nurses, governesses and secretaries. It also raised £250,000 in the seven years prior to the war, to further its effort to aid children and women among the refugees.[6]

The CBF's resolve to encourage and to finance immigration to Palestine, and the endorsement of this plan by Rabbi Baeck and his colleagues in Berlin, gave impetus to the speedy establishment of vocational training and retraining schemes in Germany and in countries of temporary asylum. Graduates of these programmes would augment the skilled agricultural and industrial labour force on their arrival in the new country. The CBF acknowledged that some who participated in these programmes might immigrate to countries other than Palestine, but recognized that their training would stand them in good stead in any country of settlement. The CBF's first agricultural training and retraining centre was established in St Albans, Hertfordshire, and in 1934 some 200 young persons were already in training there.[7]

Osmond d'Avigdor Goldsmid gave enthusiastic endorsement to the CBF's decision to regard Palestine as the pre-eminent destination for German Jews and for the CBF's income. At a meeting at the Henry Street Settlement in New York, he told his audience that practical experience, not theories, had shown 'that the best way available money could be employed, with the best hope for the reconstruction of the lives of many of the refugees, was in Palestine'. For these reasons, he said, more than half of the CBF's income was spent there.[8] In fact, almost £225,000 was allocated to Palestine for the benefit of German refugees in the first three years of the CBF's operation. Included in this sum were the CBF's contributions to the Keren Hayesod.

These moneys were designated for the purchase of land, construction of housing for adults in urban areas and those who joined agricultural settlements and other facilities in kibbutzim (agricultural settlements), and agricultural and industrial training. The Ben Shemen children's agricultural settlement of the Youth Aliyah, a new concept in the non-institutional care of orphans, whose foundation in the 1920s by the German Zionist Siegfried Lehmann had been made possible through a substantial contribution to the Jewish National Fund by Berthold, Wilfred Israel's father, was also aided by the CBF, as was the Hebrew University and the Technological Institute in Haifa (the Technion), both of which provided employment for refugee scholars and support for those who had not secured academic positions.[9] A small, but influential number of German Jewish intellectuals who were dedicated Zionists had immigrated to Palestine in the 1920s, and they provided an anchor for German refugee scholars and professionals who arrived after 1933.[10] The CBF also allocated smaller sums to the Women's International Zionist Organization, the Palestine Corporation and the World Maccabi Union.[11] Indeed, except for its financing of the JRC's operations and agricultural training centres in Britain, refugee committees on the continent, and appropriations for emigration and repatriation expenses in Germany, the balance of the CBF budget was allocated to programmes designed to aid refugees in Palestine through development there of the country's Jewish infrastructure.

Notwithstanding its enthusiastic and generous financial support for immigrants to Palestine, the CBF kept a low profile on this activity, seeking, no doubt, to avoid provoking anti-semitic responses in the British press at a time of high unemployment and concomitant poverty at home. As a result, the CBF's substantial financial endowment of Palestine's infrastructure in the 1930s has gone unrecognized. For similar reasons, the JDC was reluctant to broadcast its financing of projects in Europe. James Rosenberg, a member of the JDC's Executive Committee, told the CBF that because of the economic depression in the United States and the upsurge of anti-semitism there, the JDC deemed it unwise to publicize the large sums it sent to Europe for aid to Jewish communities.[12]

The CBF and the JDC

The first formal contact with the JDC took place in July 1933, when Judge Irving Lehman (brother of Herbert H. Lehman, then Governor of New York State) and Dr Bernhard Kahn attended meetings of the CBF Allocations Committee and laid the groundwork for co-operative effort for the benefit of German Jews.[13] JDC board members were already known to the CBF through their extended family connections (Felix Warburg, JDC's chairman, was married to Otto Schiff's cousin, Frieda Schiff) and banking interests.[14]

The JDC, known affectionately by its beneficiaries as the 'Joint', was conceived in 1914 as an ad hoc organization, but became firmly established after the First World War. The major American-Jewish philanthropic agency, the JDC had distributed millions of dollars in aid to Jewish communities in eastern Europe. This support enabled Jewish institutions devastated during the First World War to be rebuilt, community organizations to be re-established and the needy in their midst to be supported. The CBF, on the contrary, created as a temporary organization in response to the German-Jewish crisis, had determined that its resources would not be allocated for relief of the needy in Germany, who were seen as the responsibility of the German-Jewish community.[15] Again, the two agencies differed in their approach to the German-Jewish crisis. Throughout the years before the pogroms in 1938, the JDC did not regard emigration aid as a mandate, whereas from its inception the CBF had embarked on a programme that would ultimately decimate the Jewish community in Germany.

Members of the JDC's Executive Committee were not Zionists, nor were they tolerant of them, and they were troubled by the influence that Chaim Weizmann and the Zionists were seen to have on their British friends, particularly since the CBF had decided that most of its funds would be spent for immigration to Palestine and support of its Jewish institutions. Felix Warburg told d'Avigdor Goldsmid that 'the ideals and hopes of the Zionists notwithstanding, the paltry number of [immigration] certificates issued by the British government, and the threatened uprising of the Arabs, made it untruthful and unfair to hold up Palestine as a solution to the problem of emigration from Germany'.[16] None the less, Professor Jehuda Bauer, the JDC's historian, has suggested that the

JDC suffered 'a split personality' because in some measure financial aid for German-Jewish immigration to Palestine was provided through support of the Palestine Immigration Office in Berlin. This in its turn was part of the Zentral Ausschuss and the Hechalutz (pioneer movement) which operated in Austria, France, the Netherlands and Poland.[17] While the CBF and the JDC did not always agree on issues of policy, Dr Kahn helped nurture a constant flow of information between them. It was not unusual for the CBF to allocate funds to the JDC in support of projects of mutual interest, or to finance them on a shared basis, and this co-operation with the JDC grew as the years progressed.

The Cohen Report on refugees in Europe

As soon as the CBF began operations, an almost overwhelming number of requests for financial aid was received from refugee committees in countries on Germany's borders. These countries, with limited Jewish populations, suffered under a deluge of thousands of refugees, many of whom were of Polish origin. In response to these committees' pleas for help, Simon Marks suggested that a survey was needed to determine the direction and the extent of the CBF's European aid programme. He followed this through by making available to the CBF, at no cost, the services of Joseph L. Cohen, an economist in his employ who, like his mentor, was an ardent Zionist. Cohen would appraise the refugee situation in Europe and draw up a plan for the development of schemes for refugee resettlement.[18] The survey would be timely, because the CBF also wanted to provide an informed contribution to the International Conference for the Relief of German Jewry, which was scheduled to be held in London in October.[19]

Joseph Cohen held discussions with community leaders in Austria, Czechoslovakia, Denmark, France, the Netherlands, Poland and Switzerland. He also met with members of the Reichsvertretung in Berlin.[20] On his return to London, Cohen reported that, while the European picture looked good on the surface, Jewish community organizations were already finding refugees who were without financial resources a burden. He reported that refugees in France were allowed to seek employment, while others with capital were permitted to set themselves up in business. Czechoslovakia's liberal policies had enabled 400 refugees to obtain employment. In the Netherlands, the refugee committee attempted to contain the random movement across its border with Germany, by notifying the appropriate community office in Berlin when jobs were available. Suitable applicants were then sent to fill them.

But as a result of the thousands of refugees who had entered these countries, their refugee committees found it financially impossible to provide each individual with more than basic subsistence, and then only for short periods. Cohen was told that some refugees left the continent for England, because the JRC was reputed to be more generous in its financial support. Cohen observed that both committees and refugees were aware that while it was desirable, it was practically impossible in Europe's depressed economic climate, to find employment opportunities in customary occupations. In countries other than France, it was difficult to secure government authorization to accept employment. As a consequence, numbers of refugees travelled from one country to another in search of resettlement opportunities, and when these efforts proved fruitless, many of them returned to Germany.[21]

Cohen was also made aware that it was not unusual for sympathy for refugees to be replaced by a hardened attitude towards them. He suggested that this lack of compassion stemmed from the fact that refugees were not as flexible as their committees would have wished; they did not adjust readily to the lowered standard of living that their small relief grants imposed. He acknowledged that, if refugees accepted retraining in agricultural or manual pursuits, that too would carry the onus of a lowered standard of living. He ventured that refugees who could not be placed in employment, or those among them who were not prepared to retrain, and those who were not 'worthy objects of charity', a category he did not define, would be better off in Germany. None the less, he said, those who opted to go through the retraining process were more likely to make good immigrants.[22]

Undoubtedly this was so, but retraining as agricultural or industrial workers was not a path easily undertaken by individuals, many of whom, until recently, had been members of an established middle class, and had enjoyed skilled and professional occupations. There was also the fact that most Jews from Germany, native born or of Polish origin, were not Zionists and did not regard settlement in Palestine as their goal. In these early days too, their hesitancy to retrain was surely linked to the belief that the situation in Germany might improve, and that they would be able to return to their areas of former residence; or that visas to the United States and other countries would become available, and that they would be able to join relatives and friends. None the less, Joseph Cohen's report served to strengthen the CBF's resolve to fund training and retraining for those who would immigrate to Palestine or to other destinations.

Immigration to Palestine

Dr Chaim Weizmann's response to German-Jewish immigration to Palestine differed in public and in private. In public, he did not share the CBF's enthusiasm for it; there were few German Jews who possessed the agricultural and other skills most needed, and in short supply in Palestine, or who were committed Zionists. Chaim Weizmann maintained that Jews in Poland, long suffering under the yoke of anti-semitism and widespread poverty, had a far greater need for sanctuary. From his standpoint, they warranted priority in the queue, more especially since they were the main constituents of Zionist organizations in Europe and were prepared to join agricultural settlements. Chaim Weizmann wanted controlled immigration of dedicated and agriculturally trained Zionists. In 1933 it would have been difficult to dispute the fact that the economic and political situation of Polish Jews was far less secure than that of Jews in Germany. Nevertheless, significant numbers of Jews there were not seeking Palestine immigration certificates. Chaim Weizmann told the Zionist Executive, in 1935, that the movement had to choose between immediate rescue of Jews and the broader project of Jewish national redemption. As leader of the Zionist movement, Chaim Weizmann favoured the latter.[23]

Notwithstanding Chaim Weizmann's public posture, he was, in fact, pleased that German Jews were choosing to settle in Palestine, more especially since the CBF was generously financing the movement of many of them. He assured Dr Hanke, of the Keren Hayesod in Jerusalem, that as a result of the CBF's decision to sponsor German-Jewish immigration to Palestine, 'well over £100,000 had flown into the country as a result of the first Appeal' and that another £70,000 had been allocated following the second. These moneys, he assured Dr Hanke, did not include sums that the CBF spent for immigration expenses, or the payments made to hachsharah (agricultural training) outside Germany.[24]

The regulations of the British Mandatory Government for Palestine permitted Jews without means, who were sponsored, to immigrate. In addition, immigration to Palestine was open to all Jews who were able to provide evidence of financial assets. Persons with not less than £1,000 could obtain 'capitalist' immigration certificates. Although not publicized, it was not unusual for the JRC to provide prospective immigrants with loans to enable them and their families to leave Germany, and settle in Palestine as capitalists.[25]

Members of the professions seeking to immigrate to Palestine needed evidence of capital amounting to £500, while skilled craftsmen were required to produce £250. Individuals with a secure income of not less than £4 a month were also eligible to apply for immigration certificates. Several persons were able to enter Palestine on the basis of one certificate, since each male immigrant was entitled to include his wife and children.[26]

Chaim Weizmann publicly voiced his displeasure at the prospect of German Jews with capital choosing to settle in Palestine. These capitalist newcomers would be of no benefit to Palestine, he declared at a CBF meeting. Indeed, he said, they would prove to be a liability. Hospitals, schools and other social services would have to be provided for their use, creating a burden that would negate the CBF's financial contribution to the Keren Hayesod.[27] But here again Weizmann privately revealed his true opinion of moneyed German immigrants when he confided to Simon Marks that 'without doubt the prosperity [of Palestine] of these past three years has been largely due to the influx of men and money from Germany'. Indirectly, he said, the enterprise and initiative of German Jews had created openings for immigrants from poorer countries. He also conceded that, if the stream of German immigrants were to slacken, 'Palestine would suffer an economic set-back whose political and moral consequences would be incalculable'.[28] Yet, when Osmond d'Avigdor Goldsmid learned that only one-third of available immigration certificates would be allotted to German Jews without financial resources, and that only one-fifth of that number would be allocated to those who had already left Germany for countries of temporary refuge, Weizmann did not reassure him. He advised d'Avigdor Goldsmid that the remaining two-thirds of certificates had to satisfy the requirements of all other Jews in the world. With a defiant air, he told the CBF that there was plenty of room in Syria for Jewish emigrants and that the government there would welcome them.[29]

The German government not only encouraged Jews to leave the country at this time, it looked with special favour upon their immigration to Palestine. A boycott of German goods had not been mounted there, and the import of goods manufactured in Germany was made possible through a Transfer (Havara) Agreement, which had been arrived at between Jews in Palestine and the German government. It was backed by the Jewish Agency.[30] The agreement enabled German-Jewish immigrants to Palestine to deposit a specified sum from blocked German assets (usually the equivalent of £1,000 or more for each person) in a German bank, against which a German exporter shipped goods to Palestine. The exporter was then paid with money in the immigrants' blocked accounts. When the goods were sold in Palestine the proceeds were deposited in an authorized bank, which then paid the immigrants. The Jewish Agency's response to criticism of this arrangement was that not only did it save Jews and their money, but by importing capital into Palestine, the country was able to absorb other immigrants who were without means.[31] Between 1933 and the end of 1937, the total amount of capital transferred under this Transfer Agreement was calculated to have been some £4,400,000.[32] When, in June 1934, the German government reduced the amount of currency that emigrants were permitted to export, the Transfer Agreement remained in effect and Jews who immigrated to Palestine continued to benefit from its provisions.[33]

Palestine remained at centre stage. In an interim report to the Conference for the Relief of German Jewry in October 1933, the CBF was pleased to note that, in addition to support for refugees in Britain, it had made funding available to refugee committees throughout Europe for the establishment of agricultural and vocational training centres.[34] In fact, from 1933 to 1935, the CBF allocated more than £50,000 to France and the Netherlands alone, in which countries the greatest number of refugees had sought asylum, for the establishment of agricultural and vocational training centres. The Netherlands government made land and buildings available for this purpose at 'Werkdorp' in Wieringinmeer on the Zuider Zee, and a number of refugees were trained there. Refugees who had made their way from Germany to Danzig and to Poland were also aided by the CBF through funds allocated to the JDC.[35]

The Jewish Refugees Committee

The JRC estimated that some 3,800 refugees had entered Britain before the end of 1933, by which time some 300 of them had received permission to accept temporary or permanent employment. Although a majority of the refugees were transients, the CBF Allocations Committee was pleased to report that 'by dint of the most careful management' the £20,000 allocated to the JRC in 1933 enabled the needs of refugees to be met through to February 1934.[36]

While most refugees in Britain were able to maintain themselves, there were those whose resources were depleted during the months in which they awaited Ministry of Labour decisions on employment, or awaited visas and overseas transportation. The JRC cared for and housed a number of them at the Jews' Temporary Shelter and at other locations. Yet it needed another £29,000 to meet its expenditures before the end of 1934, by which time 5,600 refugees had registered, although not all of them sought financial aid. As in 1933, a majority were transients, and the JRC was able to help a number of them complete plans to immigrate to Palestine, South Africa, South America, the United States and other countries.[37] Joseph Cohen negotiated with the Colonial Office in an attempt to secure entry permits to some of the British colonies, but he was advised that before names of potential immigrants could be forwarded to their administrators, the CBF would be asked to guarantee that they would not be permitted to become a charge on public funds in those territories – a commitment that the CBF was not in a position to undertake. Similarly, when Otto Schiff contacted the Ministry of Labour with a view to sending refugees to British Dominion countries, he was asked the length of time during which the JRC would hold itself responsible for each refugee, and whether it would be prepared to finance the return transportation to Britain for those economically unable to adjust.[38] Such financial commitments were beyond the capacity of the CBF.

In 1935, when a total of some 3,800 refugees had registered with the

JRC, its funding for the year amounted to £25,000. At that time Otto Schiff estimated that 3,000 refugees were still in Britain, some 1,100 of whom had not registered with the JRC. They were assumed to have established themselves in business and to be of independent means.[39]

Not unlike the movement from one country to another on the continent, many German Jews who travelled to London and were unable to obtain government permission to accept employment, or find opportunities for immigration, returned to Germany. The JRC listed 890 refugees who had been repatriated in 1935, some of them aided in this move by the JRC. Most, commented Otto Schiff, were college students or graduates, 'with which the world seems to be overstocked'. With certain exceptions, he said, they would need a lengthy process of retraining before immigration possibilities could be found for them. It was, without doubt, less costly to repatriate them than to maintain them in London.[40] Others were supported during their first months in the British job market. Otto Schiff was opposed to granting financial aid to students who were hoping to complete their music education. He believed that they would have problems in securing employment when their training was completed. The Academic Assistance Council was not swayed by Schiff's reasoning, and it provided grants to gifted artists for graduate study.[41]

The Academic Assistance Council

The Academic Assistance Council (AAC) was established in May 1933, by Sir William Beveridge, director of the London School of Economics and Political Science (LSE), of the University of London, and by the British academic community, 'to aid refugee scholars ousted from employment in Germany because they were Jews, non-Aryans or held political opinion inimical to the German State'. Britain's most eminent and world-renowned physicist and Nobel Laureate, Lord Rutherford, was pleased to serve as the AAC's president. Professor A.V. Hill, a celebrated physiologist and Nobel Laureate; Sir Frederick Kenyon, director of the British Museum; the economist John Maynard Keynes and a host of other distinguished scholars and celebrated public figures joined in the AAC's endeavours. Walter Adams, a lecturer at London

University, later director of the LSE, was appointed secretary to the AAC, whose immediate goal was to secure university placements in Britain or in other countries for these refugee scholars.[42]

The British academic community was most liberal in its support of the AAC, and responded generously to their German colleagues' needs, contributing from their salaries on a regular basis. Simon Marks provided an initial contribution of £2,500 and the CBF allocated £2,500 to the AAC as soon as funds were available. It continued its support throughout the AAC's lifetime.[43]

The limited number of universities and other research institutions in Britain were able to offer the refugee scholars only a small number of appointments. In an effort to ease this problem, the CBF provided funds for stipends to enable academic institutions, industrial laboratories, hospitals and other institutions to make research facilities available to refugee scholars until internal or other funding could be procured, or until the scholars emigrated. In 1933 alone, the CBF allocated more than £8,000 for these purposes, and the Haendler Charity added a further £4,000.[44]

The Joint Foreign Committee of the Board of Deputies and the Anglo-Jewish Association created a Jewish Academic Committee to provide grants to academically trained professionals, university professors and teachers, specializing in Judaic studies. However, this committee was disbanded following consultation with the JRC, and a professional committee was created in its stead, thus eliminating duplication of the AAC's efforts.[45]

Within a span of three years, 57 refugee scholars had been placed in permanent posts, while 155 were in temporary positions. Oxford University's Clarendon Laboratory employed a number of renowned refugee scientists, and it was soon to secure a worldwide reputation in recognition of their research. Sir Lawrence Bragg, at Cambridge University, helped several refugee scientists to secure positions. In 1937, when it was evident that a more permanent organization was needed to cater for a continuing stream of academicians coming not only from Germany but also from Austria, Italy, Czechoslovakia and other countries, the Society for the Protection of Science and Learning (SPSL) was organized, into which the AAC was absorbed. The CBF continued its support of the SPSL as it had the AAC.

The British war effort was later to reap benefit from the research undertaken by refugee scientists.[46] It has been argued that, had the British government not restricted employment of refugees, nor made a condition of their entry early re-emigration, the skills of many more scientists would have proved invaluable to British scientific and industrial achievement, more especially when war was declared.[47]

The CBF also aided graduate students who were accepted by universities so that they might complete advanced degrees, and others who hoped to secure British medical qualifications. Ernest Chain, who later shared a Nobel prize with Alexander Fleming and Howard Florey for their work on penicillin at Oxford, was among these students. A small number of students received financial aid from the International Student Service, which the CBF also helped fund.

Scholars who remained in Britain made enduring contributions to the country's scholarship and to its scientific achievement, as evidenced by the number who were appointed Fellows of the British Academy or the Royal Society, and by those who were awarded Nobel prizes.[48] Many more lent lustre to the academic scene in the United States and other countries of asylum, which reaped the benefit of Britain's restrictive immigration policy. Some scholars immigrated to the American continent simply to achieve physical distance from Europe and from Nazi Germany. Many other refugees made similar moves, and more would have done so had the immigration laws of the United States and other countries been less restrictive.

Physicians and dentists

The British Medical Association was not sympathetic towards refugee physicians, and throughout the pre-war years it failed to extend a professional helping hand. Lord Dawson of Penn told the Home Secretary, Sir John Gilmour, that there might be room for a few doctors of special distinction in Britain, but he thought that 'the number that could usefully be absorbed or teach us anything could be counted on the fingers of one hand, and these could quite well be accommodated at research posts at universities, etc.' He was quite convinced, he said, 'that most of the persons whose admission was sought on the ground of their special qualifications were quite ordinary people who wished to earn a living by practice here'.[49]

Lord Templewood (formerly Sir Samuel Hoare), who was the Home Secretary at the time of the Austrian Anschluss, noted in his biography that on more than one occasion his 'humanitarian sentiments' were unpleasantly shocked when he attempted to admit Austrian doctors and surgeons. The British medical profession, he noted, was unimpressed by the worldwide reputation of the doctors of Vienna, and assured the government that British medicine could gain nothing from them. Templewood said that he would have admitted the Austrian medical schools *en bloc*. During the war, he continued, the refugee doctors soon proved how much the country had gained from them 'and how much greater it might have been if professional interests had not restricted' their scope.[50] However, despite professional opposition from the British medical fraternity, a number of German and, later, Austrian doctors acquired the British licence that enabled them to establish themselves in Britain or in countries of the British Empire to which they immigrated. The JRC issued weekly reports on the employment of small numbers of physicians as general practitioners or in diverse medical specialities in institutions throughout Britain. Furthermore, an agreement with Italy and Japan provided that physicians licensed in Britain might practise also in those countries. Refugee dentists were more fortunate than doctors: those holding German diplomas were permitted to practise in Britain without additional training.[51]

JRC records also reveal the ingenuity of its staff in wielding individuals' employment qualifications at consuls in efforts to secure entry permits to their countries. When visas to the United States and other countries were ultimately secured, the JRC was unstinting in its payment or loan of money to cover overseas transport and the all important shipment of baggage and household goods from storage points in Europe or Britain to ports in countries of destination.[52] Indigent refugees were also provided with funds with which to support themselves during their first weeks in countries of immigration. Osmond d'Avigdor Goldsmid was a keen advocate of this practice. It was not merely a question of furnishing ship tickets for Brazil or South Africa, which were expensive enough, he declared, but 'to send a refugee overseas without any resources is not only cruel, but exceedingly unwise. No country welcomes destitute immigrants'.[53] This generosity of spirit and of financial support was not questioned by the Allocations Committee. The smooth movement to countries of immigration in this early period mitigated against a swelling of refugee numbers in Britain, and minimized problems that their continued presence might have caused.

The JRC's correspondence with Jewish social welfare agencies abroad was extensive, and liaison with the United States and other consulates time consuming, and beyond the capacity of the limited staff that it was prepared to employ. Volunteers were always ready to assist, and an Emigration Department, in which they helped staff, was created within the JRC. As in other areas of the JRC's activities, refugees with suitable background and experience were employed, with permission of the Ministry of Labour, and their efforts were evident. They helped institute a system of record keeping that proved invaluable; one that still provides data required for compensation claims against the Austrian and German governments.

German Jews with financial means and business contacts experienced little difficulty in obtaining government permission to re-establish themselves in Britain. As potential industrial innovators and employers of British labour, they were welcomed. They were beneficiaries of substantial tax concessions when they established factories in economically depressed areas of the country.[54]

Just as he had done in earlier years at the Jews' Temporary Shelter, Otto Schiff defined the policies of the JRC and dealt personally with individuals who presented special problems. At his weekly Friday afternoon meetings with officials at the Home Office, he continued to plead the cause of those whose stay in Britain required clarification. In addition, he was ever prepared to provide a letter to the Home Office, the Ministry of Labour or the Board of Trade to smooth the path for some in matters of employment, verify the legality of the residence position of others, or aid in securing favourable consideration for permanent residence. British businessmen supported Schiff's efforts and helped refugees to make contacts in the commercial world. A number of them were employed or received training for employment by these means.[55]

Members of the JRC and other volunteers not only augmented the staff, but also served as case workers. Such 'hands on' social service by men and women of independent means was not unusual in the 1930s when academic education for social work was still in its infancy in Britain and few employed in the profession were graduates.[56] In those years Toynbee Hall, a settlement house in the East End of London, was one of several providing a training ground for socially conscious university graduates. Norman Bentwich and Leonard Montefiore were among the student volunteers trained at Toynbee Hall.[57] Norman Bentwich, the son of a distinguished Zionist who had removed his family from England to Palestine, was a Professor of Law at the Hebrew University, Jerusalem. He had served as Attorney General on the staff of Sir Herbert Samuel, the first High Commissioner for Palestine, when he occupied that position from 1920 to 1925. Bentwich now devoted his time and energy to the rescue and resettlement of German Jews. His constant travels for the CBF took him not only to countries throughout Europe, but also to South Africa and Australia. In the tradition of their forebears, members of the JRC continue to attend case conferences, now working with professional staff, but reserving for themselves final decision making regarding financial disbursement in individual cases.

Prior to passage of the 'Nuremberg Laws', the JRC aided in the repatriation of young women who had completed secretarial courses at business schools in London. There was a demand in Germany for the services of bilingual secretaries, and well-paid positions in Jewish enterprises awaited these young women on their return.[58]

In January and again in July 1935, Constance Hoster, a member of the JRC who ran a commercial school, reported that several young women who had 'perfected themselves in English correspondence have been successful in finding situations in Germany, particularly in cases where the girls have homes in Germany to which they can return'.[59] In February 1935 Otto Schiff noted that there were a number of girls 'who have left Germany for no particular reason and could at any time return to comfortable homes, yet stand in the way of those who really need to earn a living, but cannot do so in Germany' – a reference, perhaps, to young women from rural communities, where harassment of Jews was unrelenting.[60] In March 1935, when a young woman reported that she was returning to Germany to accept a position in Cologne, the prudence of her move was not questioned. Otto Schiff was convinced that 'girls who can at any time return to Germany should not be encouraged to seek positions in England, but be advised ... to return home', where their parents were happy to receive them.[61] Encouragement of repatriation diminished only when Germany decreed that women would require labour permits before being allowed to take up employment on their return, and reports reached the JRC that some returnees had been held by the Gestapo.[62]

It was not unusual for the JRC to advise would-be immigrants not to come to England. In 1936, 105 Jews were helped, at their request, to return to Germany.[63] A major factor in this movement was the difficulty in securing Ministry of Labour approval to accept employment. As German passport-holders they could re-enter Britain without visa formalities and, despite the passage of the Nuremberg Laws, neither they nor the JRC appear to have viewed their situation with alarm.

Jewish Resettlements Limited

Loans were sometimes provided by the JRC or by the loan-granting agency, Jewish Resettlements Limited, which the CBF established in January 1935. Its directors were Sir Robert Waley Cohen, serving as an independent chairman; his cousin Hannah F. Cohen, OBE, a trustee of the Haendler Charity; Leonard Montefiore; and Otto Schiff. Jewish Resettlements' working capital of £6,000 was provided by the CBF, the American Jewish Reconstruction Foundation (financed by the JDC and the Jewish Colonization Association) and the Haendler Charity.[64]

Refugees were permitted to borrow as much as £200. These loans also served to guarantee advances made by others. Such credit, which could not have been secured from other sources on the personal recognizances of the borrowers, enabled individuals to launch businesses, buy into partnerships or establish themselves professionally. A small number of refugee physicians and dentists were able to buy into medical and dentistry practices and purchase equipment.[65] Loans were also made to sculptors and artists, dressmakers, decorative paper merchants and entrepreneurs, some of whom were already in business and in need of a boost in order to survive the early stages of repayment to creditors. All loans were encumbered with interest at the rate of 3 per cent. The Jewish Resettlements organization continued to function until 1960, and it helped many refugees to become established in Britain. Almost all of them repaid in full the money loaned to them.

In 1936 the Home Office reported that 'several thousand desirable, industrious, intelligent and acceptable persons have been added to the population', bringing with them 'considerable capital, and established industries which have already given employment to more British subjects than the total number of refugees from Germany who are now living in the United Kingdom'.[66] Two years later the Home Secretary, Sir Samuel Hoare, told the House of Commons that refugees had provided employment for 15,000 persons; and that they had largely transferred the fur trade from Leipzig to London and to Paris.[67] Refugees had not only created employment opportunities in economically depressed areas, but established new industries whose products had formerly been imported from Germany. Britain was cognizant of their contribution.

The HICEM

The CBF was one of the agencies that financed the HICEM, established in 1927 by the Hebrew Immigration Aid Society (HIAS) of New York, and by the Jewish Colonization Association. The original purpose of the HICEM, whose name was an amalgam of HIAS, the Jewish Colonization Association and Emigdirect (a migration organization that had ceased to operate), was to help needy Jews in Europe to locate countries of immigration and to provide them with legal and technical advice. From 1933 its efforts were extended to Jews from Germany. Before the end of 1939, the HICEM had aided the immigration of some 50,000 refugees from Germany at a cost of £542,855. The CBF contributed £92,285 (17 per cent) of this amount, the balance of which came from the Jewish Colonization Association (43 per cent), the JDC (38 per cent) and other organizations. As countries in Europe were occupied by the Germans, the HICEM established offices in Lisbon and in Casablanca, and in the years of the war was able to arrange the immigration of several thousand more refugees.[68]

The JRC and its several welfare and emigration services functioned almost routinely until November 1938. Businessmen, legal and other professional members of the Jewish community continued to respond to calls for their participation in efforts to help individual refugees establish themselves in the new setting. They thus eased some of the insecurity which resulted from the removal from the home milieu, and enabled a number of refugees to resume gainful employment. Other refugees who planned to emigrate to third countries were secure in the knowledge that the Jewish communities had been alerted to their pending arrival, and were ready to receive them.

5

The Calm Before the Storm

DESPITE THE PASSAGE OF legislation that deprived Jews in Germany of their political status, the number of refugees arriving in England in 1934 did not swell. Sir Osmond d'Avigdor Goldsmid was of the opinion that a majority of Jews in Germany no longer felt threatened and were able to live with the restrictions placed upon them. Using the inflow of refugees as his barometer of their condition, d'Avigdor Goldsmid, who now expressed confidence that the worst offences against Jews in Germany were at an end, predicted that refugee committees in countries of Europe might soon be able to close their offices. He reasoned further that, since it was no longer necessary for German Jews to become refugees while completing their emigration plans, it would be cheaper to support them in Germany rather that in other countries.[1] d'Avigdor Goldsmid was not alone in believing that the situation of Jews in Germany had improved. It was a view that prevailed despite knowledge that Jews were still under pressure from the Nazi regime to emigrate, and that large numbers of Jewish students were being expelled from public schools and institutions of higher education. In fact, the CBF agreed to make an exception to its policy of funding only those programmes benefiting potential emigrants, and allocated £10,000 to the Reichsvertretung for Jewish elementary and secondary schools in Germany, in which many former state-school students were enrolling.[2]

Harry Sacher (Simon Marks' alternate on the Allocations Committee) contended that support of Jewish institutions in Germany was the responsibility of the Jews living there, an argument with which the CBF generally agreed.[3] Sacher also maintained that, as soon as the economic position of Jews in Germany stabilized, their circumstances would improve and 'the present acute situation of [Jewish] children in ordinary German schools would diminish in severity'. Sacher firmly believed that their position would then be better than that of the Jews in Poland and Romania, who suffered endemic persecution and poverty. It was dangerous, he observed, to mortgage the entire charitable resources of the Anglo-Jewish community for the sole benefit of Jews in Germany.[4] But the Jews in Germany were still living under the Nazi regime and they were the CBF's *raison d'être.*

Otto Schiff, who was in contact with individuals in Germany, vacillated, contributing a word of caution yet expressing confidence in their long-term future. While observing that the position of Jews there was becoming steadily worse, and that small German-Jewish bankers were being forced out of business, he voiced optimism on the refugee situation. He announced that he was negotiating with the Home Office for permission to bring 500 Jews to Britain, and he assumed that, if he was successful in this endeavour, the German refugee problem in England could be brought to a close before the end of the year.[5] Schiff did not identify the intended immigrants, but since he was interested in Jews College in London and in religious education, it is possible that they were students who were preparing for the rabbinate.

Notwithstanding the optimism of several individuals regarding the status of Jews in Germany, the pledge to the Home Office that no refugee would become a charge on public funds hung heavily on the CBF's shoulders. This concern is evident in the reaction to a rumour that the arrival of a number of young German Jews was imminent. A newly enacted German statute that discriminated against the continued employment of men under 25, in favour of those who were heads of families, was the source of their concern.[6] The CBF was of the opinion that these young men would be economic rather than religious refugees, and as such should not be entitled to JRC aid. Such a distinction had not before been voiced. Schiff and his colleagues appear to have lost sight of the fact that German law discriminated against Jews, and that the economic condition of these men was, in part, a result of increasing Nazi pressure on the employment of Jews.

Otto Schiff suggested that the Home Office should be advised that the Anglo-Jewish community would accept responsibility for refugees arriving after 10 September 1934 only if they were fleeing religious persecution. Under the terms of the pledge to the Home Office, however, the Anglo-Jewish community would be honour-bound to support all refugees. Schiff had obviously concluded that persecution was no longer a factor of Jewish life in Germany. Therefore, if Jews were not being attacked or discriminated against, there was no valid reason for them to leave for London.[7]

Schiff's view of the situation of Jews in Germany was not shared by Leonard Montefiore, who cautioned against the action he suggested. But Harry Sacher and Lionel Cohen, both of whom were alarmed at the possible consequences of a flood of young men seeking financial aid from the JRC, backed Schiff's recommendation, adding that the Home Office should also be advised that, unless a competent authority in Germany certified that new emigrants were victims of religious persecution, the Anglo-Jewish community would not accept responsibility for their maintenance. The seeming lack of comprehension at the CBF of the Nazis' intent to rid Germany of Jews cannot be censured. These men did not possess visionary powers. Fortunately, another calm voice was heard. Selig Brodetsky counselled that no action be taken until the substance of the German measure was known.

Without waiting for this detail, Selig Brodetsky, Lionel Cohen, Harry Sacher and Otto Schiff were appointed to a sub-committee to consider the possible ramifications of the German statute for the JRC. The four men agreed that there should be a limit on those eligible to be covered by the pledge to the Home Office. While they believed that the Anglo-Jewish community had a responsibility for Jews in Germany whose lives were in jeopardy, they felt differently about those who were unemployed or those whose businesses had been adversely affected by the Nazi regime. They reasoned that, since Jews were no longer being persecuted, there was no reason for them to leave Germany for England, and that they would have to adjust to the political parameters set by the Nazi regime. Therefore, those who made the journey to London would now be classified as economic rather than as religious refugees, and they would not benefit from JRC support. As a result of this thinking, Otto Schiff concluded that the time was not yet ripe for a visit to the Home Office.[8]

Neville Laski was not appeased by Schiff's recommendation and suggested that the four signatories to the guarantee to the government, of whom he was one, should also meet to discuss their future strategy.[9] A proposal that a delegation travel to Berlin to examine the German statute was contemplated, but it was rejected in favour of an invitation to the Reichsvertretung and to the Zentral Ausschuss to send representatives to London to discuss the CBF's concerns.[10] Both organizations responded favourably, and Dr Otto Hirsch, Lola Hahn-Warburg and Dr M. Kreutzberger attended a CBF meeting on 11 December 1934. Dr Hirsch, who was a senior officer in the Ministry of Interior in the government of his native Württemberg until he was dismissed by the Nazis, was much respected as a 'great gentleman, deeply cultured, a great Jew'. Formerly the chairman of the Reichsvertretung, he now served as its director.[11]

Dr Hirsch immediately put minds to rest when he informed the CBF that the statute on the employment of young men applied to all German workers under 25. It constrained dismissal by employers until alternative employment was offered, either in government labour camps or in land service. This intelligence calmed earlier fears of an inrush of young men, and there was no further mention of action on the pledge to the Home Office.[12]

However, in contrast to opinion in London, Dr Hirsch painted a grim picture of the position of Jews in Germany. He reminded his audience that, when President Hindenburg died (2 August 1934), the power of the President and of the Chancellor had been vested in the man who had written *Mein Kampf*, and although an amnesty had been proclaimed, the deteriorating economic condition of Jews was unabating. Many were still being held in concentration camps and a number were known to have been murdered. Jews were excluded from membership in the German Labour Front (trade union organization) and as a result they were ineligible for employment in many occupations. In Berlin alone 14,000 Jews, of whom 5,000 were under 25, were unemployed. The position of Jews in small towns and villages was far worse than it was for those in large urban areas, said Hirsch. Only if they were fortunate enough to be included in a training programme organized by the Reichsvertretung, which would fit them for eventual immigration to Palestine, could they dream of escaping their tormentors. Jews in large urban areas could help each other and certain types of employment and commercial enterprise were still open to them.[13] In the aftermath of Dr Hirsch's visit, the subject of economic refugees appears to have lost its appeal and it was not pursued further.

The Saar region

While at the meeting in London, Dr Hirsch referred to the plebiscite in the Saar region, which, in accordance with the Treaty of Versailles, was due to be conducted by the League of Nations on 13 January 1935. Since the Saar region was under the control of an International Commission and visas were not required to enter the territory, it served as a ready refuge for Jews from Germany. In co-operation with the JDC, the CBF was providing funds for the support there of those in need. Dr Hirsch was pessimistic about the outcome of the plebiscite for the Jews living there, and his misgivings were well founded. The result was an overwhelming vote for reunion with Germany, and when on 1 March 1935 the Germans moved into the territory, many hundreds of Jews left to seek asylum elsewhere.[14]

Harry Sacher assured Dr Hirsch that his report had been sympathetically received, and that it would be considered when the CBF decided on a third appeal. Notwithstanding, Dr Hirsch's statement regarding the deteriorating condition of Jews in Germany appears to have been forgotten. Subsequent discussions suggest that, since German Jews were no longer being vigorously persecuted, they had ceased to provide a stimulus for Anglo-Jewish community action. Members of the CBF seemed ambivalent about their continued involvement in an organization whose purpose appeared to have lost direction.

The CBF fund-raising appeal of 1935

The Anglo-Jewish community had responded generously to the CBF appeal launched in 1934, and had contributed cash and pledges totalling £176,000.

In 1935 the movement of refugees into Britain was again desultory. A majority of them were transients, *en route* to third country destinations. Small numbers stayed a while, hoping perhaps for employment, and when none was obtained, they formed a steady flow of repatriates. Jews living in Berlin and other large urban areas were still able to engage in business and industry, the professions and the arts, without serious harassment, and employment with Jewish businesses, particularly in the textile, leather and military goods industries, was also readily available.

In the absence of increased pressure on Jews to leave Germany, the CBF anticipated that moneys it had in hand would cover the requirements of the JRC and other commitments for 1935, and that a third appeal would not be necessary.[15] It was as though members of the CBF had isolated themselves from reality; that they had not heard Dr Hirsch's warning. Even Lavi Bakstansky, who had contacts with Zionist organizations within Germany, saw fit to advise the Keren Hayesod in Jerusalem that the CBF had sufficient funds available to cover its needs in 1935 and that any residual refugee problems in Britain could be taken over and dealt with by the Board of Guardians, or by the Jews' Temporary Shelter. He also informed his contacts in Jerusalem that the Rothschilds opposed a third CBF appeal, although they were contemplating supporting one for the Jews' Temporary Shelter for its work with transmigrants.[16]

The complacency with which the CBF viewed the position of Jews in Germany is difficult to comprehend. CBF Executive members frequently visited Germany and were apprized of the continued harassment, especially of Jews living in smaller urban areas and in rural communities. They also met with refugee committees in countries surrounding Germany and were told of the many refugees who continued to arrive in their countries.

For some at the CBF, however, doubt regarding the future status of Jews in Germany did exist, and it was ultimately agreed that an appeal should be mounted in 1935 to raise moneys for a possible future contingency. The financial commitment to the Keren Hayesod, and projects already authorized in Palestine, also needed to be funded. Anthony de Rothschild was pragmatic. While he appeared to have little stomach for another appeal, he thought that it might be wise to have money in hand should a need arise. He advised the CBF Executive that 'they at New Court and their friends would each subscribe £5,000', as they had in each of the two preceding years, and that other groups would be prepared to make similar contributions. Lord Bearsted, chairman of the Shell Oil

Company (launched by his father, Marcus Samuel, on whom the hereditary peerage was first bestowed) and managing director of the family-owned Montagu Samuel bank, also promised £5,000 – a sum he too had contributed in each of the past two years.[17] Similarly, an equal amount was expected from the Bernard Baron Charitable Trust. Simon Marks pledged £10,000 from members of his family, with the proviso that £5,000 of that figure be added to the contribution to the Keren Hayesod. With these contributions as a base, Anthony de Rothschild predicted that, if an appeal were launched, it would probably realize at least £100,000 – a sum which was in fact raised.[18] He thought that such an amount would adequately meet anticipated needs, and he emphasized that neither he nor his brother would take an active part in a fourth appeal that might be launched in 1936. But again, he voiced a wavering concern, adding, 'provided of course that the situation of Jews in Germany did not become catastrophic'. If there were pogroms in Germany, he said, then the matter of an appeal in 1936 would have to be reconsidered. He acknowledged that, even without additions to their number, there would still be refugees in Britain in 1936, and he made a condition of his participation in the appeal, the setting aside of money contributed in 1935 to cover the needs of the JRC in 1936, thus obviating the need to solicit the community again in that year.[19] With this reservation noted, an amount of £15,000 was set aside to cover potential JRC needs in 1936. Otto Schiff, too, still expressed the hope that the budget of the JRC would be reduced in the following year.[20] The acumen of even these keen observers of the German scene appears to have been dulled by the absence of generalized persecution.

At a meeting of the CBF Executive at New Court, a question was raised regarding financial support for Jews in Poland, whose situation was reported to be growing more precarious as a result of increased anti-semitic activity.[21] At an earlier meeting, when Sir Robert Waley Cohen raised a similar question, Leonard Montefiore said that he regarded the problem as 'such an enormous one that it would be impossible for the Committee to consider it', more especially since there were already two or three organizations whose sole purpose was to aid Polish Jewry. Anthony de Rothschild was of like mind. While the CBF had 'done a very great deal to alleviate the position of the German Jews', he said, 'Poland was quite another proposition'. Restating CBF policy, he noted that it was to assist German refugees in Poland and Polish Jews in Germany, but to refrain from involvement in the Polish-Jewish problem, which was seen as economic, rather than political.[22] Neville Laski later advised Felix Warburg that both the Rothschilds and Lord Bearsted had told him that they regretted being unable to take an interest in the eastern European Jewish problem in addition to their concern for German Jews, and that following the CBF's 1935 appeal they would have to give more of their energies to aiding Jewish and non-Jewish charities in Britain.[23] Notwithstanding the views expressed at the CBF, the appeal in 1935 was conducted with vigour. Lady Erleigh, Leonard Montefiore, Otto Schiff, the Chief Rabbi Dr Herz, the Rev. M.L. Perlszweig, Harold Laski, other supporters of the CBF within the community and well-known political figures travelled the length and breadth of the country to address potential contributors. Meetings were held at synagogues and fund-raising activities were organized by members of the Women's Appeal Committee.[24]

The doubts and hopes of individuals notwithstanding, the CBF was confident of its assessment of the position of Jews in Germany, and concluded that it could look forward to a winding down of its activities in support of German Jews.

It was at this juncture that Rabbi Morris Lazaron, of Baltimore, Maryland, was invited to address a CBF Council meeting. It was the end of May, when the rabbi arrived in London from Germany following a three-month stay there at the invitation of Max Warburg.[25] Rabbi Lazaron informed his audience that, despite their worsening situation, he was convinced that a majority of German Jews had no desire to leave the country 'because they consider themselves Germans'. His host in Germany was certainly among those who had no intention of leaving. So firm were Jews in their decision to stay, said Rabbi Lazaron, that they were prepared to cope with new employment restrictions by retraining for occupations from which they were not barred.[26] This intelligence was confirmed some months later following a visit to Berlin by Norman Bentwich. In a letter to Felix Warburg, he told of his admiration for the Jews who tolerated the political and social limitations that the regime imposed upon them, and how impressed he was 'with the courage and dignity with which the Jews in Germany endure their prison'.[27]

Early in 1935, Jews in Germany were made aware that a new definition of German nationality was under consideration. If enacted, it would deprive all Jews of German citizenship.[28] Even this eventuality, which would eliminate Jews from the mainstream of German society, did not cause the majority to abandon their loyalty to the Fatherland, or to seek to emigrate.

This final indignity was delivered on 15 September as part of the body of statutes known as the Nuremberg Laws. Jews were deprived of German citizenship (*Staatsburgerschaft*), which was now reserved for persons of Aryan blood. Jews would be classed as 'belonging to the state' (*Staatsangehöriger*), not as citizens. Marriage between Jews and Aryans as well as extra-marital relations between them was forbidden, and Jews were prohibited from employing female Aryan servants under the age of 35. All remaining Jewish civil servants were to be removed from their posts by the end of the year. For those Jews accustomed to hoisting the German flag, this was now prohibited, but they were permitted to fly the Jewish colours.[29] Effectively, Jews were now excluded from German social and political life. While they might continue to organize activities within the Jewish community, they were clearly excluded from those available to the wider population.

In 1933 most Jews had been eliminated from employment in the civil service, from holding public office, from fields as diverse as journalism, radio and farming, from teaching, theatre and films. In 1934 they were banned from trading on the Stock Exchange. If Jews in Germany had nurtured hope of a relaxation of anti-Jewish activity, it was shattered, for now they were pariahs in the land of their birth. A viable existence there would prove a most difficult proposition. The CBF viewed these developments with alarm and agreed that they would have to embark on a new course of action for the benefit of Jews in Germany.

6

The Emigration Programme and the Council for German Jewry

THE NEW COURSE OF ACTION agreed upon by the CBF, and by Rabbi Leo Baeck and the Reichsvertretung, was the promotion of large-scale emigration of young adults, discussion of which had been mooted for some time. The CBF Executive envisaged an orderly transfer from Germany to Palestine, to which country the emigrants could proceed with comparative ease, and to other countries, for which visas or entry permits would be secured.

Some months earlier, Max Warburg had recommended that Jewish communities enter an arrangement with the German government whereby 'a certain number of Jews should leave Germany every year so that within 10 to 15 years their number in Germany would be halved'. At that time Dr Otto Hirsch was vehemently 'opposed to the theory of an evacuation of the Jewish youth of Germany' and Max Warburg's suggestion was not pursued.[1] Max Warburg had also attempted to establish a 'liquidation bank' which would be funded by Jews in the United States and in western Europe. This bank would arrange the transfer of Jewish assets to countries other than Palestine, in the manner of the Havara Agreement, but here again Warburg's plan was opposed by Jews in the United States and by those in Britain.[2]

Now, at the end of 1935, the CBF was planning to sponsor the dispersion of the youth of this old-established and culturally integrated Jewish community, a venture which a majority of Jews living in Germany had themselves not even begun to contemplate. They were ready to weather anti-semitic onslaughts and the indignity of their newly legislated political and social position, as their forebears had through the millennia. They did not view emigration as a choice. They believed that they would survive in Germany. This confidence was nurtured by speeches of prominent Nazis which emphasized the feasibility of continued Jewish life within Germany. These speeches were carried in the *Central-Verein-Zeitung* (Central Community Times), the organ of the Hilfsverein der deutschen Juden (Aid Association of German Jews). Wilhelm Frick, the Minister of the Interior, asserted that the Citizenship Law and the Law for the Protection of the Race, and the regulations for their implementation, were not intended to harm Jews on the grounds of racial origin. He stressed that Jews would not be deprived of continuity of life as a community. Dr Hans Frank, of the Academy of German Law, argued that Jews would be able to remain in Germany and function unhindered as a Jewish body.[3] These placating speeches fulfilled their deceptive purpose for many Jews, who were later to suffer the consequence of trusting them.

The CBF Executive was not influenced by the Nazis' speeches. Their earlier complacency regarding the condition of Jews in Germany had given way to concern for their future, and emigration was now viewed as the sole means by which the lives of young German Jews could be saved. Organized emigration would enable those who participated to leave Germany without endangering themselves, or recreating the chaos of earlier random crossings into countries on Germany's borders. Planned emigration would also avoid repetition of the situation of a year earlier, when numbers of Jews who had left for France and the Netherlands returned to Germany following their brush with anti-semitism in those countries. In this era of continued high unemployment, no country looked with favour on refugees who sought employment. Local refugee committees were glad to ease tensions affecting their own communities by aiding repatriation, and they halted their support of this activity only when they learned that returnees were being incarcerated on arrival in Germany.[4]

The CBF's emigration scheme was introduced at New Court on 7 November 1935, when Lionel and Anthony de Rothschild invited Edward Baron, Lord Bearsted, Osmond d'Avigdor Goldsmid, Simon Marks, Lionel Montagu, the Rev. Perlzweig, Sir Isadore Salmon, Otto Schiff and Fred Stern to meet James McDonald, the League of Nations High Commissioner for Refugees (Jewish and Other) Coming from Germany.[5] McDonald, a devout Christian and a respected American lawyer, was a personal friend of Felix Warburg. Until his appointment, he was a member of the *New York Times* and president of the American Foreign Policy Association. The JDC and other organizations in the United States had sponsored him for the post he now occupied.[6] On McDonald's appointment in September 1933, Felix Warburg had cabled Otto Schiff and written to Osmond d'Avigdor Goldsmid of his delight 'to have so useful and versatile a man appointed who ... will be helpful in working out our problems'.[7] Chaim Weizmann, who was in regular contact with McDonald, helped persuade him to employ Norman Bentwich as his deputy director.[8] Under Weizmann's spell, noted Bentwich, McDonald became an enthusiastic Zionist.[9] During his tenure (1933–5), McDonald earned the esteem of leaders of Jewish refugee agencies on both sides of the Atlantic.

The CBF and the JDC were members of the permanent non-governmental Consultative Council of the High Commissioner for Refugees. They also occupied a special position in relation to the High Commissioner's office for, as a result of a private agreement with Germany prior to its withdrawal from the League of Nations in October 1934, the administrative costs of the High Commissioner's office were borne not by the League, but by voluntary agencies treating with refugees. In effect, the budget of that office was provided by the JDC, the CBF and the Jewish Colonization Association, with lesser amounts coming from the United Palestine Appeal and other agencies.[10]

During his frequent visits to Berlin, James McDonald met with members of the Reichsvertretung and he was well briefed. He was now invited to present his assessment of the position of Jews in Germany. He began by repeating the advice he had given in 1933, when he addressed the Joint Foreign Committee of the Board of Deputies and the Anglo-Jewish Association.[11] Even at that early date McDonald advised his audience that the outlook for the majority of Jews in Germany was hopeless, and he urged emigration aid, especially for the young people. As on the earlier occasion, McDonald told the meeting at New Court that the situation of the Jews in Germany was dire, and that they needed help to enable them to emigrate. He observed that, in consultation with Jewish communities and governments in a number of countries he had visited, he had been made all too well aware of the very limited resettlement possibilities on offer. He contended that, to his knowledge, Palestine presented the most realistic possibility for immigration of any magnitude. He cautioned, however, that Palestine needed immigrants with skills relevant to an agricultural society rather than those required in an urban and industrial economy, for which the majority of German Jews were equipped. He reasoned, as the CBF had done since its inception, that if large numbers of German Jews were to be integrated into the economy of Palestine, they would need to undergo a comprehensive and accelerated programme of training or retraining while still in Europe. McDonald urged that the number of those trained be geared to an anticipated rate of movement from Germany, so that those who had completed courses would emigrate with little delay and enable others to enter the training programmes. Simon Marks had also conferred with Rabbi Leo Baeck, who advised him that 'emigration must be the principal constructive activity' for the Jews in Germany.[12]

Simon Marks had already held discussions with McDonald on his proposed emigration scheme. He had also met with Lola Hahn-Warburg and Wilfred Israel when they visited London, both of whom were involved in the programme of the Youth Aliyah movement, which aided the immigration of young people to Palestine.[13] All had reached the same conclusion: that emigration was the only hope for the future of German-Jewish youth.

The CBF plan of emigration was discussed again two weeks later at the home of Lord Bearsted, when Lionel Cohen, Osmond d'Avigdor Goldsmid, Simon Marks, James McDonald and others were present. Until now Lord Bearsted was not a visible actor on the CBF scene, although he was one of its major financial supporters. Simon Marks had already confided to Chaim Weizmann that he regarded Lord Bearsted as the 'most resourceful personality, by far, to emerge from the non-Zionist Anglo-Jewish leadership'. Lord Bearsted, he said, also understood 'the overwhelming importance of Palestine as a land of immigration'. Marks reminded Weizmann that, in contrast with the United States, non-Zionists in Britain were interested in the development of Palestine, evidenced in the fact that a very large proportion of the budget of the CBF had already been spent in preparing German Jews for immigration and settlement there.[14]

Lord Bearsted told his guests that he believed that the situation of Jews in Germany was now precarious. It was as though the tensions of war were again manifesting themselves, and time was of the essence if Jews were to be rescued. Bearsted was of the opinion that the CBF should initiate its plan of emigration, and then ask the Jews in the United States and those in other countries for their support.[15] He said that he would be willing to approach 'such men as Baruch, Harkness, Rockefeller and several others' in the United States, whom he knew very well, and from whom he thought he could solicit large contributions towards the costs involved in moving the emigration plan forward. He emphasized that he felt so strongly about the plight of Jews in Germany that, if it could be arranged, he was ready to make a special trip to the United States. McDonald seized on his suggestion, and recommended that Lord Bearsted and Simon Marks visit the United States together, and meet with American-Jewish leaders, through whom they would endeavour to secure JDC support for the CBF plan.[16] Both men welcomed McDonald's recommendation. They also agreed to ask Sir Herbert Samuel to join them. Samuel, a rather remote figure, was a Zionist with a long political career in government behind him. He was the first High Commissioner of Palestine (1920–5) and Home Secretary in the British government (1931–2).[17] He would add lustre to their mission, more especially since it was known that he was soon to be named a member of the peerage.

However, before the visit to the United States could be arranged, the plan of emigration and training, and the funding that the programme would absorb, needed to be defined. Joseph Cohen, who had made several visits to Germany, was assigned the task of detailing the scheme which the three emissaries would submit to the JDC, the United Palestine Appeal and other Jewish philanthropies in the United States. The CBF would submit it to the Anglo-Jewish community and those in the Dominions.

Joseph Cohen, too, believed that Palestine offered the most realistic possibility of resettlement for Jews from Germany. He envisaged 32,000 adults, aged between 17 and 35, being settled there over a four-year period; their number adding to the 30,000 Jews from Germany who had arrived since 1933. In the same four-year time-span 2,000 children, orphans and others for whom parents were unable to provide would also be sent to Palestine. Cohen anticipated that another 32,000 young adults, aged between 17 and 35, would immigrate to other countries in the same period, half of them joining relatives in the United States. Thus, the number of assisted emigrants would total 66,000, over four years. Cohen expected that another 5,000 children under 17, accompanied by their parents, would also receive emigration aid, but they were not included in the scheme in which the JDC would be asked to participate.[18]

In arriving at his population calculations, Cohen employed the German Census figures for June 1933, to which he added the number of Jews who had remained in the Saar region following annexation. After subtracting deaths and emigrants he arrived at a figure of 438,000 Jews in Germany in October 1935. He estimated that half of this population was over 42; while those between 17 and 35, considered the most suitable age group for emigration, numbered 94,000.[19]

When presented with Cohen's proposed scheme, the CBF envisaged asking participants to contribute 20 per cent of the cost of their training, which might bring in £66,000 ($330,000) in each of the four years, while the Reichsvertretung would be invited to provide half the remaining cost, estimated at £212,000 ($1,060,000) annually. But it was soon realized that neither of these sources of income, to be contributed in local currency in Germany, could be relied on with any degree of certainty, and it was conceded that $15 million (£3 million) would have to be subscribed by Jews worldwide over a four-year period to cover the expense involved. The CBF believed that their assessment of the potential cost of the scheme was reasonable, and that with co-operation from Jews in the United States, the necessary funds could be raised and the programme instituted without delay.[20]

Encouraged by the plan before them, Lord Bearsted and Simon Marks cabled Felix Warburg in New York, on 6 December, urging that in 1936 the JDC postpone its own fund-raising efforts for the benefit of German Jews. They advised Warburg that a comprehensive plan for the emigration of 66,000 children and young adults over a four-year period, costing in the region of $15 million, which the CBF was prepared to promote, had been prepared in London. It was obvious that Lord Bearsted and Simon Marks knew little of the high powered professionalism with which Jewish institutions in the United States raised funds for philanthropic endeavours. They were not aware that the JDC was not a fund-raising body *per se*; it was financed by the Council of Jewish Federations and Welfare Funds, which raised money from Jewish communities throughout the United States. Nor did they know that these fund-raising events were executed according to nationally agreed annual timetables. By contrast, Jewish philanthropic fund raising in Britain was the work of amateurs.

James McDonald had already informed Felix Warburg of the CBF plan, and the need seen in London for speedy action in the interest of Jews in Germany.[21] Warburg responded immediately to the cable from Bearsted and Marks. He pointed out that the JDC and United Palestine fund-raising appeals were unrelated, and that decisions regarding moneys needed by each organization for its activities in the coming year had already been made. None the less, he said, a visit for consultation purposes would be welcomed.[22] Numerous cables and transatlantic telephone calls between Warburg, Bearsted and Marks followed. As a result of these preliminary communications, the plan drawn up by Joseph Cohen was redesigned and a modified version sent to Felix Warburg. Bearsted and Marks asked him to ensure that the scheme received JDC support, and advised him that Sir Herbert Samuel had agreed to join them when they visited New York.[23] With Warburg's invitation in hand and their visit confirmed, Lord Bearsted, Simon Marks and Sir Herbert Samuel, accompanied by Joseph Cohen, their honorary secretary, set sail aboard the liner *Majestic.* They arrived in New York on 21 January 1936. All four men were about to be given a lesson in American-Jewish political sagacity.

Lord Bearsted, Simon Marks and Sir Herbert Samuel visit the United States

Prior to their arrival, the JDC had organized a series of meetings for them with Jewish community leaders in major Jewish population centres, and with non-Jews interested in learning more of the problems facing Jews in Germany. As a result of the JDC's efforts, the visitors travelled extensively during their short stay in the United States. They addressed large gatherings of community leaders and other interested groups, and they received national press coverage and made five nationwide radio broadcasts. Sir Herbert Samuel also met with President Franklin D. Roosevelt, who assured him that American Consuls in Germany were sympathetic towards Jewish visa applicants, which, sadly, was not their experience. US Secretary of Labour, Frances Perkins requested that no attempt be made to dump unprepared or undesirable immigrants on the United States, and this was agreed.[24]

Lord Bearsted, Simon Marks and Sir Herbert Samuel used their visit with great effect in the interest of their cause. They met with the most influential representatives of every important Jewish community in the United States. They addressed several sessions of the General Assembly of the National Council of Jewish Federations and Welfare Funds, which was in annual session in Washington, DC, and they conferred with leaders of the JDC and the United Palestine Appeal. They made a total of 30 speeches to large gatherings at luncheons, dinner meetings and banquets in New York City, Chicago, Philadelphia, St Louis and Washington, DC.

At each of these functions the three men spoke of the dire situation in Germany, the need to sponsor Jewish emigration and training, fund transportation, provide loans for business enterprises and land for agriculturists as well as temporary relief where required and, last but not least, the monetary goals to be achieved to bring these plans to fruition. Bearsted, Marks and Samuel were adamant that their objective was not the creation of a relief scheme. German Jews, they declared, had no desire to be maintained by a charity of world Jewry, whether in Germany or elsewhere. Rather, they wanted an opportunity to rebuild their lives. The three men also made clear that it was not their intention to create a new organization, but that they sought the formation of a co-ordinated committee composed of three representatives each from Britain and the United States. The committee would use the machinery of the existing Jewish organizations: the CBF and the JDC, both of which would retain their autonomy.[25]

Before leaving London, Simon Marks had cabled Felix Warburg asking that arrangements be made for him to meet wealthy Jews who were potential contributors. He pursued this request at a JDC Board meeting at Warburg's home the day after his arrival, when he asked whether it was possible to find 25 Jews, each of whom would contribute $100,000. He was prepared, he said, to travel to meet them. Simon Marks could not have endeared himself to his American hosts when, at the same meeting, he told them 'it was probably a new experience for Americans to have an English delegation come to this country and state that they were ready to make available $5,000,000'.[26]

Simon Marks was a persistent thorn in the side of JDC Board members as he continued to ask for the names of wealthy Americans whom he might approach, more especially since the Zionist cause which he championed was anathema to them. Always ready to contribute handsomely to causes he himself favoured, Marks fervently believed that, if he met American Jews, he could persuade them to subscribe to the proposed emigration plan. He was also convinced that the American-Jewish community, far larger and wealthier than its British counterpart, was not sufficiently aware of the needs engendered by the situation of Jews in Germany, and that it could be persuaded to contribute far greater sums for their benefit.[27] Marks was undoubtedly frustrated by the institutionalized formalities and seemingly impersonal processes in raising funds in the United States, and by the JDC's lack of enthusiasm for the training and emigration programme that the CBF proposed.

Following the discussions with the JDC, a much modified version of the training and emigration programme was finally agreed. Noticeably, there was no mention in the revised document of age groups to be aided or of specific destinations, other than Palestine. Those items were omitted because it was feared that the Polish and Romanian governments might use the information to rid themselves of their unwanted Jewish populations by expelling them to countries in the West. The revised plan also made clear that the parties involved had agreed not to undertake any activity that would promote the export of German goods, whether to secure the liquidation of properties belonging to emigrants, or for any other purpose, any one of which was anathema to the JDC. This was a clear repudiation of Max Warburg's suggested scheme and of the Havara Agreement.[28]

The main object now was to 'aid the emigration of German Jews in such numbers as may be feasible and to settle them in Palestine and other lands'. It was anticipated that 20,000 to 35,000 persons would be aided annually through an alliance of the CBF, the JDC, Zionist and other organizations, which would be known as the Council for German Jewry (hereinafter the Council). The original assessment of £3 million ($15 million) to finance the scheme was confirmed, and would be secured by the Council's parent organizations in Britain and the United States (the CBF and the JDC) and by the United Palestine Appeal. Britain, its Dominions and European countries would raise £1 million ($5 million) of the total, while the United States and other countries in the Americas were expected to contribute £2 million ($10 million). It was agreed that London would be the base of operations of the Executive of the Council.[29] The plan was to be discussed with German-Jewish emissaries and with spokesmen of other organizations, all of whom would be asked to participate.[30]

The CBF's independence and its fund-raising agreement with the Keren Hayesod would enable it to participate in the proposed programme. The JDC and the United Palestine Appeal, however, whose national funding depended on their co-operation with the Jewish Federation of Welfare Funds, would each have to consult with and secure approval of that agency's General Assembly. Long-standing fund-raising agreements in the United States would have to be respected in discussion of the German emigration and training plan. The Jewish Colonization Association, which primarily underwrote agricultural settlement and emigration of needy Jews from eastern Europe through its funding of HICEM, would also need to be consulted and its participation secured.[31]

At a final meeting with leaders of the JDC and United Palestine Appeal in New York, on 5 February 1936, semantics rather than substance prevailed. It was difficult for the British deputation to convince their American hosts that the most constructive help that they could offer to Jews in Germany was sponsorship of emigration of the younger generation. Lord Bearsted was exasperated by what he regarded as the Americans' lack of interest in the programme. He regarded both the JDC and the United Palestine Appeal as being more concerned in seeing how much of the money that he and his colleagues had helped them raise for German Jews could be diverted to their own programmes. Simon Marks was in despair. In his view they were returning to England with empty hands; they had accomplished very little.[32]

Simon Marks and his colleagues could not have been aware of the underlying hostility of members of the JDC towards the Anglo-Jewish community because, unlike Jews in the United States, it had not created a national fund-raising organization to support humanitarian work among Jews in eastern Europe. In a somewhat acrimonious discussion when the moneys raised in Britain and in the United States for eastern European and South American-Jewish communities were compared, Morris Troper of the JDC reminded Sir Herbert Samuel that, in the years before the Jewish crisis in Germany, 'nobody ever heard of any assistance coming from England for the many programs carried on by the JDC'.[33] On another occasion, Troper chided Simon Marks for the same reason.[34] When Rabbi Stephen S. Wise, a leading American Zionist, returned to New York after attending a meeting of the CBF in London, he told the JDC of its success in raising funds. None the less, Wise reflected, in former years the Anglo-Jewish community had contributed 'next to nothing' at a time when American Jews were giving $5–7 million a year for the relief of Jews in Europe.[35] Ad hoc appeals had always been Anglo-Jewry's established means of response to Jewish crises whether at home or abroad.

Before the delegates left New York, Felix Warburg promised them that any moneys raised by the JDC in excess of essential needs for ongoing programmes would be allocated to the appeal for $10 million. While the three men respected Felix Warburg, they were not reassured.[36] JDC Board members did not yet share the CBF's pessimism about the future for Jews in Germany, and in consequence were reluctant to concede that emigration was important to their survival. The JDC consented to participate in the Council with reservations, for despite the parity principle, they were still wary of the Zionists' seeming influence on its British members.[37]

Felix Warburg's pledge notwithstanding, the JDC did not allocate funding for the CBF emigration plan. American Zionists were no more co-operative.[38] Although both American organizations had informally agreed that efforts would be made in the coming year to raise more money than was deemed essential for their ongoing philanthropic activities, and that the additional funds would be used for the emigration of German Jews, Lord Bearsted was angered by their seeming lack of enthusiasm for the scheme in support of which he and his colleagues had travelled to the United States.[39]

Bearsted's viewpoint was given credence at the JDC's annual meeting, which opened at the Hebrew Union College in Cincinnati, Ohio, on 23 February 1936, when its national campaign to raise $3,500,000 was launched.[40] The audience of representatives of Jewish communities throughout the United States was told of a misunderstanding concerning the proposals put forward by Bearsted, Marks and Samuel, and these were briefly reviewed. They were also advised that a formal agreement with the delegates from Britain had not been reached because the JDC budget for 1936 had been agreed by an 'Emergency Conference of responsible leaders of American communities held in Chicago on 8 December 1935 ... long before the arrival of our English friends in this country or before it was known that they planned to come here'. In fact, Lord Bearsted and Simon Marks had cabled their plans to Felix Warburg on 6 December.[41] While the JDC's Emergency Conference in Chicago had considered the hazardous condition of Jewish life in Germany, it had agreed that the funds to be raised through the forthcoming appeal would be committed, as in past years, to Jewish communities in Poland, Romania, Lithuania, Latvia, Austria and other areas of eastern and central Europe. The Cincinnati audience was advised that, if the JDC appeal for $3,500,000 for its planned programmes was adequately supported, a substantial contribution could be made towards the proposed German emigration scheme. In other words, the JDC had not intended, or perhaps felt unable, to ask its contributors for additional funding for the benefit of Jews in Germany. Instead, it was decided that the JDC Fund-Raising Committee would make personal appeals to prominent members of the Jewish community for enhanced contributions in aid of Jews in Germany. Those who would be approached were not regular subscribers to the JDC's established programme.[42]

Lord Bearsted and Sir Herbert Samuel embarked for England on 6 February 1936. Simon Marks and Joseph Cohen attended a Zionist conference in Washington, DC, and left the United States a few days later. Despite his seeming despair, Simon Marks cabled Chaim Weizmann that the visit to the United States had stimulated Zionists and non-Zionists alike. They were eager, he said, to resettle the largest possible number of German Jews in Palestine, and were ready to contribute funds for the emigration programme. He asked Weizmann to ensure that a threatened restriction of immigration and land purchase was not implemented.[43]

When the CBF delegates returned from the United States, Lord Bearsted informed the Foreign Office of the Council's plan of emigration for Jews from Germany. Officials there regarded it as 'an unattainable idea', one that would scarcely solve the German refugee problem, even if it could be achieved. But Lord Bearsted and his colleagues were not discouraged.[44]

Work of the British section of the Council for German Jewry

Immediately following their return, Lord Bearsted and Sir Herbert Samuel addressed a meeting at New Court, and Jewish communities throughout Britain were invited to send representatives to another meeting at the Dorchester Hotel in London to hear the result of the negotiations in the United States.[45] Anthony de Rothschild spoke eloquently of the scheme that had been devised together with the JDC and other organizations, and of the formation of the two sections of the Council for German Jewry.

He announced that Professor Norman Bentwich, who was well known to his audience, and Sir Wyndham Deedes, a Quaker and former chief secretary to the High Commissioner of Palestine, now one of the leaders of the National Council of Social Service, had accepted responsibility for the Council's training and emigration programme. Persuasive speeches were also delivered by Lord Bearsted, Simon Marks, Sir Herbert Samuel and Chaim Weizmann.[46] The audience was advised that the British section of the Council would assume most of the activities of the CBF, while the latter would serve as the Council's parent agency and continue to raise the funds needed for the training and emigration programme. The meeting was assured that Anthony and Lionel de Rothschild and others connected with the CBF would also be closely associated with the Council.

Lord Bearsted, Simon Marks and Sir Herbert Samuel gave no indication of the lack of accord in New York, but told instead of the undertaking by American-Jewish leaders to try to raise £2 million towards the £3 million estimated cost of the programme. They did not divulge that a formal agreement to this effect had not been reached. The inauguration of the British appeal was planned for the first day of Passover, and letters and telegrams urging similar appeals to be launched locally had been sent to Jewish communities and synagogues throughout the British Dominions. They were asked to 'make special appeals focusing simultaneously on the first day [of] Passover April 7th 1936'.[47] Sir Herbert

Samuel hoped that the joint efforts of Jews in Britain and those in the Dominions would result in £1 million being raised over the next four years and he announced that three London families had already 'come forward with a generosity which can only be described as princely ... We are bound to come to the rescue of Jews in Germany by every form of practical help' that could be provided, he said. His audience agreed.[48]

In the spring of 1936, Lord Bearsted and Sir Herbert Samuel visited Jewish communities in the Netherlands, Belgium and France to tell them of their visit to the United States and of the agreement to establish the Council for German Jewry. While on the continent they also participated in the fund-raising efforts of their hosts.[49]

Lionel de Rothschild recommended that Sir Herbert Samuel serve as chairman, with Lord Bearsted and Simon Marks the members of the British section of the Council. Although the agreement in New York had called for three members from each section, Lionel de Rothschild added a fourth: Osmond d'Avigdor Goldsmid. Harry Sacher suggested that Chaim Weizmann be consulted on the Council's composition, but Sir Herbert Samuel delivered the *coup de grâce* and invited Weizmann to join as the Council's fifth member.[50] Immediately there was a political and numerical imbalance in the composition of the Council, which did nothing to foster amicable Jewish Anglo-American relations. When Felix Warburg objected, Sir Herbert Samuel did not placate him. Since any funds to be spent jointly would have to be agreed by the two agencies, he responded, it seemed of little importance whether the Council was five Americans and three British or vice versa. He did not treat Warburg gently: 'some of the considerations which influence you do not arise here. Although there are differences of view here also, between those who are active Zionists and those who are not, for the purpose of the objects that are now being pursued those differences are ignored'.[51] Warburg offered no salutory response.

The British members of the Council were less interested in the sensibilities of their American colleagues than in getting the emigration programme under way. The beleaguered Americans also increased their members to five: Felix Warburg and Paul Baerwald of the JDC, Charles Liebman of the Refugee Economic Corporation, and Rabbi Stephen Wise and Morris Rothenberg, co-chairmen of the United Palestine Appeal. Both the British and Americans also named alternates.[52] Lionel

Montagu, designated an alternate member in Britain, was appointed co-treasurer with Frederick D. Samuel. Joseph Cohen, who had formulated the original emigration plan, was appointed honorary secretary. Lavi Bakstansky and Meyer Stephany, the joint secretaries to the CBF, were also assigned the duties attached to the Council.

As expected, the Nuremberg Laws generated an accelerated movement of Jews from Germany. Indeed, in 1936 immigrants to Palestine numbered 9,000, while 10,000 immigrated to the United States and other overseas countries. Another 1,500 were resettled in Europe and 3,800 were repatriated to countries of origin within Europe, bringing the total number of known emigrants from Germany to more than 24,000.[53] The exodus might have been greater, but in anticipation of an influx of foreign visitors ahead of the Olympic Games, which were scheduled to be held in Berlin in 1936, attacks on Jews were modified, engendering a sense of security, however false. This illusion of safety was not confined to Germany. Every lull was seized on abroad as heralding the end of Jewish persecution. In London, members of the Council of the Liberal Jewish Synagogue expressed doubt regarding the advisability of supporting the Council's 1936 appeal for funds, because they were not in favour of 'an organized exodus of Jews from Germany'.[54]

The movement from Germany in 1936 was tempered also by the Arab revolt that year against the growing number of Jewish immigrants, and a dearth of Palestine immigration certificates for those without personal finances. The Arab uprising culminated in a general strike and attacks on British troops and Jewish settlers, a number of whom were killed. Order was restored only with the arrival of British troop reinforcements. Despite this setback, the Council in London reported that its training programme in Palestine during the year had not been impaired, and it continued to authorize large sums for the development of reception facilities and for the integration into the country's economic life of German-Jewish immigrants.[55]

The Council in London was also pleased to note that increased overseas immigration in 1936 was made possible, in no small measure, by the £80,000 that it was able to provide that year for the programme. In the following year, the Council allocated £60,000 for immigration purposes, but only 3,700 Jews from Germany were settled in Palestine, a continued consequence of the Arab uprisings. Some 22,000 German Jews left for the United States and other countries overseas; 14,500 of them were financially aided by the British section of the Council.[56]

Despite their differences, there was frequent and open communication between the CBF, the JDC and other refugee organizations in Europe. Dr Bernhard Kahn regularly invited delegates from London and countries in Europe to meetings he held at the JDC offices, now located in Paris, and he was a constant and welcome participant in the Council's deliberations in London, as was Dr Martin Rosenblueth, London director of the Central Bureau for the Settlement of German Jews in Palestine. Dr Otto Hirsch, Wilfred Israel, Lola Hahn-Warburg and Max Warburg were frequent visitors from Germany, as were Max M. Gottschalk, Mr Siva and Professor E. Speyer of Belgium and Professor David Cohen and Gertrude Van Tijn of the Netherlands. All of them maintained close contact with the Council and a constant flow of information passed between them.

Following the Passover launch of the Council's new fund-raising effort in London in 1936, £730,000 ($3,650,000) was contributed or pledged before the end of the year. It was a sum not far short of the amount the CBF had undertaken to raise in four years.[57] More than £550,000 of the total was promised under covenant, and thus was payable over a period of seven years. As a result, the cash available in 1936 amounted to little more than £135,000. While this was a substantial sum, it was far exceeded by the £318,000 that the Council had committed to projects for the year. The JRC, always a first priority, the relief and re-establishment of refugees who had left Germany, funding for the Keren Hayesod, allocations to the Society for the Protection of Science and Learning for aid to refugee scholars, and other commitments all required funding in excess of the money readily available to the Council. A promise had also been made to advance capital to the Jewish National Fund 'to enable it to make an advantageous purchase of land while the opportunity existed'.[58] This commitment, too, had to be met. Faced with a heavy budgetary deficit, the Council borrowed money to cover the shortfall. Fortunately, 'benefactors of the Fund made loans to the Council free of interest'. These benefactors were, without doubt, members of the CBF who had authorized the overspending in full knowledge that they would have to secure or provide loans to cover allocations in excess of income.[59] The loans would be repayed as moneys due under covenant, and their concomitant income tax refunds were received from the government. Without these loans the Council would have been compelled to curtail its programme.

In the spirit of *noblesse oblige*, the Council did not appeal for contributions in 1937. Britain's major Jewish philanthropic organizations had postponed their fund-raising appeals in 1936, in deference to the funding needed by the Council. The Council now allowed these organizations a clear field. Although a direct appeal was not made, an unsolicited £97,497 was promised for the Council's programme. The Council committed £212,323 in 1937, again a sum far in excess of moneys pledged. On this occasion the shortfall was covered by a loan from the Rothschild and Montagu Samuel banks.[60]

Although projects generated by the Council in London or in New York continued to be funded separately, efforts on both sides of the Atlantic for the welfare of Jews in Germany, and refugees in other countries, were co-ordinated when this was possible, and duplication of effort was avoided. Both sections of the Council chartered a ship, at a shared cost of £32,000, to transport 650 Jews from Germany to South Africa before that country's new immigration law became effective on 1 November 1936.[61] The revised legislation would have required each immigrant to be in possession of a minimum of £100. London and New York also co-operated to fund housing in Palestine for children from Germany who had been sponsored by the Youth Aliyah, and they underwrote training and retraining projects for German Jews within Germany. Through their ongoing financial support of the HICEM, German Jews were able to immigrate to Australia, Argentina, Brazil and other South American countries.

Dr Bernhard Kahn now frequently attended Council meetings in London. His advice and judgement were respected, while his diplomacy helped to further co-operation between the Council's New York and London sections. Dr Kahn was pleased to report to the JDC that training and retraining programmes had greatly improved as a result of the efforts of the British section of the Council. The JDC continued to provide hard currency for the exchange clearing programme of the British section of the Council, for its projects in Germany, and the Jewish Colonization Association also participated in this endeavour. The money contributed by these organizations enabled the CBF to make additional funding available to the HICEM for immigration aid to refugees.[62]

The British section's programme of training and retraining was firmly established before the end of 1936. Even within Germany, training for agricultural employment continued to be offered through the Reichsvertretung, despite a statute that prohibited the employment of Jews on farms. Similar agricultural programmes were also ongoing in Britain, the Netherlands, France and, to a lesser degree, other countries on Germany's borders.

Those who completed training courses were transported to Palestine as soon as immigration certificates became available. As noted earlier, the movement continued despite Arab unrest, which persisted intermittently, until Britain declared war on Germany in 1939.[63] The Council noted that its loans to families to enable them to enter Palestine as 'capitalists' had enabled an entire community from Germany to establish itself as a unit.[64]

In 1936 the League of Nations appointed Major-General Sir Neil Malcolm the new High Commissioner for Refugees from Germany. Malcolm replaced James McDonald, who had resigned in December 1935, in protest at the League's ineffectiveness and worldwide indifference to the plight of refugees.[65] The High Commissioner's office was now financed by the League of Nations, a relief to the budgets of the JDC, the CBF and other contributing organizations, and Malcolm's duties were essentially limited to liaison with refugee organizations and the juridical status of refugees.[66]

At the end of 1937, except for a minority of large Jewish stores and businesses which had managed to retain their Jewish management and Jewish employees, the Jews in Germany were earning a precarious livelihood and were almost entirely cut off from economic, social and intellectual intercourse with the general community. None the less, only a small minority chose to emigrate, or were able to do so, before November 1938.

Almost all of the refugees who had entered Britain as transients since the beginning of the crisis in Germany had left for other countries by the end of 1937. Many of those who remained were awaiting visas or shipping to third-country destinations. A total of some 3,000 refugees had registered with the JRC.

Felix Warburg, who had long earned international respect for his philanthropy, humanitarianism and understanding of problems affecting persecuted Jews, and who had given tirelessly of his time and had helped stabilize and smooth relations between Jewish philanthropic institutions on both sides of the Atlantic, died on 20 September 1937. His passing was a great loss to the JDC and American Jewry, and to the relationship between American and British Jews.[67]

7

German Annexation of Austria

TO THE RESOUNDING WELCOME of thousands who lined the streets, Germany sent its Wehrmacht into Vienna at dawn on 12 March 1938. No resistance was offered, and Austria was incorporated into the German Reich without a shot being fired. Two days later Adolf Hitler arrived and took formal possession of his newly acquired territory. The feeble diplomatic remonstrances of Britain and France were ignored. Neither was ready to intervene.

The *Anschluss* (annexation) of Austria precipitated the most barbaric attack on Jews since Hitler's rise to power. Austrian Nazis immediately began an orgy of plunder. Jews were brutally and sadistically attacked; they were robbed, they were incarcerated, and many were murdered.[1] The swift and vicious action against them was in sharp contrast to the relatively slow process of economic disenfranchisement of the Jews in Germany.

The Nazis sequestered the funds and occupied the offices of the Israelitische Kultusgemeinde (Jewish community) in Vienna, where a majority of Austria's estimated 190,000 Jews lived. Jewish community leaders were arrested.[2] Before the end of March, more than 28,000 Jews in peril of starvation were being sustained at soup kitchens operating under the auspices of the Kultusgemeinde. The CBF provided £45,000 for this programme, and for aid to emigrants.[3]

Less than a week after the *Anschluss*, Adolf Eichmann, director of the Department of Jewish Affairs in the Reich Security Office, arrived in Vienna to take charge of Jewish emigration. As Eichmann later reported, 'it all went like an assembly line'. Jews were called into the Central Office and, one by one, were stripped of their property, livelihood and rights, then issued with a passport with the letter 'J' stamped on it, valid for two weeks. If the bearer had not obtained a visa from a foreign consulate in that time, he or she was subject to imprisonment in a concentration camp.[4] Jews were forced to dispose of any property that had not been stolen from them. They were also deprived of citizenship and redress under the law. Terror reigned and suicide among Jews in Vienna was commonplace.

The Council in London asked Sir Wyndham Deedes to travel to Vienna to assess the situation, and then go on to Berlin and try to arrange for members of the Reichsvertretung to help restore the services of the Kultusgemeinde. But the Gestapo, with whom Wyndham Deedes met, refused this request. It was Wyndham Deedes' impression that the Germans were bent on accelerating the liquidation of the Jewish community in Vienna; a branch office of the Reichsvertretung in Vienna might prove an obstacle to that goal.[5]

Norman Bentwich went to Vienna a short time later, where two months after the *Anschluss* the organization of the Jewish community was still in disarray. Bentwich advised leaders of the Kultusgemeinde, who had been released, that if they were able to obtain permission from the Gestapo, the Council was ready to send a representative from London to help them restore their services. Authorization was secured, and Captain B.M. Woolf, the secretary of the West London Synagogue of British Jews, was given leave of absence to work with the Kultusgemeinde and help in the restoration of its communal activities. Ruth Fellner, a JRC staff member, accompanied him.[6] Captain Woolf returned to London at the end of July; Ruth Fellner remained in Vienna to assist in the emigration of those able to secure visas.

Captain Woolf told of the terror and torment suffered by Jews in Austria. He knew of more than 200 Jewish suicides. He confirmed that the Nuremberg Laws were being rigidly enforced; that Jews were being hounded from their homes, and forced to 'aryanize' their property and sell their businesses. Those living outside Vienna, not unlike Jews in small communities in Germany, were especially vulnerable.[7]

Refugees from the *Anschluss*

Austrian Jews who chanced to be outside the country when the Germans invaded sought asylum. Numbers of them streamed into London and other capital cities. Some in Austria managed to flee to Czechoslovakia, the only adjoining country that had not closed its borders. Elderly Jews in Vienna, some of whom had hoped to join relatives abroad, were registered for emigration with the Kultusgemeinde, but for a majority there was neither sufficient time nor money to aid their departure. Most of them were later incarcerated by the Nazis and then murdered. Thousands of other Jews who were unable to leave Austria suffered a similar fate.

The Council in London, like Jewish community organizations elsewhere in Europe, was ill-prepared financially for an influx of refugees from Austria. Except for a sum set aside for refugees already in Britain, the Council's treasury was almost depleted. Lionel and Anthony de Rothschild and Lord Bearsted immediately agreed that their banks should provide loans to the Council to enable the JRC to care for an added number of refugees. Council members also reluctantly conceded that a blanket pledge to care for all Jewish refugees, including those who might arrive from Austria, could not be continued, and Otto Schiff was authorized to write to the Board of Deputies, and to Sir Samuel Hoare at the Home Office, advising them of this decision. Schiff wrote to each of them, advising them that the Council was no longer able to maintain the undertaking given in 1933: that no refugee would be allowed to become a charge on public funds. In view of events in Austria, Schiff wrote, that commitment had been reviewed by the Council, which had reluctantly concluded that the pledge could no longer be sustained for an untold number of new arrivals. This decision, Schiff noted, had been taken with regret. The Council's budgetary constraints rendered it unable to continue an unlimited financial liability for a large influx of Jews expected from Austria, more especially since the Council retained responsibility for the refugees from Germany already in Britain. The JRC would, of course, do its best to care for all refugees who found themselves stranded, and exceptions would be made for refugees recommended by the Home Office or the Ministry of Labour, after prior consultation with Schiff's Committee.[8]

Schiff's advice to the Home Office appears to have had little effect on the number of Austrian refugees who were permitted to enter Britain, presumably on their own recognizances or on guarantees from individuals. Among the latter, many failed to honour their pledges, and despite the Council's notification to the Home Office, many privately sponsored refugees were maintained by the JRC. In addition to the loans secured from the Rothschild and Montagu Samuel banks, both also provided overdraft facilities for a period of six months, during which period the Council would have to try to raise funds in the community.[9]

Simon Marks was concerned that the movement of emigrants from Germany might be affected if funds raised for the German programme were diverted to victims of the *Anschluss*, and he asked the Council to release the moneys that had been set aside for future contingencies, so that they could be put to immediate use. He also recommended that the Council 'take a bold step forward' and begin another fund-raising appeal for Austrian Jews. The Council heeded Marks, and that appeal was conducted simultaneously with one already initiated for the benefit of German Jews. The solicitation for the Austrian refugees yielded £170,000. Both appeals and their resulting incomes were soon merged. In addition, the Reichsvertretung opened its training facilities and emigration programme to Jews from Austria.[10]

The Council's withdrawal of its pledge to the government was to have an immediate and profound effect on refugee policy at the Home Office, where it was decided that action was needed to stem a greater inflow from Austria and also from Germany of persons whom the JRC could no longer guarantee to support.[11] Concern at the Home Office was heightened by the fact that Austrian nationals held passports that would ultimately become invalid, thus rendering deportation impossible if such action were deemed desirable. While additional precautions were necessary to deal with a potentially large influx of refugees, it would be difficult to take effective action to ensure their financial status at ports of entry.[12] Such measures had not, of course, been necessary while the Anglo-Jewish community's guarantee had been in effect. It would not be practical, the Home Office observed, to refuse entry to persons who were apparently respectable and who stated that they were coming for a short visit to friends, relatives or business acquaintances. The Home Office also contended that, even when there were reasonable grounds for refusing entry to an alien, to do so at the last stage of a long journey might entail great hardship, while subsequent deportation when funds were exhausted could mean even greater adversity and prove well-nigh impossible. For these reasons, it was decided that the only satisfactory method of control would be to require visas for all aliens holding German or Austrian passports. This would obviate the risk of their being refused entry on arrival at a British port.[13]

The matter was referred to the Cabinet, and a sub-committee, which included the Home Secretary, the Foreign Secretary, the Minister of Labour and the President of the Board of Trade, was asked to consider the matter. The sub-committee was reminded of the importance of adopting as humane an attitude as possible, while at the same time avoiding the creation of a Jewish problem in Britain. It was noted also that admission should not be refused to suitable applicants: the test for admission being whether or not an applicant was likely to be an asset to the United Kingdom. Prima-facie unsuitable candidates would be small shop-keepers or retail traders, artisans and persons likely to seek employment, agents and middlemen, minor musicians and commercial artists, and the 'rank and file' of doctors, lawyers and dentists. Exceptions would be made for individuals in this category who could demonstrate that they were in special danger and represented exceptional cases meriting political asylum, or who could rely on some source of support in Britain while arrangements were being made for their future. Such individuals could have their cases referred to the Home Office for instructions.[14]

The German government was affronted by the imposition of visas for its citizens who were on regular visits to Britain for business and other purposes, and the German Chargé d'Affaires in London attempted to nullify its effect by offering to deny passports to Jews or to invalidate travel to Britain on passports already issued to them. Sir Neville Bland at the Foreign Office was not averse to collaborating with the Germans on this proposal, but officials at the Home Office stoutly refused to revoke their decision to demand visas for all German citizens.[15] For many Austrian Jews, however, the Home Office definition of 'prima-facie unsuitable candidates' to whom entry would be refused rang a death knell.

Another was almost brought about by the JRC staff member who had remained in Vienna after Captain Woolf had returned to London. In an attempt to help Jews hoping to flee from Vienna, she took some pieces of their jewellery with her to London. The items would have been confiscated by the Austrians if the emigrants themselves had attempted to take them out of the country. On arrival at Croydon airport, a search of her luggage revealed the jewellery, which had not been declared. Customs officers decided to bring charges, observing that the publicity the case would receive would have a more deterrent effect on other potential smugglers than a monetary penalty.

Otto Schiff was appalled at the consequences that press coverage of the case might have for refugees attempting to leave German territory, more especially since the staff member's name was known to authorities there as the JRC's accredited representative. At a meeting with Customs officials, Schiff informed them that press coverage of the case would prove disastrous for thousands of innocent people attempting to emigrate. The mere mention of the staff member's name would also seriously prejudice negotiations in progress with German government officials for the establishment of an office in Vienna to facilitate the emigration of refugees, which had the support of the British government and the State Department of the United States. Ernest N. Cooper of the Aliens Department at the Home Office and R.M. Makins at the Foreign Office supported Otto Schiff's stance, and so advised the Customs office. The case was referred to the Chancellor of the Exchequer, who permitted it to be withdrawn, despite the fact that it had already been placed before a magistrate for action.[16] By their sympathetic gesture, government officials had averted a possible crisis situation for potential refugees.

When the British government followed the advice of its Home Office, and reinstituted the requirement that all Austrian and German passport-holders obtain visas before seeking entry to Britain, a visa agreement with Germany made in 1927 was abrogated and a bitter blow delivered to Jews still living in the Greater Germany.[17] The reimposition of the visa requirement received wide coverage in the British press. As might have been expected, comments on the advisability of an 'open-door policy' on refugees ran the gamut from ultra-conservative to liberal in tone, the former often accompanied by statements related to an incitement of anti-semitism. The theme that, if limitation on numbers were not imposed, the anti-semitic governments of Poland, Hungary and Romania might take this opportunity to expel their Jewish populations was often repeated.

In its advice to Consuls, the Home Office authorized visas to be granted immediately to distinguished persons – namely, those of international repute in the field of science, medicine, research or art – provided there was evidence that the applicant would be assured of hospitality from friends or colleagues in Britain; and to students who were refugees if they had been admitted to a British university or college for at least a two-year course and had adequate funds for the period of their stay. Students of the non-refugee class, with no Jewish or non-Aryan affiliations, could also be granted visas without referral to London. While a small number of Jews might benefit from this ruling, those in Vienna who continued to face mass arrest and brutal detention were faced with a dilemma. An irony of the condition of being granted a passport was that it required Jews to declare that they would never return and would forfeit all property to the state. For those not prepared to give these assurances, passports could not be secured. Without passports the British Consul could not issue visas to seemingly 'de facto' stateless persons.[18]

The conference at Evian-les-Bains

It was at this time that President Franklin D. Roosevelt appeared to offer hope of relieving the problems confronting the Council, when he proposed sponsorship of an international conference to consider the question of refugees.

Only ten days after the *Anschluss*, President Roosevelt invited 33 countries, including Britain and its Dominions, the Scandinavian countries, Belgium, France, Italy, Switzerland and twenty Latin American republics, to join in efforts to aid 'political' refugees from Germany and Austria. Italy and South Africa declined the invitation. Roosevelt made it clear that no country would be expected or asked to receive a greater number of immigrants than was permitted under its existing legislation, and that private organizations alone would be expected to bear the costs of the programme. This should have alerted the invitees to the fact that Roosevelt would not ask the United States Congress to bend its own immigration laws in a humanitarian gesture towards refugees, despite his reaffirmation of the role of the United States as a haven for the politically oppressed. Roosevelt's stance was doubtless influenced by the fact that there were 10 million unemployed in the United States and that 'an explosion of unprecedented anti-semitic fervor' was prevalent throughout the country.[19] The United States Congress was also committed to a policy of political isolationism.

The British Foreign Office viewed Roosevelt's invitation with some distrust, and imposed as a condition of British participation the exclusion from the agenda of discussion of Palestine as a country of rescue. Since Roosevelt considered the entire Middle East a British sphere, this assurance appeared to present no obstacle. The British Foreign Office also thought that the constitution of the conference might in itself provoke increased persecution of Jews and a new wave of emigration, and expressed the fear that refugees would come not only from Germany, but also from Poland and Romania.[20]

The conference convened at Evian-les-Bains on the French shore of Lake Geneva, on 6 July 1938. Switzerland had declined to serve as host. The Germans allowed representatives of the Reichsvertretung to attend. Hungary, Poland and Romania, with a Jewish population of almost 5 million between them, had not been invited, but they sent observers. The Council and several other major Jewish philanthropic and political organizations in London delegated Norman Bentwich to deliver their submission. It set forth their consolidated views, and detailed efforts made on behalf of refugees and Jews still in Austria and Germany. All those represented by Bentwich hoped that some relief for persecuted Jews would result from this international gathering.

It was soon clear, however, that Jewish refugees were low on the humanitarian agendas of all countries. The vastly underpopulated British Dominion of Australia stated blatantly, 'as we have no real racial problem, we are not desirous of importing one'. New Zealand was of similar mien. A few months later, however, prompted by the Australian-Jewish Welfare Society which undertook to care for Jewish refugees, the Australian government announced that it had revised its stance and would grant 300 landing permits a month.[21] The Canadian government was ready to accept only agriculturists in possession of substantial capital. Since few Jews were moneyed farmers, only a modest number of them gained entry.[22] Various regions within Britain's African colonial empire, which harboured far smaller Jewish communities than either Australia or Canada, had been investigated as possible areas of refuge, but none was reported to have territory suited to the settlement of large numbers of Jewish refugees. Countries in South America were rejected for similar reasons. In Europe, France was overburdened with 200,000 refugees of many national origins and political conflicts. The Netherlands, which already sheltered a refugee population of 25,000, offered itself as a country of temporary sojourn, and Denmark reaffirmed its willingness to continue to admit refugees to the limit of its capacity. The United States agreed to accept the full annual quota from Austria and Germany permitted by law (27,370), but its Consuls did not fulfil Roosevelt's assurance, given in 1936, that they were sympathetic towards Jewish visa applicants, and the quota was not filled until 1939.

With the exception of the countries cited, none was willing to modify its stance on immigration and alleviate the plight of Jews seeking sanctuary. A single positive gesture came from the San Dominican delegate, who said that his country would accept large numbers of Austrian and German agriculturists.[23]

The only other constructive outcome of the conference at Evian was the creation of the Inter-Governmental Committee on Refugees. Headquartered in London, it replaced the League of Nations Refugee Office. George S. Rublee, a 70-year-old American with broad international law experience, and a friend of President Roosevelt, was appointed the Inter-Governmental Committee's director. His responsibilities included discussions with the Germans on an orderly movement of refugees which might enable them to take part of their property with them. The Germans, however, were not interested in Rublee's mission.[24] He tried to negotiate with them on behalf of Jews, but any concessions he might have wrung from them could not be put into operation before war was declared in 1939. Rublee retired immediately, and he was replaced by Sir Herbert Emerson, who already held the post of High Commissioner for Refugees at the League of Nations.

Representatives of organizations concerned for the welfare of Jews in Austria and Germany, and for refugees in countries throughout Europe, left Evian in the knowledge the conference had signally failed to meet the needs of those being hounded by the Nazis. Lord Bearsted had accurately predicted that the meeting would be 'chiefly occupied with passing the buck'.[25]

8

Germany Tightens the Screw

ON 6 JULY 1938, the very day that the conference was convened at Evian, the German government made clear its intent towards Jews still living in Germany. It decreed that on 12 November Jews would be barred from owning retail stores; after 31 December they would be prohibited from engaging in service industries.[1] Another decree ordained that the licences of Jewish physicians would expire on 30 September; until this time they had been permitted to treat Jewish patients. Yet another decree, of 27 September, prohibited Jewish lawyers from practising their profession after 31 December 1938.[2] Some who were affected by these decrees decided that the time had come for them to complete emigration plans. Others, ever optimistic, remained in the belief that their situation could not degenerate further. The cautious among them secured British visas – just in case a move became necessary.

The Sudetenland

The acquisition of the Sudetenland in western Czechoslovakia was next on Hitler's list of territories to be ceded. It was surrounded on three sides by the German Reich, and was home to some 3 million Germans and 20,000 Jews. As at the time of the *Anschluss*, neither Britain nor France was anxious to confront Germany over the issue. Appeasement, therefore, was the order of the day. During the summer of 1938, Prime Minister Neville Chamberlain flew to Germany three times in fifteen days to confer with Hitler on the future of the Sudetenland. The Czech government was not invited to participate in the discussions. It was following

Chamberlain's third meeting with Hitler that Britain, France, Germany and Italy concluded a Four-Power Agreement, whereby the Sudetenland was ceded to Germany. Czechoslovakia, which had had no voice, now had no option but to accept their decision.[3]

Following Chamberlain's last meeting with Hitler, he returned to England promising 'peace in our time'. The British people were ecstatic, relieved because the war that had appeared imminent had been avoided. 'No conqueror returning from a victory on a battlefield has come home adorned with nobler laurels than Mr Chamberlain from Munich', gushed the editor of *The Times*, 'and the King and people alike have shown by the manner of their reception their sense of achievement.'[4] But as the British people were soon to learn, the treaty was duplicitous; war had only been put on hold. In March 1939 the Germans occupied Czechoslovakia's remaining territory and established German hegemony in central Europe.

Czechoslovakia's 200,000 Jews were now to be tyrannized and their communities dismembered. When Czech citizens sought refuge in Britain, the British government, in a seeming act of contrition, voted a fund of £4 million for their relief. Czech Jews who secured entry to Britain were able to share in the benefit of that fund.

German expulsion of Polish Jews

The Polish government in Warsaw eyed developments in Austria, Czechoslovakia and Germany with interest. It anticipated that, following the German occupation of Austria, thousands of Polish Jews living in Vienna, and others in Berlin, Leipzig and other German cities, might attempt to return to Poland. This was a movement the Polish government was determined to discourage at all costs. It decreed, therefore, that Poles would lose their citizenship if they had not visited Poland for five years and had not renewed their passports by 29 October 1938.[5] The German Foreign Office responded immediately. It seized the opportunity to try to rid Germany of Polish Jews, many of whom had been domiciled in the country for more than a generation. The Gestapo was ordered to round up as many of them as possible. On the night of 27–8 October, some 17,000 Polish Jews were arrested, transported to the Polish border and forced to cross it illegally. A number managed to get away and were able to join relatives in Poland or to return to Germany, but some 7,000 others were driven into the derelict hamlet of Zbonszyn in a no man's land on the Polish–German border, where the conditions in which they were forced to exist were intolerable. The Polish-Jewish community and the JDC swiftly came to their rescue and attempted to ease their situation.[6]

Among the Polish Jews who had been expelled and were now in Zbonszyn were the parents of seventeen-year-old Herschel Grynszpan, who was living in Paris. Enraged by what had happened to his parents, he shot and fatally wounded Ernst vom Rath, the third secretary of the German Embassy.

Kristallnacht

Frustrated because economic and social intimidation alone had not expedited the emigration of Jews, the Germans now seized the opportunity to force them to leave the Reich. They responded to the assassination in Paris with an orchestrated maniacal pogrom against Jews and Jewish property in Austria, Germany, the Sudetenland and Danzig, even though the latter territory was not yet occupied by the Nazis.

Kristallnacht (the night of broken glass) began on the night of 9–10 November 1938 and continued for three more days. Jewish property that was still in private hands – more than 195 synagogues, hospitals, homes for the aged, orphanages, schools, libraries and other communal buildings; industrial plants and privately owned shops, stores and houses – was looted and many of the public buildings were gutted by fire. Thousands of Jews were manhandled, maimed or killed in their homes and on the streets. Many more were incarcerated and tortured. Austrian Nazis, not to be outdone by events in Germany, joined in the carnage with a vengeance. All of Vienna's 21 synagogues were torched and 18 of them were completely destroyed. This rampage against the Jews and their institutions was followed by a Machiavellian imposition of a fine on them of RM1 billion (£80 million) to pay for the damage inflicted by the Nazi hordes.[7]

The pogroms ended any thought of Jewish survival under the German flag. Jews who had never planned to leave their homeland had finally been robbed of any illusion that they might survive in Nazi Germany. Panic emigration followed. The one concern now was for personal safety. Jews who were already in possession of British visas, acquired earlier as a form of insurance, now put them to use. Together with those able newly to acquire visas, they fled to Britain. Astoundingly, a number of visa-holders, still hoping for a change in their fortunes, did not leave. Their fate can only be imagined.

The British public responded to *Kristallnacht* with revulsion. The British government reacted by easing entry restrictions on refugees. Within days, there was tremendous growth in the number of Jews who sought sanctuary in Britain, an upsurge in arrivals that continued until the outbreak of war.

As in earlier crises, the Anglo-Jewish community was in no way prepared for the onslaught of thousands of new refugees, many of whom were without financial means. None the less, the Council immediately informed the Home Office that the advice given after the *Anschluss* – that it was unable to maintain the guarantee, lodged in 1933, that no refugee would be permitted to become a charge on public funds – was no longer valid.[8] How the newcomers would be cared for was not a question anyone cared to pose.

The small JRC staff, which until now had dealt with a limited and orderly procession of individual refugees, during what must have been remembered with nostalgia as halcyon days, was soon faced with a challenge for which it had not been possible to prepare, and with which it was unable to cope. Its several departments were hastily expanded and new ones created. But the scene at Woburn House can only be described as chaotic, as the hastily enlarged JRC staff and corps of several hundred volunteers, none with prior experience in counselling people in distress, were besieged by more than a thousand visitors a day, seeking help for themselves or for family members still trapped inside Nazi-occupied territory. Newcomers needed housing, some required medical attention, others hospitalization. JRC volunteers and doctors among the refugees answered the call for these and a multitude of other services. Thousands of personal requests for intervention at consulates, mountains of incoming mail, hundreds of phone calls and other types of basic service requested by those besieging the staff at Woburn House were beyond the capacity of the JRC. Staff and volunteers worked tirelessly for inordinately long hours in an effort to cope, but the demands on them were insatiable and they were the recipients of much acrimony from frustrated and frightened people.[9] Simon Marks made professional personnel available to the JRC from Marks and Spencer headquarters, and they attempted to bring order from chaos, but several weeks were to pass before a semblance of organization could be achieved.

In the midst of the upheaval, the Council had no option but to appeal once again to the Anglo-Jewish community for funds to sustain the newly arrived refugees. As in the years since the beginning of the German-Jewish crisis, the community responded unhesitatingly and donations in cash and pledges under covenant totalled £260,000. As in all calls for help when catastrophe struck, the Bearsted, Simon Marks and Rothschild families responded with extraordinary generosity.[10] But all the moneys received were insufficient to meet the needs of the refugees. Only one option remained, which was to secure another loan against future income from pledges under covenant. Anthony de Rothschild and Lord Bearsted secured a gigantic loan of £356,000 from the Prudential Assurance Company, which, together with the interest due, was guaranteed by the Rothschild bank. The loan enabled the Council to repay its outstanding debts to the Rothschild and Montagu Samuel banks, totalling £220,000, leaving £136,000 in the Council's treasury.[11]

The Council was now able to sustain the basic needs of refugees, who continued to arrive from the continent in their thousands. Some 13,000 (8,000 from Germany and 5,000 from Austria) among those who arrived before the end of 1938 registered with the JRC. In the eight months of 1939 prior to the onset of war, some 55,000 new refugees registered with the JRC, exclusive of the 15,000 whom the Ministry of Labour had permitted to enter the country as domestic servants.[12] The Council continued to provide financial aid to those still attempting to emigrate from Austria and Germany. Only when war was declared, and remittances to enemy-occupied territory were prohibited by the government, did funding for projects in Europe cease.

It was towards the end of 1938 that Dr Otto Hirsch, who had been assaulted and then incarcerated when he accompanied Rabbi Leo Baeck to the Reich Chancellery in the wake of *Kristallnacht*, was released and returned to his post.[13] Dr Hirsch was now very concerned for his senior staff members, who remained at their posts at the Reichsvertretung despite the emigration opportunities that were open to many of them. He asked Norman Bentwich, who visited him in Berlin, if the Council could assure them that, if they stayed on for another six to nine months, they would receive visas enabling them to enter Britain. A number of rabbis who had remained in their communities had been given this assurance and they had only recently left Germany. Bentwich was able to assure Dr Hirsch that the Council readily agreed to his request. The Council arranged for the Home Office to issue visas 'in the event of an emergency' to the persons Dr Hirsch listed. Hirsch was also assured that they would be accorded special treatment when they arrived in England, and that a sum of money, which the JDC readily agreed to share, was being earmarked for them. But Dr Otto Hirsch, Cora Berliner, Dr Paul Eppstein, Hannah Karminski, Julius Seligsohn and other outstanding Jewish civil servants, who chose to stay at their posts in Berlin, were to die at the hand of the Nazis.[14] Rabbi Leo Baeck also refused to leave his congregation, and in 1943 he was incarcerated. He survived internment in the Theresienstadt concentration camp, and was reunited with his daughter and her family in London when the war ended.[15]

The *St Louis*

On 13 May 1939, four days before the British government issued its White Paper on Palestine, the *St Louis*, a ship of the Hamburg America Line, set sail from Hamburg bound for Cuba, with 930 Jewish passengers aboard. Officials of the shipping company had allowed the vessel to depart even though they were aware that Cuba had nullified the visas of all but 22 of the Jews aboard. The 22 visas had been verified on payment of an additional fee. Cuba was to be a temporary sanctuary for 734 of the passengers who were documented and awaited visas to the United States, a wait estimated at from three months to three years. When the *St Louis* sailed into Cuban waters the 22 legitimized visa-holding passengers were taken ashore; the Cuban government refused permission for the ship to dock.

The captain moved his vessel into United States waters and dropped anchor off the coast of Florida while representatives of the JDC negotiated with Cuban government officials on behalf of his passengers.[16] The JDC was prepared to pay the Cuban government an 'official ransom' of $500,000, but Cuban politicians hoped to extract almost as much again in bribes.[17] The JDC's income was not equal to the possible Pandora's box that bribes to government officials would open. There was always the possibility that payment to the Cubans would encourage other Latin American governments to make similar demands. Reluctantly the JDC had no option but to withdraw.[18]

The national press in the United States published countless columns sympathetic to the hapless passengers aboard the *St Louis*, but no American civic or religious organization joined the JDC in its efforts to save them. Neither President Roosevelt nor the United States Congress was moved to attempt to offer a lifeline to those aboard. Roosevelt could have issued a presidential directive and granted the passengers temporary refuge – a gesture he made in 1944 when 982 refugees were brought from Italy to the United States and interned there for the duration of the war.[19]

When the JDC's bargaining with the Cubans failed to elicit the desired result, the captain of the *St Louis* was compelled to head his ship back towards Germany. In Europe, Morris Troper, acting for the JDC, began urgent negotiations with Max Gottschalk in Brussels, Gertrude van Tijn in the Netherlands and Jules Braunschvig in Paris, in efforts to secure permission from their governments to land some of the ship's passengers, instead of returning them to Germany. The JDC agreed to underwrite all the expenses that would be incurred for their maintenance in each of the three countries. As a result of these efforts, the governments of Belgium, France and the Netherlands responded favourably, and between them they authorized two-thirds of the ship's passengers to land.

While the drama of the *St Louis* was unfolding, Paul Baerwald and Harold Lindner of the JDC, both members of the American section of the Council for German Jewry, were holding discussions with their British colleagues in London on plans for a Co-ordinating Foundation, which had been approved of by President Roosevelt. The Foundation would correlate efforts of individuals and philanthropic organizations to improve the conditions of Jews and non-Aryans still in Germany and to assist in their orderly emigration.[20] When the *St Louis* steamed out of American waters, Otto Schiff in London was invited to arrange a meeting with British government officials which he, Baerwald and Lindner would attend. Paul Baerwald had already given the American Ambassador in London, Joseph Kennedy, a letter of guarantee for the maintenance of those who might be allowed to disembark in Britain. In fact, the JDC had already allocated $500,000 in support of all the passengers aboard the ship.[21]

Paul Baerwald, Harold Lindner and Otto Schiff met at the Home Office with Sir Alexander Maxwell, E.N. Cooper, Principal Officer of the Aliens Department, and Lord Winterton and A.W.G. Randall of the Foreign Office. Sir Herbert Emerson and Robert T. Pell, director and deputy-director respectively of the Inter-Governmental Committee for the Resettlement of Refugees, were also present.[22] Paul Baerwald informed those assembled that the Belgian, French and Netherlands governments had each been provided with a guarantee of maintenance for the *St Louis* passengers whom they had agreed to accept, and that a similar assurance for those who might be allowed to disembark in Britain had been lodged with the American Ambassador. It was evident during the discussion that followed that not all government officials agreed that German refugees aboard the *St Louis* should be permitted to land in Britain. However, they were overruled by Sir Alexander Maxwell, who announced that he would advocate that up to 350 of the passengers be accepted by Britain, a recommendation which the government readily endorsed.[23]

By the time that the *St Louis* sailed into European waters, it had been agreed that Belgium would accept 214 passengers, the Netherlands would admit 181, and 224 were to be landed in France. The 288 remaining passengers (one had committed suicide), would land in Britain. Those destined for France and Britain were transferred to a small cargo vessel, the *Rhakotis*, which docked at Boulogne and in Southampton on 21 June.[24] Those who landed in Britain were registered with the JRC, which would provide for their care throughout their stay.

Two other ships sailed to Havana carrying illegal immigrants: the SS *Flandre*, a French ship with 96 refugees aboard, and the SS *Orduuna*, under British registry, which carried 40 passengers. Their passengers, too, were refused permission to land in Cuba, and the vessels returned to Europe. Again, paralleling the experience of passengers aboard the *St Louis*, they were permitted to disembark in Belgium, Britain, France and the Netherlands.[25] Fate was kinder to the passengers who landed in Britain. Many of those who disembarked in continental Europe did not survive the war.

Illegal immigration into Palestine

The Germans continued to press relentlessly for the emigration of Jews from their territory. It was reported that Hitler had decided that the emigration of Jews should be promoted by all available means. If illegal immigration into Palestine would embarrass the British administration and cause difficulties between Britain and the Arabs, whom the Germans favoured, so much the better.[26] Even before Britain had acquired the Mandate for Palestine, Jews had made the long land trek from eastern Europe to Palestine without the benefit of legal sanction. In the early summer of 1939, it was apparent that the British government planned a pro-Arab compromise, when its White Paper on Palestine, issued on 17 May 1939, decreed that within the following five years only 75,000 Jewish immigrants would be allowed to enter the territory. The rate of entry was fixed in six-monthly quotas, following which no further Jewish immigration would be permitted without Arab consent. In effect, the rescue of Jews from the Nazi onslaught was to be severely limited, and Zionist aspirations were to be thwarted. To counter the effect of the White Paper, a clandestine emigration operation was mounted by the Histadruth (General Jewish Federation of Labour), which was funded by private individuals and various Zionist organizations. The Gestapo was well aware of this operation.[27] In the wake of *Kristallnacht*, the Reichsvertretung also favoured this activity.[28]

Simon Marks was well informed on the number of illegal immigrants reaching Palestine. He told Morris Troper, who succeeded Dr Bernard Kahn when the latter immigrated to the United States, that between 3,500 to 5,000 illegal immigrants had reached Palestine during the last quarter of 1938. Troper made what he considered 'discreet' comments in letters and in a memorandum to the JDC in New York, regarding attempts by Simon Marks to involve the JDC in the funding of the illegal movement, which was anathema to that organization as it was to the Council in London. At a meeting with Lord Samuel, in February 1939,

Troper naively asked him whether the Council would make funds available for illegal immigration into Palestine. Lord Samuel assured him that such a request would not be entertained.[29]

Those responsible for the illegal immigration movement responded to the British government's White Paper by accelerating the numbers of Jews they assisted in reaching Palestine. The British government retaliated by temporarily suspending all Jewish immigration into the territory.

Despite the British government's action, the illegal movement to Palestine of German and other Jews continued, and thousands who might otherwise have perished at the hand of the Germans were saved. A report by Sir Harold MacMichael, the High Commissioner for Palestine, revealed that between 1 April 1939 and 30 September 1942, 38,002 immigrants arrived in Palestine: 18,521 of them were legal; 19,481 had arrived without legal sanction.[30]

Dissolution of the Council for German Jewry

The use of the word 'German' in titles of Jewish organizations in Britain proved onerous following Britain's declaration of war on Germany. The Jewish Refugees Committee, which had been renamed the German Jewish Aid Committee in January 1938, in order to remove the stigma of the appellation 'refugee' from those among them who had lived in Britain for several years, now reverted to its original name (JRC).[31] At a meeting in London on 26 September 1939, the Council for German Jewry also decided to remove the word 'German' from its name and asked the JDC for its approval. In response, the JDC suggested that, since the United States was still a neutral country, the American members should be withdrawn from the Council, or not be re-elected to it. They would, however, continue to co-operate in its activities. Thus was the Council for German Jewry disbanded.

The name of the Council in London was appropriately changed to the Central Council for Jewish Refugees (hereinafter the Council), whose efforts would now be concentrated on those who had found asylum in Britain.[32]

9

The Worsening Situation of Jewish Children in Germany

PARENTS OF MEANS IN Germany had long been accustomed to sending their children to Britain to be educated, a practice which accelerated following the German government's decision to disrupt the schooling of Jewish students. The JRC attempted to help lessen the financial burden created for these parents, and instituted a Schools and Training Sub-Committee whose purpose was to seek out free and reduced-fee places for children from Germany.[1]

The German Act Against the Overcrowding of Schools and Universities mandated that, after 25 April 1933, Jewish students were to comprise a maximum of $1\frac{1}{2}$ per cent of the number of Aryans enrolled, while those admitted before the measure was enacted were to be dismissed where their number in a school exceeded 5 per cent of its total registration. As in the Law for the Reconstruction of the Civil Service (1 April 1933), Jews who served the Fatherland in the First World War were recognized, and minor exceptions to the regulations were permitted for students whose fathers were front-line soldiers in that war and for those whose parents, married prior to enactment of the law, had one Aryan parent or two Aryan grandparents.[2]

Jewish students permitted to continue in attendance at state-run schools often suffered verbal abuse and physical attack, not only from fellow students, but also from teachers. Following a visit to Germany in 1937, Joseph Cohen reported that Jewish children in attendance at state schools in country districts were made to sit by themselves and were not permitted to participate in lessons. Christian children were forbidden to speak with them. Jewish children were excluded from games and sports and were not allowed to bathe in pools used by other children.[3] Students barred from attendance and those for whom it was no longer a viable proposition were in a seemingly hopeless situation, particularly in areas where there were insufficient children to warrant a Jewish school. Their middle-class parents had sent them to state schools, often hoping thereby to enhance their prospects of securing places in universities when they were older. Now their aspirations of higher education for their children were shattered. In an attempt to ameliorate the basic education problem, the Reichsvertretung extended placement available at existing Jewish schools in large communities. Similar facilities were provided for children in some rural areas and in small communities.[4]

Until the months leading up to the war, school fees and other expenses for children at school in Britain could be paid in Germany through the Exchange Rate Mechanism, which, in co-operation with the Reichsvertretung, the CBF had established in 1934. Under this arrangement, parents deposited the Deutschmark equivalent of the cost of their children's school fees and maintenance with the Reichsvertretung, and in exchange the CBF paid those charges in pounds sterling. The moneys received by the Reichsvertretung were put towards the expenses incurred in its programme of training for agricultural and industrial employment of potential emigrants, and for emigration aid. Thus, the children's parents, the Reichsvertretung and the CBF were able to finance their respective activities without providing the German government with hard currency. Late in 1938, when many parents had lost their sources of income, or had been forced to leave Germany and were no longer able to reimburse the Reichsvertretung, the CBF accepted responsibility for payment of the children's fees, thus enabling them to continue their education without disruption.[5]

American-educated Anna Essinger, headmistress of the Herrlingen (boarding) School in the Schwabian Jura mountain region, was apprehensive about the future education of Jewish children in Germany. Essinger was filled with foreboding when, following the German government's boycott of Jews on 1 April 1933, repercussions were evident even in the small village that housed her school. Essinger concluded that 'Germany was no longer a place in which to bring up children in honesty and freedom' and, already aged 54, she decided that she would remove her school and its students from their home base. Essinger lost no time in doing so. With the support of friends in England, she applied to the

Board of Education and the Ministry of Labour for permission to establish a school there. Neither the Board nor the Ministry objected to the education plan she presented, and when she had secured the approval of the Home Office to bring students and personnel to England, Anna Essinger signed a seven-year lease on Bunce Court, a large manor house in Otterden, Kent. In August 1933 she moved there together with 71 of her students and almost all of her staff.[6]

The number of German students at Bunce Court and at other boarding schools in Britain grew appreciably following enactment of the Nuremberg Laws. Not all were children of Jewish parents; some were non-Aryan Christians whose parents were at political risk, or were under arrest. Local families in Otterden supported Anna Essinger, and during school holidays they would often invite her students to stay with them. Local families were later instrumental in helping siblings and parents of these children to find refuge in Britain.[7]

The Inter-Aid Committee for Children from Germany

Immediately following enactment of the Nuremberg Laws, the CBF invited the Save the Children Fund (SCF) to support its appeal for hospitality from schools and families in Britain for non-Aryan Christian and Jewish children at risk in Germany. But at that time the SCF was not prepared to co-operate, fearing that 'the Fund might very easily be left with a number of children on its hands'.[8] Some months later, however, the SCF reversed its stance. It was following this decision that on 24 March 1936 the CBF, the SCF, the Society of Friends and other agencies concerned for the welfare of children organized the Inter-Aid Committee for Children from Germany with the 'special object of looking after Christian children of Jewish Extraction'.[9]

The Inter-Aid Committee, on which Sir Wyndham Deedes served as chairman, functioned as a sub-committee of the SCF, its financial backing provided in large part by the CBF, with lesser amounts coming from the SCF, church dioceses, synagogue organizations, the Women's Appeal Committee for German and Austrian Women and Children, and individual contributors.[10]

In co-operation with the Reichsvertretung and the Society of Friends in Germany, the Inter-Aid Committee sought out children whose anti-Nazi parents had been arrested or were in danger of incarceration, or were Jews suffering particular harassment at the hands of the Nazis. The Jewish children brought to Britain under Inter-Aid Committee auspices were financially supported by the CBF.[11]

Within months of the formation of the Inter-Aid Committee, a small number of individuals who had sponsored children on their personal recognizances attempted to renege on their obligations by asking the JRC to accept financial responsibility for the youngsters in their care. Neither Otto Schiff nor the JRC was amused. They agreed to advise these sponsors that the JRC would provide maintenance for the youngsters for two weeks, following which they would be returned to their parents in Germany. Otherwise, said Otto Schiff, 'we shall have large numbers of children being sent over in this way and left on our hands'.[12] The threat to those concerned was sufficient, and they resumed their obligations.

It can be assumed that Otto Schiff reported these incidents to the Home Office and asked for its support, for he was soon able to inform the JRC that the Home Office had ruled that unaccompanied German children would no longer be admitted for the purpose of education unless families, approved by the Home Office, would undertake to be financially and morally responsible for them.[13]

As knowledge of the work of the Inter-Aid Committee became known to privately owned boarding and day schools in Britain, many of them generously offered reduced-fee or free places to children from Germany. Private families also offered accommodation to children who could not be housed in school facilities.[14] None of these benefactors sought publicity. Consequently, although the Inter-Aid Committee helped some 471 children, 45 per cent of whom were Christians, to gain admittance to British schools prior to November 1938, its efforts and the generosity of the schools and families concerned were almost unknown to the general public.[15]

The plan to rescue children

Few in Britain, even within the Anglo-Jewish community, had met German-Jewish refugees, whether children or adults, especially since many of them were concentrated in a small area of north-west London. Following *Kristallnacht*, this was to change. BBC radio and the national press broadcast vivid accounts of the Nazi rampage and the destruction and looting of Jewish orphanages and schools, and other communal property. Wilfred Israel, in Berlin, pleaded with the Council for help in saving the lives of children. Poignant stories of bands of children, many on the verge of starvation, roaming the countryside, touched the heart of the British public. Neville Chamberlain's recent promise of 'peace in our time' seemed hollow and deceptive in the face of these events.[16]

Jews in Germany, as in Austria some months earlier, were confronted with the knowledge that there was no longer a future for them unless they left the country. The realization of their plight was devastating. Parents who had never thought of being separated from their progeny now felt unable to ensure their safety, and while many could not immediately arrange their own departure from Germany, their anxiety for the children was unbounded. The Council in London shared their apprehension. Children were, after all, the future of the community.

The Council estimated that there were some 60,000–70,000 children in Austria and Germany who needed to be brought to safety. If large numbers of unaccompanied children were to be transported to Britain, an agency dedicated to their needs would be essential. The mandate of the Inter-Aid Committee was far too limited for such an enormous undertaking, while its funding was totally inadequate. It was apparent to all those concerned that the Council was the only organization in Britain with the will and the potential fund-raising ability to shoulder this mammoth task. In its haste to install a plan of action, no attempt appears to have been made to seek out experts to recommend the best means by which so great an undertaking might be handled. Nor was it deemed necessary to convene a committee that included representatives of both the orthodox and non-orthodox Jewish communities, who would participate in the selection of families to host children, especially those from orthodox religious backgrounds. Members of the 'cousinhood' had long been used to dominating the boards and executive committees of communal institutions. It probably did not occur to them that wider involvement would encourage greater community participation in the plan of rescue. While every effort would be made to place Jewish children with Jewish families, where their religious and dietary requirements would be catered to, these arrangements would be made following the youngsters' arrival.[17] The Council's major concern at this stage was the rescue of the greatest number.

Helen Bentwich (née Franklin), wife of Norman Bentwich and a niece of Lord Samuel, a political activist and a member of the important Education Committee of the London County Council, was asked to organize a plan for the evacuation of children from Germany. Dennis M. Cohen, who was chairman of the Emigration Department of the JRC, was invited to join her in formulating the scheme of rescue.[18]

It is to their credit that, within a few days, they presented the rescue plan that they had drafted.[19] They envisaged bringing 5,000 children to Britain in groups of 200–500 and housing them in summer holiday camps located along the south coast of England, which were vacant during the winter months. They anticipated, quite erroneously, that a majority of children would be ten years old or younger. The public at large would be invited to offer to accommodate these children and a system of inspection of potential foster homes would be instituted. The minimal standards set by the London County Council for foster homes for British children, in regard to sleeping accommodation, etc., would apply in the housing of the refugees. When the bona fides of individuals offering foster care for children were approved and as children left the reception camps to join foster parents, other youngsters would be brought over from the continent. Rescue was paramount.

With seemingly little discussion, the Bentwich–Cohen plan of rescue, endorsed by James McColl, a Member of Parliament, and by Major Geoffrey H. Langdon, a businessman affiliated with the JRC, was approved by the Council with the recommendation that the scheme be operated in co-operation with the Inter-Aid Committee.[20] Until this time the Inter-Aid Committee had dealt with children on an individual basis. Now, through its liaison with the Paulusbund, the Reichsvertretung, the Kultusgemeinde and the Friends Service Committee in Vienna and Berlin, it would be especially helpful in locating numbers of non-Aryan Christian children.

The Bentwich–Cohen plan anticipated that the Council would obtain Home Office approval for the admission of children and young persons, up to the age of seventeen; and that all children would be educated and trained for employment in demand in Britain, or in countries to which they might immigrate. In compliance with British immigration regulations, each child would be medically examined and its good health confirmed before leaving Germany or Austria. The Council hoped that an adequate supply of teachers and social workers would accompany the children from Germany and Austria, but if that were not possible, refugees already in Britain would be invited to fulfil those needs. The Bentwich–Cohen plan was accepted as proposed, and it was to provide the basis of operation of the Movement for the Care of Children from Germany (hereinafter the Movement), by which the Inter-Aid Committee was soon subsumed.

A sub-committee, chaired by Lord Samuel, whose members were Helen Bentwich, Dennis Cohen, Rebecca Sieff and Gladys Skelton, the secretary to the Inter-Aid Committee, was instituted by the Council to assume responsibility for the children's programme. Lola Hahn-Warburg joined them soon after she arrived from Germany. The Rothschild and Montagu Samuel banks again provided the Council with loans, which enabled the rescue scheme to be activated.[21]

While the plan was being formulated, the Council called an emergency session and invited Anglo-Jewish community leaders to attend. The main topics of discussion were the pressing need to bring children to safety, and the havoc and suffering caused by *Kristallnacht.* It was agreed that a national appeal to the 'non-Jewish public in the non-Jewish press', the first such appeal since the beginning of the German-Jewish crisis, would have to be launched to help finance the rescue mission. It would be signed by Lord Samuel and the Earl of Selborne. Another appeal to the Jewish community was scheduled to appear in the Jewish press that week.[22]

Government approval of the rescue scheme

The participants in the emergency session, which was held on 14 November, agreed that it was imperative for a delegation to meet Prime Minister Chamberlain without delay, so that their apprehension regarding the position of Jews in Germany might be conveyed to him, and approval secured for the plan to rescue children. On the following day (15 November), Lord Samuel asked Chamberlain to receive a delegation whose members would include Lord Bearsted, the Chief Rabbi, Neville Laski, Lionel de Rothschild and Chaim Weizmann.[23] Neville Chamberlain responded immediately, agreeing to meet them in the House of Commons at 5 o'clock that evening.[24]

Lord Samuel told the Prime Minister that, while those present realized that Britain alone could not be called upon to protest the outrages, they hoped that in concert with other countries the government would make diplomatic representation to Germany. In response the Prime Minister said that he saw no chance of the British government exercising any effective influence on Germany in regard to its persecution of Jews. Indeed, he thought any representation by Britain might make the situation of the Jews in Germany even worse.[25]

Lord Samuel then described his delegation's primary concern, asserting that while he was not proposing that Britain's doors 'should be widely thrown open' to the 300,000 Jews who were potential emigrants from Germany, he was asking the Prime Minister to consider, as a matter of urgency, permitting the entry of children and young persons to the age of seventeen, whether Jewish or Christian, for whom organizations in the Anglo-Jewish community would give a collective guarantee of support. The children would be educated and trained with a view to their ultimate re-emigration.[26] In response, the Prime Minister indicated that the request was a matter for the Home Office to decide, but he said that he was prepared to support any suggestion regarding the children which that department approved. Lord Samuel also urged the Prime Minister to ensure that the government assigned additional staff to both the Home Office and British Consulates throughout the expanded Germany, so that the accumulated backlog of applications for visas might be more expeditiously handled.

Chaim Weizmann reminded the Prime Minister that the Jewish community had been refused permission to bring 10,000 children from Germany to Palestine. Now Weizmann asked only that the government permit 1,500 children, and 6,000 young men, whom the Germans had incarcerated and whose release could be secured, to enter the territory. The Prime Minister was not stirred by Weizmann's appeal. He committed himself only to 'benevolent interest' in the matters before him and, in bringing the meeting to a close, asked his visitors to discuss their concerns with the relative government officers at the Home, Foreign and Colonial Offices.[27]

On the following day (16 November), the Cabinet evaluated the Prime Minister's meeting with Lord Samuel and his colleagues. Ministers were of the opinion that Chamberlain had been less than sensitive in his treatment of the delegation. They were concerned because his responses to their requests would be open to criticism, particularly in the United States, where Britain's policy of appeasement of Germany had been widely criticized. Lord Halifax, the Foreign Secretary, suggested that American opinion might be more favourable if Britain gave a lead that would force the United States itself to take some positive action. In response, the Prime Minister suggested that Jewish refugees might be permitted to use Britain as a temporary refuge (a category not covered by Britain's immigration laws), and the Home Secretary agreed to consider this proposal. The Cabinet also discussed the capacity of the Dominions to absorb immigrants and the economic implications that were involved, but it made no recommendations for action, except to draft a statement on the decision which the British government 'proposed to take immediately to deal with the Jewish problem'. At the same meeting, Lord Halifax asked his colleagues if an appeal might be launched in Britain to persuade people to support the immigration of elderly Jews who, he said prophetically, would endure a terrible fate if left in Germany. Lord Halifax's concern does not appear to have been generally shared by his Cabinet colleagues, and the Prime Minister said it 'might be considered later'.[28] However, Sir Samuel Hoare, the Home Secretary, was persuaded by Lord Halifax's concern, and it was agreed to admit, without limit, persons over the age of 60, provided that their support was guaranteed for life by a responsible person or organization. Nathan Laski (father of Neville Laski) indicated that the Manchester Jewish community was ready to enlarge its Home for the Aged and contribute towards the maintenance of 50–60 elderly refugee relatives of its members. The Home Office was further prepared to admit other individuals whom the Council indicated had a fair prospect of emigrating within eighteen months of their arrival in Britain.[29]

Another week was to elapse before Lord Samuel and members of the Council were able to meet the Home Secretary. They were accompanied by a representative of the Inter-Aid Committee, and by Bertha Bracey and Ben Greene of the Society of Friends, who had just returned from a visit to Berlin, where they were involved in helping Christians leave German territory.[30] The Home Secretary told his visitors that the government would give them its full support, and that he would facilitate their rescue efforts. He repeated this promise when he addressed the House of Commons during a debate on the position of refugees that same evening, the positive tone for which was set by a long and impassioned speech delivered by Noel Baker, on the situation of Jews in the Greater Germany. The Home Secretary informed the House that children whose maintenance could be guaranteed either by voluntary agencies or by individual sponsors would be admitted without restriction. He placed no upper limit on their number. 'Here is a chance', he said, 'of taking the young generation of a great people, here is a chance of mitigating to some extent the terrible sufferings of their parents and their friends.' This was certainly a different attitude towards Jewish refugee children from that adopted by the United States Congress.[31]

Following the Home Secretary's statement in the House of Commons, the Home Office immediately simplified admittance procedures for unaccompanied refugee children up to the age of seventeen. Most importantly, the children would no longer require German government travel documents or visas from British Consulates. Instead, the Home Office would provide a two-part identity card for each child which would serve as a travel permit; one half would be retained by the Home Office, the other by the Inter-Aid Committee, which was authorized to issue them. Each card, to be presented to an immigration officer on arrival in Britain, would record the child's personal data and have his or her photograph attached.[32]

The Movement for the Care of Children from Germany

The voluntary agencies now regrouped under the mantle of the newly formed Movement for the Care of Children from Germany with Lord Samuel and Sir Wyndham Deedes as co-chairman. When they retired in April 1939, Lord Gorell, a former minister of the Crown, soldier and educator, served in their stead until the Movement ceased to function in 1948.[33] Lord Gorell's committee now included representatives of the

Jews, the Nonconformists and the Roman Catholics, and since he admitted to being none of these, he accepted the role of representative of the Church of England. Lady Reading (formerly Viscountess Erleigh) was the committee's deputy chairman. Elaine Laski, and Lola Hahn-Warburg were the most active of the committee's members, and both women continued to serve the needs of the refugee children long after the Movement ceased to function as an entity. Sigmund Gestetner and Rabbi Maurice Swift were the other Jewish representatives on the committee. The Rev. Canon George L. Craven (later Monseigneur, and then Bishop) represented the Roman Catholics and the Rev. William W. Simpson spoke for the Nonconformists.[34] F.W. Lindgren served the Movement as its accountant and Helen Bentwich was its honorary secretary during the first six months of its operation.

As originally envisaged, the Movement undertook to care for both Jewish and non-Aryan Christian children and provided medical insurance for them – an extension of its pledge to the government that no child would become a charge on public funds. The Movement also agreed that children would emigrate from Britain before they were eighteen, or on completion of training, which the Movement promised to provide.[35]

In anticipation of the children's arrival, vacant holiday camps on the south coast of England were rented as planned. The response to the appeal in the British press was generous. People across the economic spectrum and numerous philanthropies, religious organizations, denominational schools, training centres and a diversity of other organizations sent contributions, all wanting to succour the most helpless of the Nazi victims. Offers of help came also from individuals who had received the brochure distributed by the Movement calling for sponsors for children, and from others who responded to advertisements placed in the Jewish and national press by desperate parents in Germany and in Vienna, or by friends or relatives in Britain who were themselves unable to accommodate a child. The prospect for the rescue of a large number of children looked sound.

The Movement had set itself a formidable task. Even before its life-saving operation could begin, a vast, hastily assembled and inexperienced staff, composed mostly of volunteers, was besieged by heart-rending appeals for help from parents in Austria and Germany and frantic relatives already in Britain. A suite of offices were rented at 69 Great Russell Street in Bloomsbury, where the staff attempted to cope with the many hundreds of visitors each day, and to answer thousands of letters and telegrams and innumerable telephone enquiries. In the midst of the tumult, contact had to be maintained with the Reichsvertretung in Berlin and with the Kultusgemeinde in Vienna, both of which were charged with selecting, documenting and assembling the children.

In Germany, the Reichsvertretung co-ordinated the lists of children that were submitted by Jewish community organizations, the Paulusbund and the Friends Service Committee, whose workers were spread throughout the country. In Austria the Friends Service Committee co-operated with the Kultusgemeinde and helped locate children of non-Aryan Christians who were at risk. As far as was possible, all the children were chosen according to the urgency with which it was deemed necessary to evacuate them: orphans who had been made homeless, teenage boys who would be released from concentration camps if immediate emigration plans could be demonstrated, boys in danger of incarceration, children whose parents were in danger of imprisonment or had been incarcerated, and other youngsters for whom there was no visible means of support.

A few days before the rescue operation was to begin, a rumour reached London that 500 homeless children were gathered on the German–Dutch border.[36] The Council asked Norman Bentwich to investigate the situation and he left immediately for Amsterdam. There he met Gertrude Van Tijn, Mrs Karmarsky, Mrs Grunewald and others who represented both the Dutch Committee for Jewish Children and the Committee for non-Aryan Children from Germany. The rumour proved to be false, but Gertrude Van Tijn assured Bentwich that the German authorities did not prevent unaccompanied children from crossing the border. On the contrary, she said, 600 youngsters had already done so, and they were being cared for in facilities provided by the Dutch government. Accommodation was being prepared for another 800 youngsters whose unauthorized arrival was anticipated before the end of the year. A small number of stateless children, probably of Polish origin, had also crossed the border and the government was anxious for them to emigrate without delay. Bentwich arranged for them to be absorbed into transports carrying German children *en route* to Britain. Bentwich also learned that a number of Dutch families had offered to accommodate children from Germany, but since the government expected them to emigrate with little delay, they were housed together in hostels.[37]

Gertrude Van Tijn also told Bentwich that her committee had received appeals from Jewish children's organizations in Hamburg and in Breslau for help in evacuating youngsters who were at risk. Bentwich's immediate response was to telephone Max Hamlet, the former manager of the Warburg Bank in Hamburg, who was in close contact with the Jewish community organization there and knew the extent of the problem. Hamlet confirmed that there were such children in Hamburg and in Breslau, and on Bentwich's assurance that the youngsters would be received in England, Hamlet agreed to arrange for 300 of them to leave for England via Hamburg during the course of the coming week.[38]

Confident that the youngsters would leave, Bentwich returned to London, only to learn that ferries from Hamburg berthed in Hull on the east coast, a port far less accessible to London than the port of Harwich, at which ferries from the Hook of Holland docked. The routing of the children would have to be changed. Bentwich contacted Max Hamlet again and asked him to cancel the evacuation via Hamburg, advising him that it would be rescheduled through the Netherlands. Bentwich also informed the Reichsvertretung of developments. He then called Dennis Cohen, the co-author of the rescue plan, and asked if he would travel to Berlin without delay to assist in assembling the first transport. Cohen would act as a contact with the British Consulate if difficulty was encountered in securing permission for the children to leave on the travel documents provided by the Home Office.

Dennis Cohen needed no persuasion and, together with his wife, left for Berlin on the following day. The Reichsvertretung, with its usual efficiency, had already successfully negotiated with German immigration and transport officials, who had approved the use of the British travel documents and the route of travel from Germany to the Netherlands. Railway carriages had also been reserved for the children's use. The youngsters destined for the first transport had already been selected by the Reichsvertretung and their personal data entered and photographs affixed to travel documents provided by the Home Office. Certificates of good health were also attached. Documentation for the first group of children was complete. Members of the Reichsvertretung staff performed a herculean task in ensuring that children and their parents or guardians were kept advised of arrangements for their departure, and directions for boarding the train in Berlin or at a stopping point *en route* to the German–Dutch border. With these formalities settled, the Reichsvertretung now began to assemble the children and Dennis Cohen was pleased to inform London by telephone that the first *Kindertransport* was being readied to leave Germany.

Gertrude Van Tijn had promised Norman Bentwich that members of the Jewish and Christian children's committees in the Netherlands would meet trains carrying the children when they crossed the German–Dutch border, accompany them to the Hook of Holland, and ensure that they were embarked on ferries leaving for Harwich. The Netherlands committees fulfilled this promise with magnanimity until the war halted the children's evacuation movement.

10

The Movement of Children from Germany Begins

IN ONLY THREE WEEKS following the pogroms of *Kristallnacht* in November 1938, the Council in London had organized reception facilities and secure placement for a large number of refugee children. In Germany, almost miraculously, and with only 24 hours' notice of the date and time of their departure, the Reichsvertretung assembled 200 children, the youngest of whom was only seven. Among the youngsters were a number who had been living in the Children's Home in Fehrbellinerstrasse, or in the Ahawah, Auerbach and Reichenheim orphanages in Berlin; others had been in a Jewish girls' secondary school. All of these the Nazis had plundered or razed to the ground. Several were German-born children of Polish fathers; others were children of parents who had been deported to Poland. Some were children of German parents whose fathers had been incarcerated. Others were teenaged boys from Hamburg and Breslau, included in the transport because they were in immediate danger of incarceration.[1]

This diverse group of youngsters, accompanied by eight teachers, left Berlin for the Hook of Holland on 1 December 1938. When the train pulled out of the railway station, parents who had accompanied their children dispersed silently, not wishing to draw attention to themselves, and all of them wondering whether they would ever see their offspring again. Many children had been led to believe that they were off on a holiday and were happy to be on the train. It was a harrowing experience for those who knew why they were leaving, and who feared that they might be removed by the guards at the German border. But after an uneventful journey overnight, the train arrived in the Netherlands. There the children were welcomed by members of the Children's Refugees

Committees, who, true to their word, smoothed their path, provided hot drinks and food, and helped them embark on the ferry *Prague* which awaited them in the harbour. Movement staff and volunteers in London were informed by telephone of the children's progress.

Some hours later, Geoffrey Langdon, together with other volunteers and Movement staff, greeted this first *Kindertransport* on its arrival at the port of Harwich. A children's home, in Broadstairs in Kent, had been loaned to the Movement to house the youngest children; the holiday camp at Dovercourt Bay, just two miles distant from the dock at Harwich, and another at Pakefield, near Lowestoft, were still in the process of being made ready when the *Prague* docked.[2] It was Friday, 2 December. There was joy and relief in the knowledge that the first rescue mission had been accomplished without incident. The eight teachers who accompanied the children were compelled by the German government, as were future escorts, to return.

When the youngsters arrived, the Chief Rabbi, Dr Herz, wrote to Lord Samuel, not to congratulate him on the rescue of the first 200 children, but to remind him that a supply of kosher food was made available to the camp only through the efforts of Rabbi Solomon Schonfeld acting on his behalf. The Chief Rabbi also informed Lord Samuel that he was incensed to learn that Dennis Cohen had arranged for the next group of children to leave Berlin on Saturday, 10 December, 'a step strongly defended by Mr Norman Bentwich'.[3] Travel on the Sabbath was anathema to orthodox Jews.

A day before the first group of children arrived in England, the Council Executive had met to discuss recent events in the Greater Germany. They feared that the Nazi government would soon 'take such steps as would lead to the practical extinction of Jews in Germany' – a foreboding that persuaded the Council to try 'to get as many Jews as possible out of Germany immediately'.[4] A sense of urgency rather than impiety had certainly been dominant in Dennis Cohen's decision to arrange the day of departure for the second transport. The Chief Rabbi, for his part, wished to avoid orthodox Jewish children being compelled to desecrate the Sabbath, especially when their travel did not appear to him to be urgent. Following intervention by the Chief Rabbi, Rabbi Baeck in Berlin was advised that the second transport would not have to leave before Monday, 12 December, a change in plan for which he was most appreciative.[5] The Movement took heed and, where possible, planned transports for days other than the Sabbath. Kosher food was also made readily available at the reception centres.

Before returning to London from Amsterdam on 26 November, Norman Bentwich was introduced to Gertruida Wijsmuller-Meijer, a Christian member of the Netherlands Children's Refugee Committee, who spoke fluent German. Bentwich told Mrs Wijsmuller-Meijer of the dire situation of Jewish children in Vienna and of the Council's anxiety regarding their safety if they were to remain. He asked her if she would travel to Austria and attempt to secure permission for children there to leave for England. Bentwich explained that this would necessitate an approach to Adolf Eichmann, head of the Jewish Office of the Gestapo. Members of the Friends Service Committee in Vienna were providing support to the Kultusgemeinde, but it was judged best that an outsider should intervene with Eichmann.

Gertruida Wijsmuller-Meijer, a seemingly fearless woman, the wife of a Dutch banker, agreed to approach Eichmann, and she flew to Vienna. One less courageous might not have acceded to Bentwich's request, especially since he had not provided her with a document designating her the Council's intermediary.[6]

Adolf Eichmann was not easily persuaded of Gertruida Wijsmuller-Meijer's bona fides. However, she eventually won him round, and he agreed to permit unaccompanied children to leave for England. He ordered that the first group leave Vienna a week later, on 10 December, the Jewish Sabbath.[7]

On leaving the meeting with Eichmann, Gertruida Wijsmuller-Meijer telephoned Lola Hahn-Warburg in London, who assured her that the Movement would receive the children. The staff of the Kultusgemeinde and members of the Friends Service Committee immediately began the task of selecting and registering youngsters. Despite the short notice given them, they were able to document and make ready 630 children, the youngest of whom was only two-and-a-half years old. On the evening of 10 December, after conclusion of the Sabbath, the children left Vienna's suburban Huttledorf railway station on a ten-coach train.[8] The large number of youngsters crowded on to this first transport is probably explained by the Kultusgemeinde's fear that Eichmann might not permit another to leave.

When the children arrived in the Netherlands on the morning of 12 December, members of the Dutch committees were there to greet and nourish them. All but 100 were helped to embark on the *Prague*, which again was docked ready to leave for Harwich. Three days later, when the next group of youngsters *en route* to England arrived from Germany, the 100 children held back from the first transport from Vienna joined them aboard the ferry bound for Harwich.[9]

Those responsible for planning the children's transports from Germany and from Austria worked without respite. In little more than four weeks they had documented and assembled 1,950 children and arranged their movement to the Hook of Holland, from where they had been ferried to Harwich. It is difficult to conceive how in those first weeks of the Movement's operation, it was able to receive so many children and arrange for their care.[10] Working from the offices at 69 Great Russell Street in London, the volunteers and limited paid staff brought some order to their efforts, despite the seeming confusion.

The Movement had not been in a position to consider a children's rescue organization in Bohemia or Moravia before these areas were occupied by the Germans. Fortunately, Nicholas Winton, a 30-year-old English stockbroker whose German-Jewish parents immigrated at the turn of the century, had business dealings in Prague. In January 1939, Winton undertook to rescue children whose parents were prepared to entrust them to him. Winton established an office in Prague, and the Movement provided him with children's travel documents. Through his valiant efforts and those of other volunteers, including the school teacher Trevor Chadwick and a colleague employed at the preparatory school run by the Chadwick family, Winton was responsible for the rescue of 664 Czech children. Chadwick, who remained in Prague for several months, co-ordinated his efforts with the Movement in London and secured many guarantees from sponsors in Britain, thus aiding in the rescue.[11]

Winton located numerous families in Britain who were willing to sponsor children from Czechoslovakia, and when their documentation was completed he dispatched the youngsters by train, or by plane, to London. On arrival there, the cost of their maintenance was borne by the Czech Trust Fund, which had been established by the British government. The German and Austrian youngsters among them were aided by the Movement. In his search for sponsors and faced with distraught parents hoping to save their children, Winton and the parents accepted offers of accommodation from Christian missionaries working in Czechoslovakia. The Barbican Mission to the Jews helped save a number of children 'from tyranny and death', but its purpose in so doing, as the Mission itself noted, was 'not merely humanitarian ... it is to glorify our Master and lead souls to him. It is our first and foremost intention to give these children a true Christian home ... and give them an opportunity to know the Lord Jesus as their Saviour.'[12] As a result of their proselytizing activities, a number of these children, whose parents did not survive the war, were lost to Judaism.

Arrival in Britain

When ferries or ships carrying children from Germany and Austria arrived at Harwich or Southampton, representatives of the Movement boarded and 'docketed' each child with a label, thus confirming its new 'refugee' status. Children living in towns in northern Germany were sometimes able to board transatlantic liners in Hamburg without having to join transports travelling via the Netherlands. These youngsters disembarked when the liners docked in Southampton and were met there by Movement representatives.[13] Government medical officers examined children as they landed and marked the labels provided by the Movement. Customs officers stamped the date of arrival on the Home Office travel documents. This was the extent of the immigration formalities. In general, the children's luggage was not searched, and when dutiable articles were declared no duty was imposed.

Children with relatives, family friends or other sponsors in Britain who had agreed to bear the total cost of maintaining children, and others who were Movement grant recipients of 12s 6d a week toward a child's support, presented no problem. The credentials of sponsors had been investigated and accepted. These guarantors would already have been notified of the date and time of arrival of the children for whom they would care, and of the railway station, usually Liverpool Street, in London, where they would meet. The Movement would also advise relevant committees in areas of children's destinations. Guarantors or their representatives would assemble in a waiting room at the station until trains arrived. They would then be asked to acknowledge, in writing, responsibility for the children they had vouched to support; they would be introduced to the youngsters whose care they had undertaken, and together sponsors and children would set off for the sponsors' homes, perhaps in London or its environs, or a town or village that might be located some hundreds of miles away. This experience alone must have traumatized children, particularly those who had no common language in which to communicate with their hosts. Even if the hosts were members of the children's extended families, the children's recent experiences at the hands of the Nazis must surely have scarred them. For most of the children there was also a cultural divide. They had been raised in a German ethos, which was very different from the one most of them were about to encounter. It was a painful and difficult period for most of these young refugees. That so many of them appeared to adjust to the totally different and alien environment into which they were thrust reveals something of the resilience of the human spirit.

When 'unguaranteed' children, those without sponsors, completed Customs formalities, they were escorted from the harbour and driven to the reception centres, sometimes accompanied by the chaperones who had been allowed to travel with them from the continent. The largest of these centres was the summer holiday camp at Dovercourt Bay, which Anna Essinger was invited to administer. Together with some of her teachers and older students at Bunce Court, she attempted to create an orderly and serene environment for the newcomers at the camp. Local residents and stores in Dovercourt and Lowestoft showered the children with gifts of clothing and toys, and doctors and dentists among them offered their services without cost to the Movement.[14] The Movement had taken the precaution of insuring the children 'against 72 serious illnesses and mishaps'.[15]

But Dovercourt and Lowestoft were summer holiday camps and the huts (grandiosely called chalets) that housed the youngsters were unheated. Despite makeshift attempts at heating, the children were uncomfortably cold during most of the time they were there. Other physical accoutrements, parental assurance and basic comforts of home were also lacking, but an advantage of the camp setting was that the children still had each other with whom they could communicate and share the experience, which made adjustment to the new setting a little less traumatic.

Offers to accommodate 'unguaranteed' children had to be codified and then investigated by local committee representatives to ensure both their suitability and the financial security of the head of the household. The committees were created to locate families throughout the country who were ready to open their homes to individual children, and the committees also monitored the children's progress. No child could be sent to a home that had not been visited and approved of by a representative of the Movement, usually a member of one of the almost 100 local committees, whose number was to double within a short time.

There was no shortage of potential foster parents ready to care for the younger children.[16] Those who offered to accommodate the 'unguaranteed' children among them were a disparate group, but there was a prevailing trend in the type of child all of them preferred: 'Nearly everybody wanted a small child – a blue-eyed, fair-haired boy or girl', a child under ten years of age.[17] There was no difficulty in placing those children.

The Movement had assumed that there might be a problem in finding families ready to foster teenagers, a majority of whom among the boys had been sent to England because they were most at risk, and this was indeed the case.[18] Appeals in the Jewish press for middle-class sponsors for these youngsters brought only limited response from both the strictly orthodox and those who were not rigorously observant Jews.[19] While there was generous financial support from the Jewish community for the rescue of children, the same spirit of beneficence was not manifest when foster families were needed to care for the teenagers among them, as a result of which observant Jewish children sometimes found themselves cared for in Christian homes.

Some teenagers found themselves in somewhat exalted surroundings, cared for in groups on the estates of wealthy Christian and Jewish families. Others were accommodated in Quaker boarding schools and some were fostered by Quaker families. But these teenagers were an exception. The JRC housed other teenagers in hostels – a generic term often used to describe one or more houses where a number of youngsters were accommodated – some supervised by the B'nai Brith or the Agudath Israel, both offering food in compliance with orthodox Jewish law, or by the Movement and refugee committees in Birmingham, Cambridge, Glasgow, Leeds, Liverpool, London, Manchester, Oxford and other areas.

Many offers to foster children were received from Christian and Jewish families whom the Movement classified as 'working class'. In the prevailing economic depression the Movement felt compelled to refuse them, reasoning that if the wage-earner lost his job he would no longer be in a position to support the child. There was also the knowledge that the majority of children came from middle- and upper-middle-class homes and the Movement hoped to place them with families of similar background.[20] The paucity of offers from 'suitable' sponsors for older children in the first weeks of the Movement's operation resulted in a diffusion of funds from the primary goal of rescue to one of maintenance for youngsters already in the country. This lack of sponsors caused the Movement to call a temporary halt to the inclusion of unguaranteed teenagers.[21] However, when the Reichsvertretung advised the Council that 150 boys between the ages of fifteen and seventeen would be released from concentration camps if their emigration was assured, approval was immediately given for them to be brought to England.[22] Notwithstanding, the lack of Jewish sponsors and the never-ending shortage of funds to sponsor the children's movement from the continent continued to blight the Movement's life-saving operation in the short time available before it was halted by the war.

The Baldwin Fund

On 8 December 1938, Lord Baldwin (the former Prime Minister, Stanley Baldwin) made an impassioned radio appeal to the public at large, for contributions in support of refugees. The appeal, sponsored by *The Times*, was carried simultaneously in the United States.[23] Baldwin stressed that the Jewish community was caring not only for Jewish, but also for non-Aryan Christian refugees. Compared to their effort, he said, the Christian contribution towards the aid of refugees until this time had been insignificant. He explained that many refugees now arriving in Britain were unaccompanied children of the Christian as well as of the Jewish faith, and he urged support of his appeal.[24] The response, from more than a million people throughout the British Isles, was indeed outstanding.

Together they donated some £522,000. Government officials were not unmoved by the appeal, for they enabled people of moderate means to contribute through a scheme whereby sixpenny saving stamps could be purchased at Post Offices and books filled with 40 stamps delivered to the Baldwin Fund for redemption.[25] A separate 'Mother's Day' appeal, in May 1939, raised a further £23,000.[26]

The Baldwin Fund, of which Lord Victor Rothschild was a trustee, was aware of the extraordinary expenditures being incurred by the Movement, and at the end of January 1939 it made an emergency allocation of £30,000 to the Council.[27] The Baldwin Fund ultimately awarded the Council a total of £237,000, the major portion of which was allocated to the Movement for the care of children.[28] These moneys were carefully husbanded, and they sufficed to maintain a large number of children until October 1941, at which time the Home Office undertook to bear a major portion of the cost of their support.[29]

Early in February 1939, the Council authorized 1,500 fully guaranteed children to be brought to England, on the understanding that those aged sixteen would be trainees, for whom the German Jewish Aid Committee (formerly the JRC) would be responsible. Its Training Department would place these youngsters in employment or in training situations and would maintain contact with them until they immigrated or reached the age of eighteen.[30] By this administrative formality the Movement was relieved of responsibility for the care of many of the older children.

Also in February 1939, the Council decided that the Movement's hastily organized procedures needed to be systematized, and its expanding activities co-ordinated. A review had become necessary because accommodation in transit centres was not being made readily available for children still awaiting evacuation from Austria and Germany. The camp at Lowestoft had been vacated in December 1938 when a storm at high tide had forced its evacuation. Two hundred and fifty of the children from Lowestoft were accommodated temporarily at the St Felix Girls' School in Southwold, whose staff generously forfeited their Christmas vacation to care for them. Fifty of the boys were then housed in a Salvation Army home at Harwich and a small number of girls at the Cliff Hotel. Others were accommodated at Dovercourt and in hostels.[31]

The Movement's treasurer, Berthold S. Kisch, undertook the review of the Movement's activities and organization. On completion of his study he recommended that volunteers, particularly those handling individual offers of sponsorship for 'unguaranteed' children, be replaced with salaried case workers and other officials. A professional staff, he observed, would also systematize efforts to secure additional offers and guarantees; they would decide the allocation of children to individual homes and hostels, and would maintain a routine of inspection. If children were unhappy with host families, they would be relocated. In short, noted Kisch, from the moment contact was established in Germany or another country, responsibility for each child should rest with the professional staff until each was settled in his or her new home.[32] It is to the credit of the Council that, despite pressures from volunteers who preferred their own often arbitrary methods of placement, and despite the added costs involved, Kisch's recommendations were soon instituted and a more structured organization developed.

The Movement was incorporated as a company with limited liability in April 1939, and an Executive Committee replaced the sub-committee.[33] Sir Charles Stead, a retired member of the Indian Civil Service, was appointed executive director, a position he held until the outbreak of war, when he was replaced by Dorothy Hardisty, the secretary to the Movement. Dorothy Hardisty served the children devotedly and firmly throughout the war years until she retired in 1948, when the Movement was disbanded and its activities were absorbed by the JRC.[34]

In an effort to conserve its funds, the Movement decided that from April 1939 guarantors would be asked to deposit £50 to cover the re-emigration costs for children aged twelve and older. This was intended to protect the Movement against the prospect of having to pay the cost of overseas transportation, since the children were expected to leave the country by the time they reached the age of eighteen. However, the £50 deposit requirement was soon rescinded when it was realized that it gave preference, on transports to England, to children with friends or relatives ready and able to make this payment. It was retained, however, for sponsors of nominated children. The Council emphasized that no child had been prevented from leaving Austria or Germany because a deposit had been lacking.[35]

Short-term sponsors

Among potential foster parents were those who were prepared to care for children for periods of two to three years, but who did not wish to commit themselves for longer terms, particularly since the end of the German crisis could not be foretold. The Movement had not considered acceptance of these limited-term guarantees, because it could not vouch for the availability of funds for the children's support when the guarantees expired. The issue was thrust to the forefront when the Movement hesitated to accept an offer, to maintain 100 children for a period of three years, from the Refugees Committee in Birmingham.[36] Berthold Kisch cautioned that refusal of the offer would have grave consequences, not least of which would be to discourage public interest in rescuing children, and a possible diminution in contributions to the Movement. He urged that 'it ought to be possible to devise some means whereby no reliable offer of any kind remains unutilized'. Heeding his counsel, and despite the fact that the Movement could not predict its future funding, it agreed that all offers of temporary sponsorship, for periods of not less than three years, would be accepted. The Council immediately authorized the transport to England of 200 younger children whom short-term sponsors were ready to receive.[37] A small number of older children, who had been housed in hostels, also profited from this decision, when they were moved to private homes. Another 150 children without individual sponsors benefited when the Council made funds available for the construction of dormitory accommodation at Bunce Court.[38] In addition, fully guaranteed sponsorships were accepted for a further 500 children.[39] But war was approaching, and a continued shortage of sponsors for teenagers was a factor in limiting the number who reached Britain before war was declared.

In anticipation of their immigration to Palestine, a number of teenagers joined agricultural training centres, which were financed by the Council, the Women's and Children's Appeal, and the Youth Aliyah Movement.[40] A substantial financial infusion for the Youth Aliyah programme had come from Eddie Cantor, an American-Jewish actor, who toured England for sixteen days in July 1939 and raised £100,000 for its operation. Some teenagers had begun agricultural training while still in Germany and moved easily into these centres in Britain, where, at the outbreak of war, some 500 boys and girls, aged between fourteen and sixteen, were in residence.[41]

The Movement was aware of the educational aspirations of a majority of the children, but it was in no position to finance them. Although it recognized that children from educated families could not be compelled to become members of the 'working classes', the Movement none the less decided that, in keeping with the limited educational aspirations of a majority of parents in Britain, refugee children, like their British counterparts, would become wage-earners, or apprentices. There were foster parents and regional refugee committees whose generosity enabled children to continue their schooling beyond the age of sixteen, but the number who profited was limited. None the less, refugee youngsters attended night school, after paid employment during the day, out of all proportion to their number, and many of them won competitive scholarships and gained admission to technical colleges and universities.[42] Hosts and members of university faculties in Cambridge and Oxford encouraged refugee children living among them to continue their education.

In the six weeks between 5 July and 23 August 1939, Samuel Echt and Else Itzig were able to escort 124 children, the youngest of whom was seven, from Danzig to England.[43] The Movement also secured places in specialized institutions for handicapped youngsters, including a group from the Jewish School for Deaf and Dumb Children in Berlin-Weissensee, who arrived on 19 July, accompanied by Dr Felix Reich.[44] Full co-operation was extended to the Polish Jewish Committee, which had undertaken to rescue children of German birth who had been deported with their Polish parents to Zbonszyn. George Lansbury, MP, was the committee's sponsor. The first of these children reached London on 15 February 1939, and before the outbreak of war 185 youngsters, including 25 who were stateless, arrived from Zbonszyn.[45]

When the camp at Dovercourt was abandoned at the end of March 1939, the teenagers still housed there were transferred to hostels. Some were maintained by the B'nai Brith; others wholly or in part by the Movement or Jewish Refugee Committees in different areas of the country. In the months leading up to the war, the number of hostels was expanded. In August 1939 the B'nai Brith had almost 900 children in its care, some in hostels, others in schools or with individual families in London, or in the provinces.[46]

One hundred boys and a number of teachers from the ORT school in Berlin arrived in Britain four days before the onset of war, and they were housed, temporarily, at the Richborough Camp until facilities were made available in Leeds. The school's plant and machinery, which had been supplied from England, was scheduled to follow them, but this plan was foiled by the advent of war.[47]

On the day that the youngsters from the ORT school arrived in England, Sir Charles Stead advised the Home Office that, until further notice, the Movement could accept no more children. Until this time, contact with the Home Office on policy issues had been Otto Schiff's prerogative.[48] Stead's message was relayed from the Foreign Office to Sir Neville Bland, the British Ambassador at the Hague, and he was asked to inform the Netherlands government of Stead's advice, so that it might refuse permission for the usual transport of children across its border with Germany. The Home Office also indicated that Stead had told them that the Gestapo had seized eighty or more children's travel documents and were sending another party of youngsters across the Netherlands frontier *en route* to England, but evidence supporting this latter claim has not been found.[49]

News of the impending Netherlands border closure was relayed to the Reichsvertretung in Berlin, where 60 youngsters, 29 sponsored by the Movement and 31 destined for Youth Aliyah agricultural training centres, were making arrangements to travel to England. The Reichsvertretung was determined that they would leave. Communicating by telephone, the Reichsvertretung, the Council and the Youth Aliyah agreed that Stead's advice to the Home Office should be ignored. Gertruida Wijsmuller-Meijer in the Netherlands was told of this development, and she agreed to meet the youngsters at the Dutch–German border. The Reichsvertretung, now well-experienced in dealing with the transport authorities, was able to board the youngsters on a train bound for Cologne. From there another train took them to Cleve on the German–Dutch border, where Gertruida Wijsmuller-Meijer awaited them aboard a bus that she had hired for the journey to the Hook of Holland. The frantically conducted telephone conversations between London, Berlin and Amsterdam, and their successful conclusion, revealed the spirit in which those concerned for the rescue of children had worked. At the Hook of Holland, a steamship whose departure had been delayed to await their impending arrival conveyed the youngsters to Harwich, where they arrived on 1 September. Those sponsored by the Youth Aliyah left immediately for the agricultural training centre at Gwrych Castle, north Wales, where they received a joyous and enthusiastic welcome. The Movement provided housing for the remaining children.[50]

In the nine hectic months from December 1938 to the outbreak of war, the Movement had registered 9,354 of the children it had rescued. Almost 90 per cent of them professed the Jewish faith. Ten per cent were Christian members of Catholic or Protestant churches. Several hundred other children who were brought to Britain by the Movement were sponsored by independent agencies who did not register them with the Movement. Tragically, further transports, including one of 180 youngsters in Prague, were unable to leave Europe during the last days before the war began.[51] Sir Charles Stead, who had not been happy in his position with the Movement, left abruptly as soon as war was declared – a move that Lord Gorell noted without regret.[52]

Dramatic escapes

A small number of children on the continent were able to escape the Germans when war was declared. Providentially, Italy did not enter the war for another nine months, so that 77 youngsters, sponsored by the Youth Aliyah, were able to proceed from Trieste to Palestine aboard the *Galilea*, an Italian ship. The Jewish Refugees Children's Committee in Amsterdam arranged passage for 100 German and Austrian youngsters on another Italian ship of the Lloyd Triestina line. They had been promised Palestine immigration certificates on arrival in Trieste. There is no record to suggest that they were disappointed. Other children holding Palestine immigration certificates, who were unable to leave Germany in the days following the invasion of Poland, were taken to Denmark and to Sweden, where they were placed aboard ships bound for Palestine.[53]

Another dramatic escape was experienced by refugee children in

Amsterdam following the German invasion of the Netherlands, on 10 May 1940. Aerial bombardment and airborne troops had brought the country under German control within a few days. Amidst the ensuing confusion, the indefatigable Gertruida Wijsmuller-Meijer plotted the escape of refugee children whom the government had housed in the Amsterdam Municipal Orphanage. With the help of friends, she managed to commandeer vehicles into which she crammed more than 60 of the youngsters. She drove with them to the harbour at Ijmuiden, where they boarded a coal-carrier, the *Bodegraven*, on to which many other refugees were already crowded. The ship sailed for England during the evening of 14 May. A British patrol vessel, believing that it was an enemy ship, fired on it off the Cornish coast. Fortunately, the captain of the *Bodegraven* was able to change course, and he landed his charges safely at the port of Liverpool.[54]

British government authorities housed the children, temporarily, with Christian families in Wigan, Lancashire, while they sought more permanent accommodation through the north-west regional office of the Movement. However, when news of the 'Amsterdam children', as they became known, filtered through to the Jewish community in Manchester, they decided to care for the youngsters, and provide them with a Jewish environment. The Manchester community raised funds for the children's care, and they were soon transferred to two hostels in Manchester, which the Jewish War Refugees Committee sponsored.[55]

While the exact number of Jewish refugees who fled to Britain following the German occupation of Belgium, France and the Netherlands is not known, 44 Jewish adults and 132 children from those countries, who had reached Britain before the end of 1940, had registered with the JRC.[56] In 1944 the JRC reported that 27 persons who had arrived during that year had registered with the committee, bringing to 516 the number known to have arrived since the outbreak of war.[57]

11

Children in Britain during the War

REFUGEE CHILDREN WERE still adjusting to Britain's alien environment and mores when Germany invaded Poland on 1 September 1939. Many of the children were already attending school and were conversant in the English language. Some were comfortable in the new setting and looked forward to the time when their parents might join them in Britain, or when they would travel to the United States or another country to be reunited with them. Jews were permitted to emigrate from Germany until 1941. For a small number of children this dream was fulfilled during the war years. Others had to wait until the cessation of hostilities. For too many youngsters there was to be no reunion, and the years of the war were anxious and difficult for them and for their hosts.

Evacuation begins

The fragile sense of security now enjoyed by many of the children was soon to be shattered. In the early 1930s, the British government had laid plans for the evacuation of children from cities and coastal areas considered vulnerable in time of war.[1] Bombing raids on England during the First World War were still in the conscious memory and children were to be spared similar experiences in future conflicts.

The German invasion of Poland was the signal for Britain to begin the evacuation of its children from London and other potentially vulnerable areas. Accompanied by their teachers, hundreds of thousands of school-age youngsters, cardboard-boxed gas masks and their name tags hanging by string around their necks, boarded trains together with mothers of under-school-age children and pregnant women. They all left for unknown destinations. It was estimated that before the end of September 1939 more than a quarter of the population had changed their address.[2]

The refugee children's records maintained by the Movement contained personal information, Home Office entry permits, certificates of identity and other items that were irreplaceable. The Movement, fearing possible destruction of the records by enemy action, relocated them, together with the fifteen staff members of its After-Care Department and five refugee teenagers to assist them, to a rented house in Hindhead, Surrey.[3] The Movement was also concerned that communication with London might be cut as a result of enemy action, and that difficulty would then be experienced in maintaining contact with children whose whereabouts, following evacuation, had sometimes taken many weeks to re-establish. To avoid such a possibility, twelve regional committees were created, corresponding to the twelve Regional Defence Areas into which Britain had been divided. Area refugee committees were grouped under their appropriate regional committee, and each was linked to the central office of the Movement and was asked to maintain contact with children, to visit them and to notify regional offices when problems arose, or when children were moved from one foster home to another. Billeting officers alone were permitted to sanction such moves. Local committees were also specifically instructed to ensure that children were placed in homes where they were able to receive religious instruction in their own faith, which was to be given in consultation with the nearest Jewish or Christian clergyman, who was usually in contact with the Movement, or the Christian Council for Refugees.[4]

Refugee children under the age of fifteen were not exempted from the government evacuation scheme, and many of them faced the trauma of being moved from Jewish families and hostels in communities into which they had been received only weeks or months earlier, to new surroundings and different areas of the country, where extempore arrangements often meant that there were no Jewish families to receive them, and no other refugee children with whom they might maintain contact. There had been neither the time nor the machinery to select the type of home which would accord with each child's religious background, and it is doubtful whether, had time permitted, such accommodation would have been found. Fourteen hostels and their refugee residents were fortunate enough to be evacuated as units, so their children remained together.

Many refugee children were boarded in the homes of caring Christian families, where they adjusted to their new surroundings and to their hosts. Others fared less well and felt isolated and abandoned. Among Christian hosts there were those who sought actively to proselytize Jewish children, despite their knowledge that this was prohibited by the Movement, and some of them were successful in their endeavours. British-born Jewish children faced similar upheaval and placement, but they spoke the language of their hosts and most were able to communicate with at least one of their parents.

Children who were evacuated to areas of Jewish settlement were less isolated than those in rural areas. A group of 50 orthodox Jewish boys, most of whom had arrived from Cologne, Czechoslovakia and Zbonszyn only weeks earlier, were evacuated from the Cricklewood and Dollis Hill areas of London to Bedford. There, Arnold Harris, who had moved his family from London, provided 'club' and synagogue facilities for them.[5] In Birmingham the Jewish Refugees Committee accepted an offer from the Christadelphian Ecclesia to provide a home for 20 strictly orthodox Jewish boys under the supervision of Dr and Mrs Albert Hirsch, while Dr and Mrs Samuel Echt, who had brought youngsters from Danzig to London, cared for 30 boys and girls in a hostel sponsored by the JRC.[6] A number of other hostels were established by refugee committees throughout the country and in Northern Ireland, and they were often staffed by caring couples who were themselves refugees and who provided a semblance of Jewish family life for the youngsters in their charge.

The Movement notified Jewish communities when refugee children were housed in their localities, and they were asked to contact Jewish children who were billeted in Christian homes.[7] Wartime conditions added to the difficulty of communication, particularly since much of it had to be conducted by mail, and it was often neglected. A home telephone was a luxury for a majority of families in Britain, and fuel for cars was strictly rationed during the war. The Chief Rabbi attempted to ease dietary concerns of orthodox and other dietary-observing Jewish evacuees, when he announced in a BBC national radio address that all that was required of them during the national emergency was to refrain from eating forbidden meat and shellfish. But in many homes a radio, like a telephone, was a luxury item, and there were children and others who were not aware of the Chief Rabbi's message.[8]

The placement of Jewish evacuees

Harry Sacher was troubled when, soon after the first children arrived from Germany, he learned of the possible placement of Jewish children with Christian families. He was worried that they would be influenced by their non-Jewish environment and that they might become converts to Christianity. Sacher's concern was given serious consideration at the time, but it was decided that in general such placement ought not to be prohibited, particularly since the number of children who could be rescued would depend on the offers of accommodation from families willing to care for them, whether in Jewish or non-Jewish households.[9] When Harry Sacher raised his objection in January 1939, little or no thought had been given to the possibility that Jewish sponsors would not come forward in sufficient numbers. Nor was it known that war would ensue before the end of the year, and that children would be evacuated to areas of the country where there were few, if any, Jews.

The religious education and placement of Jewish children was of concern to the CBF. In 1936 Sir Robert Waley Cohen and members of the Women's Appeal Committee had been distressed to learn that children, sponsored by the Youth Aliyah movement, were being sent to private homes and agricultural settlements in Palestine which did not observe Judaism or were anti-religious in character, and an investigation into their concern was mounted in Jerusalem.[10]

The Movement was adamant that it was the right of every child to receive religious instruction according to the faith of his or her parents, and that divergence would not be countenanced without their permission where this might be obtained, or unless a child had reached the age of discretion in matters of his or her own religious conviction. In support of its stance, the Movement created the Joint Emergency Committee for Jewish Religious Teaching, which would serve children in areas of evacuation.[11] None the less, because children were housed with Christian families, Harry Goodman and other members of the Union of Orthodox Hebrew Congregations relentlessly condemned the Movement, both in letters to the Jewish press and in a nationally distributed pamphlet.[12] So serious were the charges levelled at the Movement that, in a private letter to Lord Gorell, the Chief Rabbi 'mildly' disassociated himself from them. But there was also acrimonious correspondence on the subject of proselytization of Jewish children from the Chief Rabbi to Lord Gorell, some of which, as noted by Lord Gorell, was undoubtedly instigated by Rabbi Schonfeld, who headed the Union of Orthodox Hebrew Congregations.[13]

Lord Gorell responded to the attacks – the most recent of which had appeared in the *Jewish Chronicle* only a few days earlier – at a conference of regional committee representatives of the Movement held in January 1941.[14]

> What has struck me most in this series of attacks is that they do not give credit to the Movement at all for anything whatever that it has done. The Movement after all, for four years and more, has been responsible for these thousands of children. A great number of our workers are voluntary and I should have thought that common generosity would have thrown out some slight word of thanks, especially as the Movement has from the start set its face like flint against any form of tampering with the religion of the children. We have set as a principle that every child must, as far as possible, continue in the religion of its parents, in the hope that many of the children will be reunited with their parents hereinafter and, in any case, we are not a body concerned with changing the religion of the children. I feel, therefore, that the attacks were not only unwise, but also ungenerous.[15]

It was difficult for the Movement to remove children from unsuitable families with whom they had been billeted. In legal terms it had no authority to do so, since it was not their legal guardian, and the government had not yet appointed one to act in the children's best interest.[16] The Chief Rabbi attempted to influence the Home Office to appoint him a joint guardian with Lord Gorell, but the decision was made to appoint only one, for all the children, both Christian and Jewish. The relationship between the two men became somewhat less rancorous when the Bill 'to provide for the guardianship of infants who have come to the United Kingdom in consequence of war or persecution' was enacted into law in

1944 and Lord Gorell was appointed the sole guardian for all the children brought to Britain by the Movement.[17] Until then, the youngsters seemed caught in an almost inextricable net of conflicting rights, interests and duties, claimed not only by foster parents, but also by various committees and rabbinical and church groups.

The Movement's position was strengthened by the Guardianship Act, and it was able to take decisive action and remove children from unsuitable families, particularly those influencing them to accept baptism. A number of children were already lost to Judaism, and the Union of Orthodox Hebrew Congregations continued its attacks on the Movement.

When the Movement ceased operations in 1948 and Jewish children still in its care were made the responsibility of the Jewish Refugees Committee, the Rev. Ephraim Levine was appointed their legal guardian.

In a report prepared by the Board of Deputies, entitled *Jewish Children Brought to England*, which investigated the influence of non-Jewish placement on Jewish children, the Movement was vindicated. The report emphasized that 'considerable care was taken to bring the children to this country and place them in good homes'. It was not the fault of the Movement, the report continued, 'but of the Jewish community at large that these homes were often non-Jewish': a reflection, in large measure, on the community's lack of response to the Movement's appeal for Jewish families to foster children. The report stressed that it was imperative that the children still in non-Jewish homes be contacted and efforts made to try to move them to a Jewish environment and thus regain them for Judaism.[18] It was felt strongly that too many Jews had already been lost in the Holocaust.

Refugee children after the war

In 1945 the Movement advised the Home Office that 6,720 children, of whom 4,648 were now over the age of eighteen, were still in its care. The Home Office was asked to clarify their future position, so that they might know whether they would be permitted to remain in Britain as permanent residents, whether they would be allowed to take up employment and whether they would be granted British citizenship if they remained. The question of adoption of children by persons who had nurtured them since their arrival in Britain was also raised, the Movement emphasizing the need for the power of revocation in the event that parents were found. It also stressed the need for the government to provide overseas transportation for children whose parents or other relatives overseas were ready to receive them, so that they might build new lives without further delay. The Movement also made the Home Office aware that many of the children who were orphaned might be heirs to property confiscated or stolen from their parents by the Nazis. Although Lord Gorell was still the children's legal guardian, he was not the guardian of their property and so could not act for them in this regard. In 1947 the passage of restitution laws enabled individual claims for the restitution of property that was located in the United States or French Zones of military occupation of Germany to be filed through the legal facilities provided by the CBF. A restitution law was enacted in the British Zone only in 1949, and children's claims for property there were also filed through the CBF.[19] Only after the reunification of Germany on 9 November 1989, coincidentally the 51st anniversary of *Kristallnacht*, could compensation claims be filed for property confiscated or forcibly sold in the former East Germany.

By 1947 it was clear that a majority of the children rescued by the Movement would remain permanently in Britain. A number who had been orphaned in the Holocaust were adopted by the 'parents' who had fostered them. Some children had married, within or outside the refugee orbit, and had families of their own. Other children were reunited with their parents or other relatives in Europe, in the Americas, or in Israel when that state was created in May 1948. Again, all of them had to adjust to a new way of life in a different setting.

In an unprecedented move, in 1947 the British government offered naturalization (citizenship) to Movement children who were under 21. The Home Office simplified formalities and abandoned fees for the more than 1,300 youngsters whose parents had not survived the Holocaust.[20]

Almost all of the children sponsored by the Movement were registered in the JRC index. Fifty years after the end of the war, the index is still vital to searches by former Movement children and other refugees who continue to seek, and to find, family members now spread throughout the world.

Kindertransport Associations, through which links are maintained and reunions held, have been established by former Movement children now domiciled overseas. In June 1989, a 50th anniversary reunion, organized by Bertha Leverton, one of their number, was held in London. More than a thousand *Kinder*, their spouses and progeny from countries around the world attended and renewed their special relationship. It was a poignant experience for them and their invited guests.

Perhaps the most moving tribute to the Movement, the CBF and the British people was made by Kurt Fuchel, president of the Kindertransport Association of New York. In April 1995, following an address by the author to a gathering of 100 former Movement children, their progeny and other family members in New York City, Fuchel wrote to the CBF:

> A few days ago we celebrated the Day the War Ended, and I am moved to express my own and my fellow *Kinders'* gratitude to the CBF and the other organizations, and to the people who persuaded the British government to admit us to the UK and thus save our lives. This gratitude is the more profound as I eagerly await the birth of my first grandchild, and realize that I owe this gift, this continuity, and so much else to people like you who worked for humanitarian and just causes 55 years ago.[21]

12

Kitchener Camp at Richborough in Kent

THE COUNCIL HAD BEGUN with the rescue of children. It was now bent on helping to secure the freedom of men and teenage boys incarcerated by the Gestapo following *Kristallnacht*.

Even before *Kristallnacht*, Wilfred Israel, in Berlin, wrote to Viscount Samuel at the House of Lords, imploring him to help rescue men and boys who were being indiscriminately arrested by the Gestapo, incarcerated and physically abused. They were in mortal danger, he said.[1] Following *Kristallnacht*, Israel made a similar plea to the British Ambassador in Berlin, which the Embassy conveyed to the Foreign Office in London.[2] The Reichsvertretung was already in negotiation with the Gestapo, and Rabbi Baeck confirmed that they would release internees if they left the country without delay. He asked the Council's help in offering to accommodate men on their release. The Council readily agreed.[3]

Funding for the camp

Lords Samuel and Bearsted, Sir Robert Waley Cohen, Simon Marks and Neville Laski had already asked for a meeting with Lord Winterton at the Foreign Office, to discuss their plans for a camp that would house the released men until they completed plans for immigration to third countries.[4]

At their meeting at the Foreign Office on 7 December 1938, Lord Samuel told Lord Winterton that it was their hope that the government would provide funding for this life-saving undertaking.[5] He then repeated a threat made by the Gestapo to Rabbi Baeck in Berlin: if another assassination of a German officer took place, the Jews in Germany would be exterminated. It would not be difficult, said Lord Samuel, for extremists to 'arrange' for an assassination, the consequences of which were too grim to contemplate.[6]

Lord Winterton, known for his forthright manner, and for an irascible temper, appeared sympathetic, but he repeated a statement he had recently made to Anthony de Rothschild, when he reminded him that the governments at Evian had agreed that public funds would not be spent for the benefit of one class of refugees.[7] He said that, if government aid were granted for Jewish refugees, 'not only would this inevitably cause anti-semitism in the countries concerned, but it would also mean a demand for Spanish refugees, assistance to Chinese refugees, etc.' There was always the fear, he observed, that the moment the Germans and other anti-semitic governments found that countries were prepared to finance the migration of Jews from their territories, they would expel their Jewish populations.

Sir Robert Waley Cohen found difficulty in containing his frustration and anger at Winterton's response, since it axiomatically precluded government support for the Council's life-saving activity. It was imperative, said Sir Robert, that the government grant financial assistance for a camp. If this were not done without delay, 'all the potential refugees would be dead'.[8] Lord Winterton had no rejoinder. Further discussion ensued, but it was evident that the government would not risk German censure by financing the Council's endeavour to save Jews. If Jews were to be rescued, the Anglo-Jewish community would have to finance the effort as it had done since the crisis began.

Funding a site

Lord Samuel and his colleagues had been under little illusion regarding the government's response to their request for funding of the proposed camp, and they had already agreed that even without government aid they would establish a facility to house men released by the Germans. Lord Bearsted, a former army man with a pragmatist's eye to the matter at hand, asked Lord Winterton whether there was a disused First World

War prisoner-of-war camp which might be put at their disposal. Lord Winterton said he knew of none, but that he saw no reason why objection would be raised if one were available, particularly since it would not involve monetary endorsement by the government.[9] Winterton had already consulted with the Home Secretary and he had been assured that the Home Office would not object to camps being established for transmigrants.[10]

On 3 January 1939, Sir Robert Waley Cohen and Norman Bentwich met Sir Alexander Maxwell at the Home Office, to discuss the plans for the camp. Dr Otto Hirsch was in London and accompanied them. Dr Hirsch told Maxwell of difficulties that Jews were now experiencing in obtaining passports from the German authorities. Maxwell was sympathetic, and agreed that in such cases the men would be permitted to enter Britain on permits that the Home Office would issue. The permits would be similar to those issued to the children who were being brought to England by the Movement.

Sir Robert confirmed that the Council's plan was to select men whose ages would range between 18 and 35. In exceptional circumstances, he said, older men might be included. In a subsequent letter to Norman Bentwich, the Home Office confirmed that it would be glad to facilitate arrangements for the men to come to Britain, providing that they would neither seek employment without authorization nor be permitted to become a charge on public funds.[11] The Council was also asked to ensure, as far as was possible, that men whose prospects for immigration would materialize at a comparatively early date would be selected 'so that vacancies may be made in the camp ... and facilities thereby afforded for the admission of other selected refugees to fill such vacancies'.[12] Now that the Home Office had confirmed that it would raise no bureaucratic obstacles, the Council could initiate its plan of rescue.

The Council contacted refugee committees in Belgium, France and the Netherlands, and asked for their co-operation in accommodating some of the thousands of men whose release could be secured if they were able to leave Germany without delay. Morris Troper was approached in the hope that the JDC would contribute towards the cost of establishing the camp in England, and Norman Bentwich wrote to Paul Baerwald in support of the Council's request. In response Paul Baerwald agreed to provide the Council with $100,000 (£20,000) for the purpose.[13]

A sub-committee to locate and prepare a suitable campsite had already been organized. Sir Robert Waley Cohen, of whom Norman Bentwich said 'action follows suggestion as the thunder, lightning', served as its able chairman. This was an aspect of the Council's efforts to which Waley Cohen could relate unhesitatingly, and he gave it his best. Working with him were Harry Sacher, a director of Marks and Spencer, Frank Samuel, a colleague of Sir Robert's at the United Synagogue and managing director of Unilever, Leslie Prince, an accountant, and Norman Bentwich.[14]

The site selected for the camp was one on which Major Ernest Joseph, the architect of Woburn House, had worked during the First World War. It had housed 40,000 men and was located at Richborough in Kent, close to the port of Dover. It was now in private hands. Sir Robert Waley Cohen and Ernest Joseph negotiated a lease on the property for three years at what was considered a nominal rent of £350 a year. The sub-committee decided to renovate two camps on the site: the Kitchener Camp, which would accommodate the men and the kitchens; and the Haig Camp which would house social and educational activities. All the buildings on the site were of cement block and asbestos tile roofing. They were in a derelict condition and needed total refurbishment to render them habitable: roofs needed replacement and all the buildings required new electrical wiring, new flooring and toilet facilities, among other necessary major repairs.[15]

Restoration and refurbishment

Ernest Joseph, who was known as the 'father' of the Jewish Lads' Brigade, undertook to supervise the work of restoration at the camp.[16] He had no difficulty in persuading a number of generous building companies and individuals in the building industry to donate much of the material and equipment needed to make the camp habitable. He was also able to enlist the services of Walter H. Marmorek as resident architect and building supervisor. Marmorek, an architect who had fled from Vienna, had set up office in London. He moved to Richborough to direct the camp's labour force.[17]

The 48 huts in the Kitchener Camp, each of which would house 48 men, had to be made weatherproof, as did the kitchens and two dining halls, each capable of seating 1,500 men. Similar restoration of an administration building was needed in the Haig Camp, in which it was planned to locate a social hall and reading and writing rooms.[18]

Norman Bentwich visited Captain Frank Foley, the sympathetic British Consul at the Passport Control Office in Berlin, to confirm the Home Office assurance that the men's admission to England would be eased by the provision of block entry permits by his office. He also called on E.N. Cooper at the Home Office in London to ensure that the men would be permitted to work on the camp's restoration, since under normal conditions they would need to secure work permits from the Ministry of Labour.[19]

The first party of 100 German-Jewish craftsmen released from concentration camps arrived in England at the end of February 1939. They were immediately transported to Richborough to begin the work of renovation. As demanded by the Home Office, the Council had provided assurance, with no knowledge that it could be fulfilled, that the men would not remain in Britain permanently. It had also guaranteed that they would not seek employment outside the camp unless special permission was granted.[20] The guarantee was a bureaucratic formality at this juncture, and without it the men would not have been permitted to enter the country.

Poldi Kuh (later Captain Kew) served as foreman of the crew of craftsmen brought to Richborough from Germany. Kuh, a born leader, had been director of a Reichsvertretung retraining camp in Germany. There was no need to remind him or his workers of the urgency of their task. Together with volunteers from the Jewish Lads' Brigade, whose services Ernest Joseph had secured, and with the help of the brothers Jonas and Phineas May, a Mr Banks and other volunteers, they laboured to prepare the camp. They laid pipes, constructed a water tower, and rebuilt huts and wash-houses. They installed a drainage system and electric light. They also built concrete roads. Within a few weeks, scores of huts had been made habitable, baths and showers installed, and a dining hall and offices renovated and equipped. A gymnasium and a cinema were planned for the Haig Camp. Oscar Deutsch, a scion of the movie industry, donated the cinematographic equipment, and Mrs Lionel de Rothschild, her cousin Mrs Alfred Sassoon and a number of friends from the locality attended the opening celebration in June.[21] Through the generosity of the Unilever company, Frank Samuel was able to provide all the food and toiletries needed in the camp. This enabled the Council to maintain each of the men at a cost of less than ten shillings ($2.50) a week.[22]

The work on the camp was completed in the incredibly short space of six months. Each week, as buildings were readied, groups of men released from concentration camps in Austria and Germany arrived at Richborough. Before the end of April 1939, 1,000 men were in residence. The Council also housed 200 refugees from Czechoslovakia who had arrived in England during the Passover festival, for whom the Czech Refugee Committee had not yet been able to provide accommodation.

Although the government had simplified procedures for the men's entry, they still had to pass through British Customs. Generally, this procedure was without incident, but on one occasion a group of 127 men were detained by Customs officers when a variety of musical instruments were found in their possession, items which were dutiable unless there was evidence that their owners were musicians. In response to questions about the instruments, the men removed them from their cases, tuned them as though readying for a concert and then at a beat from their 'conductor' rendered *Tales from the Vienna Woods* to the delight of all those present.[23]

While the camp at Richborough was being made habitable, Edward Baron and Julian Layton, both long-time CBF benefactors, and Mr Gentilli, selected because he was a Christian, paid an extended three-week visit to Vienna at the Council's behest to select men for transfer to Richborough. Julian Layton, a stockbroker, had already given years of voluntary service to the Council and to the JRC and, in February 1938, had visited Germany and Austria at the Council's request. Layton had also dealt with Adolf Eichmann, whom he was scheduled to meet again in Vienna in November 1938. On the eve of *Kristallnacht*, Eichmann had telephoned Layton and cautioned him to stay away.[24]

In Vienna, Layton and his colleagues selected men between 18 and 45, who could produce evidence that they would be able to emigrate from England to third-country destinations within a 'reasonable' period of time. While conducting interviews, Julian Layton became aware that no provision had been made to rescue men who were without friends or relatives overseas able to secure entry permits or visas for them. Inadvertently, these men had not been provided for in the Council's plan of rescue. When Layton and his companions returned to London, they recommended, and the Council accepted, that men in the latter category be admitted to the Kitchener Camp at Council expense. The JRC would attempt to find immigration opportunities for them. The Council also agreed that men who had contacts overseas, especially those whose relatives in the United States had provided them with 'affidavits of support' attesting to their ability to maintain them on arrival, would be asked to obtain funds for their maintenance in the camp and for the cost of their overseas transportation. The Council would try to conserve its funds for those who were indigent.[25]

In June 1939, Dr Lowenherz of the Kultusgemeinde in Vienna advised the Council that, as a result of its intervention, 1,400 men had been released from Buchenwald and Dachau, and that 400 of them had already left Austria for Richborough. Lowenherz believed that the only hope of salvation for the others, who had no relatives overseas, was to leave for Shanghai. The cost of their travel to Shanghai, where entry visas were not required, could be paid in local currency by the Kultusgemeinde. However, the men were without funds, and Lowenherz asked Lord Reading whether the Council would provide each of them with £50 for landing money.[26] Lowenherz was not aware that the Council and the JDC were contributing to the support of indigent refugees already in Shanghai. The Council refused his request, since the men's arrival in Shanghai would only add to the number who would have to be supported.[27]

City of refuge

Few of the men who arrived at Richborough had much in the way of personal possessions, other than clothing and the tools of their trade. Some 100 of them were in poor health and had to be removed from the camp and accommodated in boarding houses.[28] Many were professional men or skilled artisans, 60 were doctors or dentists, some were industrialists and agriculturists, a few were scientists and scholars. Doctors among them with Italian qualifications, which were recognized in Britain, were permitted to practise in the camp. Some of the medically qualified men were appointed ships' doctors on British vessels. Qualified dentists set up a clinic in the camp, saving the Council large sums that would otherwise have had to be spent for dental treatment. Some men were permitted to accept employment as farm hands or as technicians outside the camp, while others employed their artistic talents to earn money. All earnings went into a common fund and each man in the camp received a small and equal amount of pocket money. If rail tickets had to be purchased for visits to consular offices or to the JRC in London, they were paid from the common fund. The camp was a self-governing city of refuge, equal in its population to the neighbouring Cinque Port of Sandwich.

The camp was rich in talent; its musicians included a former conductor of the Stuttgart Radio Orchestra. These artists formed a dance band, a first-rate orchestra, an instrumental quartet and a choir. The Royal Academy of Music donated musical scores to the camp, and the Mayor of Sandwich presented the dance band with two saxophones. Visitors who lived in nearby communities flocked to the concerts given each Saturday evening, and during the summer of 1939 both the orchestra and the dance band were in demand at events in local coastal resorts, activities which the Home Office approved. Many local residents befriended the men during the weekends, when they were free to travel outside the camp, and these newly won friends aided wives of the men, and their children, in their escape from the Nazis by securing the women's entry to Britain under the Domestic Servants' Scheme.[29] Almost all of the children of the 650 married men in the camp were brought to Britain by the Movement, and 350–400 wives entered the country on domestic labour permits. A small number of Christian non-Aryan men from Berlin and Vienna were brought to the camp, and a pastor, appointed by the Christian Committee, also took up residence.[30]

A number of teachers living in the surrounding area taught English voluntarily in the camp, and soon the men were able to produce an English-language newspaper. They also developed a popular 'university', whose courses were given by the camp's own scholars and scientists, lawyers and former community leaders.

Jewish education and religious life were directed by two rabbis, Werner van der Zyvl, a liberal, and the other a conservative Jew. The

Chief Rabbi Dr Herz hoped to assert the authority of the office of the chief rabbinate at the camp, but the Council did not accept this proposition. The Richborough Camp Committee extended an invitation to Dr Herz to visit the camp, where he was accorded a warm welcome and which he reported to the Council had been satisfactory. As an aside, he asked the Council whether in the event that he was unable to attend meetings of the Executive, to which the Council had appointed him two weeks earlier, he might send Rabbi Solomon Schonfeld as his alternate. The response was firmly in the negative. There were many issues on which the Council did not see eye to eye with Rabbi Schonfeld, an orthodox, articulate and well-educated man, who used somewhat unorthodox means to rescue rabbis, rabbinical students and other synagogal dignitaries and their families. Rabbi Schonfeld often secured their entry into Britain by assuring the Home Office that guarantees for their support were in hand, and he would then request financial aid for their maintenance from the Council. By these means, Rabbi Schonfeld aided several hundred individuals to reach England.[31]

Preparations were under way to rebuild another area of the Richborough Camp to accommodate several thousand more men, but the war put paid to these plans. Among the last groups admitted to the camp were 30 young men who had been in temporary housing since disembarking from the *St Louis*, and the 100 boys from the ORT school in Berlin, whose transport to England the Movement had arranged.[32] When war was declared, 3,500 men, almost one-quarter of whom were non-Aryan Christians and political refugees, were housed in the camp. Of the total number in residence, 2,000 had come from Germany, 1,000 from Austria and 500 from Belgium, Czechoslovakia and Italy.[33] Two hundred and twenty wives and children of men in the camp, who had lost their employment, were also housed temporarily until accommodation elsewhere was found for them.[34]

When the war began, the men in the Kitchener Camp dubbed themselves 'the King's Own Loyal Enemy Aliens'. The government classed them only as 'enemy aliens', and all of them were required to appear before Aliens Tribunals. All but two individuals were cleared as 'refugees from Nazi persecution', who could be trusted.[35] Julian Layton joined the army at the outbreak of war, and served as the Officer-in-Charge of the civilian section of the Kitchener Camp. The War Office appointed Lord

Reading, now a Lieutenant-Colonel in the army, Commanding Officer of the Pioneer Corps Training Centre (1939–41) at Richborough.[36] His staff of nine British officers and a number of non-commissioned officers were assigned to train the refugees who volunteered to join the armed services, although it took some time before the War Office agreed to allow enemy aliens to enlist. Some refugees did not volunteer because they were awaiting immigration visas; others feared that their relatives still in German-occupied territory would suffer if the German authorities learned that they had volunteered. They hoped that the government would make enlistment compulsory, thus sheltering their relatives in Germany from possible retaliation.[37] The Auxiliary Military Pioneer Corps, later the Royal Pioneer Corps, a non-combatant force, became the base for these volunteers, and the Kitchener Camp was the first training centre of the Alien Companies. The first five Alien Companies, numbering some 1,500 men, trained at Richborough, were landed in France early in 1940. When British forces made a hasty retreat before Dunkirk, these unarmed aliens were given weapons and in a very short time learned to handle rifles and machine and anti-tank guns. Good fortune favoured them, and all were brought back safely from France.[38]

During the men's absence overseas, those who had remained in Richborough had been evacuated and the camp commandeered by the army. The men who had not volunteered to join the armed forces had been interned on the Isle of Man, where, together with thousands of other refugees and enemy aliens, many of them were housed in primitive conditions.[39] In his letter to Lord Samuel in June 1939, Wilfred Israel had suggested that the men who would be rescued from Germany might be housed in 'semi-military camps, for instance ... the Isle of Man'. For a number of them, the internment camp established there was now the camp of last resort.

The men who returned from France were transferred to areas in the western region of England. One of the reasons given for the move was that, if they remained on the south coast and were captured by the Germans following an invasion, they would be treated as traitors. More than 100 of Richborough's former inmates were later employed for special intelligence, especially in the monitoring of radio broadcasts from Germany.

When the Richborough Camp was taken over by the army, Sir Robert

Waley Cohen took much pleasure in advising Anthony de Rothschild that the total cost to the CBF of renovation, equipment and feeding those housed there for the 67 weeks of its operations, from 21 February 1939 to 26 May 1940, when those who had not volunteered to join the Pioneer Corps were interned on the Isle of Man, was 13s 6d a head, per week. This figure was based on an average of 1,964 persons in residence, spread over the entire period of the camp's operation. Waley Cohen was so delighted at the low cost to the CBF that he was ready to consider similar housing for other groups of refugees. Sir Robert, however, had not taken into account the contributions of food and other provisions, which had been provided, free of cost, by generous benefactors.

13

Financial Crisis, 1939–40

REFUGEES ARRIVING IN LONDON in the weeks and months following *Kristallnacht* were traumatized, and many were in need of the financial aid and the social services offered by the JRC. So great were the demands now made on the JRC that in the first seven months of 1939 alone the Council authorized the expenditure of £250,000 for the care of refugees. The magnitude of this outlay is seen in the fact that in all of the six previous years the JRC had spent a total of £233,000 in aid to refugees in Britain.[1] Tending the needs of this extraordinarily large inflow of refugees depleted the Council's treasury. In fact, the financial position became so untenable that the Council asked Lord Reading, Simon Marks and Otto Schiff to review its implications and recommend means whereby the Council could cope with the crisis.

The onset of war, in September 1939, in no way lessened the Council's financial burden. On the contrary, nearly one-half of the refugees now seeking support were individuals whose existence was hitherto largely unknown to the JRC. Their private sponsors were unable to continue commitments to maintain them as they themselves were called into the armed forces or were conscripted into employment in war industries in different regions of the country. In addition, refugees whom the Ministry of Labour had earlier permitted to accept employment lost their jobs in war-related circumstances. Yet others, who had established small businesses, were forced into closure. Many of the 15,000 mostly female refugees who had entered Britain independently as domestic servants on Ministry of Labour permits were also unemployed, either because of their employers' changed circumstances or their sheer panic at having an enemy alien in the house in war-time.[2] Unemployment among refugees was further compounded by the fact that the government classified them as 'enemy aliens' and that they would have to be cleared by Aliens Tribunals before they could accept new employment.[3] Adding to the overwhelming financial burden that the Council now carried was the halt, albeit temporarily, to outbound shipping, which meant that many of those awaiting overseas transportation had also to be maintained. Responsibility for these many thousands of refugees was assumed by the JRC when its most vigorous volunteer workers were conscripted into some form of National Service, leaving inexperienced individuals to cope with an inordinate array of new problems. It was a difficult time for refugees and for the staff at the JRC.

With the advent of war, the government prohibited the transfer of funds to enemy-occupied territory. None the less, the Council was bent on making every effort to help Jews on the continent to find safe havens. Thus, when Simon Marks announced that 2,900 persons in Germany and Austria, including a number of Czech nationals, held Palestine immigration certificates, but were unable to depart because they were without ship tickets, the Council agreed to help.[4] Simon Marks had already been in contact with the Czech Refugees Committee in London, which had assured him that it would finance the transportation of the Czech citizens.[5] This left £25,000 to be found for tickets for the Austrians and Germans, and here again, Marks had contacted the JDC and the Jewish Colonization Association (ICA), and each had promised one-third of this sum. He asked the Council to cover the balance. The fact that the men should be rescued was not questioned, but there were no unallocated funds in the Council's treasury. Meyer Stephany, ever a splendid accountant, came to the rescue when he announced that £5,000 had been set aside for transmittal to the Kultusgemeinde for emigration purposes, but since this sum had not been remitted before war was declared, government permission would not now be given for its transfer. The £5,000 was, therefore, available. The Council authorized it to be used towards the passage costs of the certificate-holders. Simon Marks and his family undoubtedly contributed the balance needed to ensure that all 2,900 of the certificate-holders were able to leave for Palestine.[6] The void in the Council's treasury was probably plugged by loans and individual contributions from Council members.[7]

Only a few weeks later Otto Schiff, who had meticulously husbanded

Council funds, authorized payment of transportation to Palestine for 65 individuals who were being supported by the JRC. Their immigration certificates would expire within a month, on 14 January 1940. Anthony de Rothschild, who had assumed the Council's chairmanship when Lord Reading enlisted in the army, was well aware that if those concerned were to remain in Britain, the Council would have to continue to provide funding to the JRC for their maintenance. While suggesting that an attempt be made to extend the validity of their certificates, he honoured Schiff's commitment while gently admonishing him: obligations for which funds had not been allocated should not be undertaken without the consent of the Executive, he said.[8] Only a month later Schiff proposed, and Anthony de Rothschild approved, payment of passage costs (at £11 a head) for 170 immigrants to the United States.[9] Both men were aware that United States immigration law prohibited payment of ship tickets by voluntary agencies but, as on previous occasions, they chose to ignore it. At a Council meeting, Meyer Stephany stressed the need to continue to conceal this fact from the JDC, more especially since another 294 refugees who were soon to embark for the United States were in possession of ship tickets paid for entirely, or in part, by the JRC.[10] With lives at stake, rescue rather than attention to United States immigration law was the Council's maxim.

Appeal to friends in the United States

In an effort to secure permission for refugees to accept employment, which in turn would also lessen the financial burden on the JRC, Lord Reading and Otto Schiff met with officials of the Home Office, the Ministry of Labour, the War Office and the Ministry of Health to discuss the absorption of refugees into the general labour force. Many of the refugees were members of professions, others were skilled artisans, craftsmen or businessmen; all could contribute to the British economy. It was obvious at their meeting, however, that the government would make no immediate ruling in the matter of refugee employment.[11] Simon Marks, ever optimistic and generous, believed that until a government decision was reached the Council could raise another £200,000 to £250,000, which would enable it to continue to maintain those in need. But there was no assurance that the government's response would be favourable, or that its decision would be arrived at speedily.[12] Until a government ruling was handed down, however, the Council would have to maintain refugees or, at worst, refer them to local authorities for public aid. The Council did not believe it could approach the community for financial support at this time.

Government officials were appalled at the thought of Jewish refugees applying to their local authorities for relief, and foresaw an anti-semitic backlash if they were to become a charge on public funds. But anti-semitism, whether latent or overt, was endemic in British culture, and it had long been endured in its various manifestations by the Anglo-Jewish community. Of as great concern to the Council, however, was the stigma that would attach to the Anglo-Jewish community and to the refugees if they were compelled to seek public relief. Indigent Jews had always been cared for by community institutions, and public relief was anathema.

Lord Reading, Simon Marks and Otto Schiff considered the options and concluded that the Council's only alternative was to try to secure a substantial contribution from wealthy Jews in the United States. Simon Marks was convinced that, if a personal approach were made, individual American Jews would make greater contributions for the benefit of refugees – an opinion he had voiced earlier on more than one occasion. Here was a chance to put it to the test. The three men reasoned that if 'the approach were made in the right quarter in America, by the right people on this side', $1 million (£200,000) might be raised, half of which would be requested as a gift and half as a loan. Furthermore, if American support were forthcoming and the Council could place $1 million at the British government's disposal, it might make credit available to enable the Council to continue its aid programme.[13] This was an approach that had to be pursued, because no other source of major funding was in sight, and an appeal to the 'right quarter in America' appeared reasonable. In the meantime, Simon Marks provided the Council with £25,000 – a contribution he had promised in June, before war was declared.[14] Lord Bearsted and Anthony de Rothschild, 'the right people on this side', cabled Lewis L. Strauss, a member of Kuhn Loeb & Company, the New York banking house with which members of the Council had banking and family connections.[15] Strauss was a member of the JDC Board, and chairman of the American section of the Council for German Jewry. He was well informed on the critical financial situation of the British section, which had followed the inrush of refugees in the wake of *Kristallnacht.* He and his family had been house-guests at the Exbury estate of Lionel de Rothschild just before the war began. Strauss' warm letter of appreciation for the hospitality afforded them and Lionel's gift of rhododendron and azalea bushes, 'which had adapted well to American soil', might have encouraged his selection as the recipient of the Council's appeal.[16]

In their cable to Lewis Strauss, Lord Bearsted and Anthony de Rothschild informed him that 35,000 Jewish refugees had been given asylum in Britain since *Kristallnacht*, bringing their number in the country to 65,000. As a result of their need for financial aid, the Council had almost been bankrupted. Bearsted and de Rothschild feared the repercussions on the Jewish community when the Council was unable to assist them further and the refugees were compelled to seek public relief. Bearsted and de Rothschild were not approaching the JDC, because they appreciated the enormous burden it too now carried, but 'we appeal to you and your friends to provide the Council with $1,000,000 either as a contribution or half by loan and half by gift'. Such an infusion of dollar funding, they added, would also help the Council in its quest for government aid.[17]

On receipt of their cable, Strauss consulted with Paul Baerwald, Harold Lindner and other members of the JDC, before responding briefly, asking what the ICA would contribute. Lord Bearsted immediately conferred with Sir Osmond d'Avigdor Goldsmid, the president of the ICA, after which he advised Strauss that heavy losses in Poland, subsequent to the German assault, meant that the ICA could only help relieve the Council of liabilities payable to the HICEM before the end of 1939. Bearsted emphasized that this personal appeal was made in the hope that a gift would be made to the Council in dollars, a currency much needed by the British government, and that such a gift would be of special value at this time. Neither Strauss nor his associates appeared moved. Strauss insisted that they, in New York, expected the ICA to reverse its position.[18] The Americans were digging in, hoping to loosen what they assumed to be the ICA's tightly drawn purse strings.

Strauss conferred further with his JDC associates and cabled again.[19] He offered the Council a $50,000 contribution from the JDC, and an additional $50,000 as a loan, both being contingent upon the ICA's financial participation. He followed this cable with an elucidating letter.[20] It was generally agreed, he wrote, that it would be neither safe nor wise 'to establish a precedent of raising funds for overseas relief *outside* of the JDC which has pre-empted the field during the past 25 years and to which all of those, with whom I have spoken, have pledged their contribution'. In support of his argument, Strauss cited a Federal Government regulation that prohibited the raising of funds for any overseas purpose without prior permission from the US Department of State. He also referred to a recently enacted US statute that entitled contributors to registered United States charities to deduct from personal income tax their contributions amounting to 15 per cent of income. Any financial response to the British request, therefore, would have to be made through the JDC. On receiving this letter, an exasperated and forthright Lord Bearsted wrote to Anthony de Rothschild, 'It does not appear to me in any other light than that of an apology or an attempt to find excuses for doing as little as possible.'[21]

Despite the outbreak of war, members of the JDC had not modified their anti-Zionist stance. Even at this date they opposed moneys being made available to the Council because they objected to JDC funds being spent for projects that might benefit the Zionists. 'Such grants are just a way of giving money to Palestine indirectly', noted one.[22] This at a time when Palestine was the one major escape route for Jews in Nazi-occupied countries of Europe, other than the United States. Strauss confirmed the JDC's opposition to the Council's funding of projects in Palestine, and its reluctance to make up the Council's budgetary shortfall, which it believed was a result of such contributions.[23] In great measure, the JDC was still wedded to financing the infrastructure of Europe's Jewish communities. America's physical distance from Europe appears to have rendered its Jewish leaders immune to the reality of the situation of Jews in German-occupied territory.

Strauss continued to demand a financial commitment from the ICA. He wrote that he and his associates at the JDC believed that, 'no information to the contrary being available', the ICA trustees had a substantial capital fund, perhaps in the region of $10 million or more, left by a 'Jewish philanthropist' (Baron de Hirsch) which they were attempting to preserve, rather than using for the existing emergency. If that were so, Strauss noted, 'it is a travesty to think that a strict legalism should withhold these funds in a period of mass distress which has no parallel in history'.[24] Unfortunately, the ICA was not in a position to refute the Americans' assumption of its available capital and the JDC's negative view prevailed.

Lord Reading now entered the picture. He cabled Strauss and asked whether the 'Americans' would be in a position to provide passage money for 6,000 refugees who held United States immigration visas, which would enable them to leave Britain within the next six months. In the meantime, they were being supported by the JRC. Strauss responded, indicating that the JDC would consider the matter. The JDC then offered the Council a grant of £4,300 ($21,500) for each of the months of November and December (1939) and a further £4,300 to be repaid to the JDC at a later date.[25] The JDC made it clear that their offer could not be taken as a precedent and the Council was reminded that JDC funds could be used only for maintenance of refugees, since United States immigration law prohibited payment of immigrants' passage costs by voluntary agencies; a prohibition long ignored by the JRC.

The Council found this latest offer derisory. Anthony de Rothschild told Lord Bearsted of a lengthy discussion by Council members on whether it should be accepted. In the end, he said, 'Sacher [Harry] thought that it was so miserably inadequate' that they could not.[26] And they did not. Being English gentlemen, they decided that 'rather than appear impolite and reject it out of hand', they would thank the JDC, and advised them that the Council was approaching the government on the question of financial support and would communicate again at a later date.[27] More than a month later, Anthony de Rothschild announced that he had received a further cable from Strauss in which he indicated that, while the JDC Exchequer was already in deficit, they were making a fresh fund-raising drive and hoped to be able to do something for the Council in the New Year.[28] It was obvious that 'the right people on this side' had failed to impress their American friends, and there is no record of further communications regarding a loan or a gift to the Council.

Anthony de Rothschild was deeply offended by Louis Strauss' handling of his appeal on behalf of the Council, and he wrote to tell him so. 'I will not disguise from you the fact that your response to the appeal which Bearsted and I sent to you jointly was so disappointing that there seemed no point in responding to your last letter to me'.[29] In response Lewis Strauss attempted to explain the thinking behind his communications, assuring Anthony de Rothschild that they were not prompted by 'caprice, stubbornness or callous indifference to the circumstances with which you were faced', but that the American coffers were empty when the first cable was received and there was 'a general belief that the English Jewish community was rich enough to bear the burden cast upon it by the war'. It was also believed that 'the ICA was hoarding a huge capital sum in marketable or hypothecable securities which should be given or loaned from capital as private individuals were doing'.[30] Anthony de Rothschild was not impressed by Strauss' response. On 12 February 1940, he sent Lewis Strauss a copy of the documents relating to the Council's latest fund-raising effort in the Anglo-Jewish community and asked 'whether it will be at all possible for you to help us at this difficult moment'. He could have had no illusion regarding Strauss' response.[31] The 'Americans' were convinced that the Anglo-Jewish community's generosity was evidence of its unlimited wealth and they were not prepared to bail it out, particularly since such aid might benefit Palestine. The Council would now have to concentrate its efforts on securing government aid if refugees were not to become a charge on public funds.

Negotiations with the Home Office

Even while the non-productive transatlantic communications were in progress, Lionel de Rothschild, Otto Schiff and Clare Martin, the latter representing the Christian Council for Refugees, had met Sir Osbert Peake, MP, Parliamentary Under-Secretary to the Home Office, and presented him with a memorandum that set forth the financial position and future needs of the Council and of the Christian refugee agencies.[32] Victor Cazalet, a member of the Parliamentary Committee on Refugees, whose aim was to influence the government and public opinion in favour of a generous and comprehensive policy on the refugee question, and to stimulate interest and provide information for Members of Parliament and the general public upon the question, had suggested this move to Anthony de Rothschild, following his discussions of the Council's situation with Sir Herbert Emerson, the High Commissioner for Refugees.[33]

Emerson's response had been entirely negative. He believed that it would be difficult to induce the government to provide funds to voluntary agencies.[34] Otto Schiff had also approached Emerson who, reported Schiff, had at first been unhelpful, indicating that the community had no right to apply to the government for financial aid. At a subsequent meeting, however, Emerson appeared to have had second thoughts, and was now willing to help.[35] It is possible also that Emerson had discussed the Council's financial problem with the Rev. Henry Carter, CBE, Chairman of the Joint [Christian and Jewish] Consultative Committee for the Christian Council for Refugees, and Carter had provided Emerson with an insider's view of the tremendous financial burden that the Council had carried since 1933, in caring for Jewish and non-Aryan refugees.

A week after his earlier meeting with Sir Osbert Peake, Otto Schiff had another meeting with him at which Lord Reading was present. Peake told them that nothing could be done without the approval of Parliament – an approach that the Home Office was anxious to avoid. Peake had, in fact, asserted that no financial help could be expected from the government and that, if the Council's funds were exhausted, then there was no alternative but for refugees to apply for public assistance.[36] This was not the response that Reading and Schiff had anticipated. It was not only disconcerting, it was also unacceptable. Large numbers of refugees were congregated in the three north-west London boroughs of Golders Green, Hampstead and Hendon, which bore a marked similarity to the middle-class neighbourhoods they had left in Germany. The political repercussions that would result if these boroughs were asked to shoulder an undue portion of the financial burden of support for refugees, who were both German and Jewish, were not difficult to contemplate. At a meeting of the Council in November, Sir Robert Waley Cohen reminded his colleagues that when, in 1914, Belgians had fled to Britain to escape German persecution, government resources had been harnessed to assist them. It was Waley Cohen's conviction that the government should now provide similar aid for the refugees who had fled from the Nazis.[37] Anthony de Rothschild bore Waley Cohen's argument in mind.

The Council and other voluntary agencies agreed on a joint meeting with Osbert Peake, to discuss their mutual concern for the future maintenance of refugees in need. Each of the agencies was facing insatiable demands on its financial resources. When they met Peake on 30 November, Anthony de Rothschild, as spokesman, Otto Schiff and Lionel Cohen represented the Council; Bertha Bracey spoke for the Quakers; and the Rev. Henry Carter represented the Christian Council for Refugees. Sir Herbert Emerson, High Commissioner for Refugees, was also in attendance. Sir Osbert Peake was accompanied by E.N. Cooper and Sir Alexander Maxwell.[38]

Hoping no doubt to forestall a call for government support, the government officials advised those present that the Treasury had authorized the Home Office to offer a loan to enable them to continue to care for refugees. Without hesitation, Anthony de Rothschild responded to this unexpected proposal. It was anathema, he said. It would be immoral, he declared, for the agencies to accept a loan that they had no reason to assume they would be able to repay.[39] Anthony de Rothschild's firm response was doubtless equally unexpected. It was followed by a lengthy discussion, at the end of which Osbert Peake made it clear that the government could offer nothing more.

Unaccustomed to being thwarted, especially when seeking money for the support of refugees, Anthony de Rothschild was impatient with the government's dalliance. He told Sir Alexander Maxwell that 'if nothing was done by the Government, the Organisations would be compelled ... to close down on Monday next ... or a week later', at which time the refugees would have to be maintained out of local rates. There was finality in this statement, more especially since the largest number of refugees, by far, were being cared for by the Council.

Home Office officials were possibly unprepared for Anthony de Rothschild's response, and the threat it implied. In a more conciliatory tone, Sir Alexander Maxwell indicated that the government might be prepared to make a grant to the agencies, which would equal the sum they would raise from contributors.[40] It was now clear that government officials had been testing the agencies' resolve, and had concealed the latest offer in the hope that it would not have to be made.

Anthony de Rothschild, now assuming the driver's seat, was careful to exploit Maxwell's suggestion that government funding might be forthcoming. If the government would backdate its offer to the beginning of September 1939, and credit the voluntary agencies for the approximately £150,000 that they had expended from that date until 30 November, he said, they would be able to continue their activities until the end of February 1940. For their part, the voluntary agencies would then attempt to raise between £150,000 to £200,000, and provided the government contributed a like amount, they would be in a position to continue their efforts until August. Government officials knew, full well, that most of this money would be raised by the Council. Anthony de Rothschild made it clear, however, that the voluntary agencies were not prepared to commit themselves financially beyond the end of February – a position that they had doubtlessly agreed upon prior to the meeting. Their united stance must certainly have awakened the government officials to the fact that they no longer faced malleable supplicants. Anthony de Rothschild added that, if his plan were accepted, the Council would borrow £25,000 which the Rev. Henry Carter and the Christian Council for Refugees had offered to enable its services to be maintained for another two weeks, following which it would be forced to close down.[41] But government officials were not yet convinced that the Council was in such dire financial straits that it needed to borrow money from the Christian agency. They, like the Jews in the United States, had undoubtedly assumed that the generous support of refugees by British Jews was evidence of the community's unbounded wealth.

Immediately following the meeting, Anthony de Rothschild wrote to Sir Osbert Peake. He restated the Council's financial position and reminded Peake of the loan of £25,000 that the Christian Council for Refugees had offered. He now advised Peake that the Council had been obliged to accept the loan, which Simon Marks and he had guaranteed, so that the JRC could continue to function until 15 December.[42] Whether the acceptance of the loan was a political ploy in an effort to force a government decision is not known. Anthony de Rothschild asked Peake for the government's decision on his proposal by 8 December. If it were negative, Rothschild wrote, the Council would have a week in which to wind up its activities.[43] It was at this point, perhaps, that Home Office officials took seriously the claim that the Council's treasury was depleted. Anthony de Rothschild kept Sir Robert Waley Cohen informed of developments *vis-à-vis* the Home Office and asked him to use his influence at the Treasury, where he had contacts, to try to obtain a satisfactory financial outcome for the Council.[44]

Despite Anthony de Rothschild's request that the government make known its decision by 8 December, it was only on that day that the War Cabinet Committee on the Refugee Problem convened. Chaired by Malcolm MacDonald, MP, Secretary of State for the Colonies, the committee heard Sir Osbert Peake's report on his meeting with Anthony de Rothschild and other voluntary agency representatives. He told his colleagues that he had reminded his visitors of the 'appalling consequences which must follow if their Organisation [the Council] collapsed and if some 13,300 Jewish Refugees were left to be maintained out of public funds ... He had emphasized that it was inevitable that in such circumstances anti-semitic tendencies in the country would be strengthened.'[45]

Sir Osbert Peake then reported that the government had considered making a loan to the agencies, 'but quite apart from the obvious objection to the British Government lending money to the Jews, the Heads of the Organization had stated that they could not honestly entertain such a proposition as they saw no prospect of being able to re-pay the loan'.[46] This intelligence was of particular concern to Malcolm MacDonald, because he anticipated mounting pressure from the Council to facilitate immigration to Palestine if government aid were not provided. This would embarrass the government, he said, since preference for immigration certificates was being given to Jewish emigrants from central Europe. MacDonald was probably referring to Czech refugees in Britain, who were being supported by the government-financed Czech Trust Fund. The only alternative in view was a scheme formulated by the Home Secretary, Sir John Anderson.

The Cabinet Committee continued its deliberations, and concluded that there were three options open to them. The first was to take no action at all. This, they were aware, was out of the question. The second was to give refugees the same treatment under the Poor Law that destitute British people received. The inherent dangers in such a move precluded this solution. The third was to accept the Home Secretary's proposal and justify it on the grounds that it was 'special' because it could not be covered by the Poor Law or any other existing government machinery. Such a move would help forestall criticism, by political opponents, of government aid to refugees.

Sir John Anderson now addressed the Cabinet Committee. For a number of reasons, which he knew all those present understood, he said, it would be impracticable to allow the 13,300 refugees in need of support to fall on local rates. By the same token, he noted, refugees could not be allowed to starve. The alternative open to the government was to provide, for a period of six months, from 1 January 1940, half the 16 shillings a week it cost the voluntary agencies to maintain individual refugees under their care. He also recommended that refugees who had been permitted to accept employment (i.e. domestic servants) be entitled, as were other workers in Britain, to apply to the Unemployment Assistance Board for financial support. Furthermore, Anderson advocated that the government pay half of the refugees' immigration expenses, which would be based on an approved scale of charges. Finally, he recommended that the government provide the refugee organizations with a flat sum of £75,000 to enable them to continue their activities while they attempted to raise additional funds to meet the anticipated share of their costs, realistically observing that £75,000 would probably not suffice.[47]

The Home Secretary had already informed the Cabinet Committee that there were some 50,000 refugees (precise figures were never available), among whom approximately 13,300 were being maintained by refugee organizations, and that the Council was responsible for 85–90 per cent of that number. The Council, therefore, would need some £15,000 a week to continue its programme of support. Children sponsored by the Movement were not included in these figures; their financial needs were being met from moneys provided by the Baldwin Fund.

Four days after the Cabinet Committee meeting, Anthony de Rothschild again reminded Sir Osbert Peake of the gravity of the Council's situation, but the Home Office had not yet finalized a course of action.[48] Only one day before the loan from the Christian Council was due for repayment, Anthony de Rothschild, Simon Marks, Otto Schiff, the Rev. Henry Carter, Clare Martin and Sir Herbert Emerson were invited to meet Sir Alexander Maxwell and Sir Osbert Peake at the Home Office. The Rev. Carter took this opportunity to press the Council's case, and left government officials in no doubt that the Council fully intended to close down operations on the following day.[49]

Government support for refugees

It was at this point that tension was relieved. Sir Alexander Maxwell announced that the Cabinet Committee on Refugees had agreed to Sir John Anderson's proposals for refugee support, which would be funded by the Treasury. The government now promised:

1. £100,000 towards the expenditures that refugee organizations had incurred since the outbreak of war. The Home Secretary had been persuaded to increase his original offer of £75,000.
2. To fund unemployed refugee domestic servants up to the full rate allowed by the Unemployment Assistance Board. The government proposed to set up an office for this purpose at Bloomsbury House, which now housed a majority of the refugee agencies. Those drawing assistance would thus be confined to one location.
3. A contribution equal to half the expenditure incurred by refugee organizations for the ongoing care and maintenance of refugees. These funds would be paid to a Co-ordinating Committee that would act as the disbursement agency, which Sir Herbert Emerson agreed to chair.

The government offer was contingent on the total grant not exceeding £27,000 a month, the expenditures being approved by the oversight Co-ordinating Committee that would be established; and the refugee organizations assuring the government that they would endeavour to prevent refugees becoming a charge on public funds. The government also agreed to pay 50 per cent of the cost of refugees' overseas transportation.

The Council estimated that it would receive approximately 85 per cent of the government grant, the balance going to the Christian Council for distribution to its members. Implicit in acceptance of the government offer was the need for the Council to raise an estimated £150,000 in the first six months of 1940 and a further £210,000 before the end of the year. After many months of despair the Council's financial burden was eased. While it would still need to conduct fund-raising campaigns, there was no further thought at this time of 'so calamitous a conclusion to seven years of devoted service and sacrifice' which would have attached to the Jewish community in allowing refugees becoming a charge on public aid.[50]

In a written statement to the House of Commons, the Home Secretary extolled the work of the voluntary agencies, emphasizing that they had borne the total financial responsibility for refugees since the beginning of the German-Jewish crisis in 1933. He estimated that they had collected and disbursed some £5 million in addition to £3 million that had been expended by relatives and friends. He then explained the government's proposed financial arrangement with the voluntary agencies, which would appoint a representative committee to exercise a general oversight of the use of the grants.[51] Sir Osbert Peake elaborated on the Home Secretary's statement when he presented the government's recommendations to the House of Commons on 22 February 1940. The government's recommendations were voted into law.[52]

The Rev. Henry Carter and Anthony de Rothschild agreed to serve as joint chairmen of the Executive Committee of the Central Office for Refugees, which was created to administer the moneys that the government would assign to Sir Herbert Emerson's Central Committee. A third office sponsored by the government was the Provincial Department of the Central Office for Refugees. Chaired by Otto Schiff, it served as the link between Bloomsbury House and the twelve Regional Councils, which in turn had oversight of some 450 committees throughout the British Isles, most of which were concerned with the welfare of children, and were eligible to receive allocations from the central fund.[53] It had been estimated that during the first six months of 1939 these committees had spent some £5,000 a week to meet the needs of their charges.[54]

Now that its basic financial difficulties had been eased, the Council could concentrate on the many problems that had been added to its agenda. Most important, it still needed to set in motion an ongoing fund-raising campaign to finance its activities.

14

War-time Activities of the Council and the Jewish Refugees Committee

Fund raising in 1940

THE COUNCIL'S FUND-RAISING appeal in 1940 was addressed to its 'most important subscribers and representatives of Anglo-Jewry'. Simon Marks and Anthony de Rothschild, the Council's indefatigable advocates, were joint chairmen, and they were supported by Lionel Cohen and Israel M. Sieff. The appeal was launched on a bleak day in February and the invited audience was not as large as had been anticipated. Those present were urged to spread the message when they returned to their home communities, for failure to achieve the appeal's financial goal was an outcome the Council was not prepared to contemplate.[1]

Anthony de Rothschild related in detail the Council's lengthy negotiations with the government on its financial crisis – a consequence of the unprecedented upsurge in the number of refugees who arrived after *Kristallnacht.* He made no mention of the failed attempts to secure funding from friends in the United States, but spoke of the months of frustration and anxiety before government officials reluctantly accepted the fact that the Anglo-Jewish community alone could no longer raise the moneys needed for the support of the refugees.

He told of the government's decision to maintain refugees on the basis of a fixed rate of a pound for each pound spent by the Council and by other agencies; information which had been broadcast to the nation a few days earlier. This financial arrangement was for a period of six months, but Anthony de Rothschild was confident that the government would extend it beyond that time. He then told of the dire circumstances of many of the thousands of refugees, for whom maintenance costs and emigration aid were expected to amount to some £275,000 before the end of the year. This was a sum over and above the subsidy that the government would provide to the Council through the Central Committee for Refugees, of which he and the Rev. Henry Carter were co-chairmen.[2] The fact that the government had undertaken to pay half the transportation costs for those able to emigrate had relieved the agency of a tremendous financial burden. Notwithstanding, it was now imperative, he said, for the Anglo-Jewish community to raise £400,000 to meet the Council's share of the funding of its programme until the end of 1940.

Not known as an effusive man, Anthony de Rothschild spoke warmly of the eloquence with which the Rev. Henry Carter had presented the Council's case to the government. It was only when the Rev. Carter addressed government officials in 'our cause', he said, that they were convinced of our insolvency.[3] Until then 'they ... did not frankly believe that this wealthy Jewish community was unable to continue to find all the necessary funds'.[4]

Anthony de Rothschild then told of the harmonious working relationship that the Council had maintained with the Keren Hayesod during the past seven years. He emphasized that throughout that time the Keren Hayesod's national fund-raising machinery had been employed to organize and collect contributions to the Council. The original contract with the Keren Hayesod had now expired, he said, and one similar could not be contemplated under war-time conditions. None the less, the Keren Hayesod had agreed to bear the expense of running the Council's 1940 appeal and, in return, the Council would contribute a total of £75,000 to the Keren Hayesod to be payable over a number of years at the rate of £3,500 a month. During 1940, however, these payments would begin only after pledges to the Council totalled £350,000. Refugees in Britain had first claim on the Council's funds, he said, and such a sum was the minimum needed for their support during the year.[5] Anthony de Rothschild did not reveal that the new agreement with the Keren Hayesod had been forged by Simon Marks only after much hard bargaining. But he did tell Lord Bearsted that the 'Zionists eventually agreed to the terms [of the agreement]. Simon Marks, I believe, had to bribe them to do so, but he wrote quite a good letter which produced such an effect on Bob Waley Cohen that the latter was almost in agreement – so you see that the age of miracles is not yet past.'[6] Anthony de Rothschild was evidently pleased that a new contract had been forged.

Simon Marks, Lionel Cohen and Israel Sieff also addressed the audience, urging them to ensure that the community supported the Council's fund-raising drive so that refugees would not be compelled to become a charge on public funds. Israel Sieff warned of the anti-semitic consequences to the community if the appeal failed to reach its goal.

These sponsors of the appeal not only spoke to the audience at the meeting on 6 February; they wrote to and met potential contributors from all sectors of the business world. Anthony de Rothschild also solicited contributions from refugees whom he knew had established themselves, as well as from banking associates.[7]

The result of all these efforts was a generous response from the Anglo-Jewish community, despite the extraordinary dislocation and dispersal of families through evacuation, enlistment into the armed services and war-related industries, and the closure or removal of businesses. Within a month almost £200,000 had been pledged, and contributions for the year finally totalled more than £387,000.[8] Refugees who were established in Britain organized their own fund-raising committee, and contributed £10,000 to the appeal.[9] The ICA, whose president was now Leonard Montefiore, donated £31,000.[10] The Jewish community in South Africa remitted £15,000 with a request that £2,000 of that sum be allocated to the appeal mounted for Jewish refugees from Poland who had found sanctuary in Britain. The Council also donated £6,500 to the Polish Fund for the maintenance of 181 Polish Jews who had formerly been domiciled in Germany and Austria.[11] The Women's Appeal Committee contributed £20,000 to the Council to enable 200 children sponsored by the Youth Aliyah to immigrate to Palestine, and donated another £1,000 to the JRC.[12]

As in past years, not all the money contributed was immediately available. In fact, only £190,000 was accessible; the balance would be received in annual instalments from payments made under covenant.[13] As a result, it was not long before the Council was again compelled to secure a loan, and once more the Rothschild bank came to the rescue.[14]

Even though the government was reimbursing the JRC for half of its expenditure, the cost to the Council of overseas transport and refugee care, and the financial agreement with the Keren Hayesod, contributed to a further deficiency in its financial position. Once more, early in the summer of 1940, the Council was again compelled to advise the government that it could not continue to operate on the basis of reimbursements which amounted to half the refugees' maintenance and emigration costs. Other voluntary agencies were facing similar financial crises and joined the Council in its negotiations. Part of their problem resulted from the fact that the government was not reimbursing them on a pound-for-pound basis, due in some measure to its own lax accounting system rather than an attempt to debase the agreement with the voluntary agencies. The Council also saw fit to remind the government that almost half the number of refugees receiving its aid, and that of other agencies, had been admitted through the intermediary of private individuals, including Members of Parliament, yet it was the voluntary agencies who were having to care for them.[15]

After weeks of further bargaining, in which Sir Herbert Emerson and the government-appointed Central Committee for Refugees participated, the government agreed that from 1 October 1940 it would cover the entire cost of refugee maintenance, at the level that would be paid by the Assistance Board to destitute persons. In addition, 75 per cent of the price of emigrants' ship tickets and of agencies' administration costs (up from 50 per cent) would be covered.[16] Under this new financial agreement, the basic cost of care for a majority of those being aided would be ensured.[17]

Government loan to the Council

An enormous financial burden was lifted from the Council. None the less, the reprieve proved to be of a temporary nature. Only six months later, it became necessary to approach the government anew. Government support did not cover the needs of an increasing number of elderly and sick refugees, or provide the balance of the cost of ship tickets for immigrants, as well as the Council's administrative budget and other calls on its finances. Documents relevant to negotiations by the Council at this time, which were undoubtedly conducted by Anthony de Rothschild, have not been found, but no voice appears to have been raised regarding 'the obvious objection to the British Government lending money to the Jews'.[18] On the contrary, Sir Alexander Maxwell noted that the Home Office and the Treasury had concurred in a reversal of 'the historic practice by which governments have borrowed money from the Jews' and had agreed instead 'that the Government will lend some money to the Jews!'[19] In an unprecedented gesture, the Home Secretary granted the Council an interest-free loan of up to £75,000: 'an amount equal to one-quarter of the expenditure on the emigration of German and Austrian refugees to, and their settlement in, any part of the world and the expenses in connection with the administration and care of refugees from Germany in this country incurred by the Central Council for Jewish Refugees [CBF]'. The Council accepted the loan in the knowledge that it could be repaid over several years from moneys received under covenant and from income tax refunds.[20]

The Council estimated that it would need between £2,500 and £3,000 each month to supplement its income. From September 1941 until December 1942, a total of £38,556 was borrowed, all of which was repaid before the end of October 1944. At that time the Council asked the government to terminate the agreement, Meyer Stephany noting that the relative documents were in safe keeping as a 'lasting record of the willingness of the government to help those who tried to help themselves'.[21] Following repayment of the loan, Sir Alexander Maxwell added a notation to the file in the Public Records Office in Kew, which reads: 'This file is historic. It records a case of HM Exchequer lending money to the Jewish Fraternity. The loan has been repaid but the tripartite agreement should be on permanent record.'[22]

Was the loan an act of contrition? Government officials had long been aware that the Anglo-Jewish community carried a financial burden for legislators and others who had reneged on their pledges to maintain refugees. In the final analysis, the burden was carried for the government. One wonders also whether Anthony de Rothschild's indomitable perseverance, as spokesmen for the Anglo-Jewish community, had at last been acknowledged.[23]

Support of refugees and payment of emigration costs, agreed by the government in January 1940, continued until July 1948. At that time the government conceded that former refugees, now seen as permanent residents, would be entitled, in common with the general community, to claim assistance from the National Assistance Board.[24]

Treatment of 'enemy aliens'

Early in 1939 the JRC moved most of its staff from Woburn House to extended office space in Bloomsbury House, the former Palace hotel, which the Baldwin Fund had provided for the major refugee agencies. Bloomsbury House was less suited as offices, since many of its rooms were small, but an advantage was the proximity to other agencies and the ease of communication.

When war was declared, Otto Schiff decided that refugee case-files, estimated to number 60,000, should be removed to safety outside London. Accordingly, JRC records and half of its staff were moved to offices in Sunningdale, Berkshire. It was there, at government request, that reports for the Aliens Tribunals were prepared on approximately 48,000 refugees who had registered with the JRC, and who were still in the country. When the task was completed in the record time of little more than two months, it was realized that it was not possible for the JRC to function efficiently from two widely separated locations. A decision was made to maintain only one. Fortuitously, Otto Schiff now chose London, where many refugees were located. The Sunningdale operation was closed and all the records were returned to Bloomsbury House. The premises in Sunningdale were later bombed by the Germans, while the London offices and the records remained intact throughout the German bombardment.

None felt the disruption caused by the war more than the refugees, many of whom had fled German-occupied territory only weeks, or even days, before Britain declared war on Germany. The declaration of war sharply focused the fact that hope of rescuing relatives and friends on the continent was virtually ended. The frantic scenes that followed *Kristallnacht* were repeated, and the largely volunteer staff of the JRC was besieged by thousands of refugees and others who flocked to the offices in a desperate last-minute attempt to try to save those left behind. It was weeks before a semblance of calm was restored.

Emigration from Britain came to a virtual standstill as shipping for civilians was temporarily halted. Refugees found themselves dependent upon the refugee agencies as their hosts were called into the armed forces, or some form of national service. It was with deep concern, therefore, that the JRC learned that the newcomers were soon to be exposed to further distress. Enemy aliens, including refugees no longer regarded as German citizens by the Nazis, were to be interrogated by government Aliens Tribunals, which were empowered to decide whether they were to be interned or freed from the restrictions imposed upon aliens in time of war.

The 120 Aliens Tribunals located throughout the country, staffed by barristers and judges, with senior police officers serving as secretaries, began operating in November 1939. At the request of the Home Office, the refugee organizations appointed liaison officers to the tribunals. With little or no knowledge of the background and distressful experiences of the Jewish refugees, the tribunals were to decide their fate, assigning them to one of three categories: category A: persons to be interned; category B: persons to remain at liberty, but subject to certain restrictions; or category C: persons to be certified as 'refugees from Nazi oppression' and freed from restrictions other than those applied to friendly aliens.[25]

The tribunals, meeting behind closed doors, were a formidable experience for the refugees, who were not permitted a lawyer, but were entitled to invite a friend. Often they were accompanied by a German-speaking member of the JRC, or a representative of one of the many refugee committees in cities and towns throughout the country. By the end of March 1940, the tribunals had examined the cases of 73,800 enemy aliens, 6,000 of whom they placed in category B and 64,200 in category C. Less than 1 per cent were assigned to category A. Several of the tribunals placed all aliens who were not recommended for internment in category B. The JRC and allied agencies protested this assignation, and the cases of the refugees involved were then reviewed.

Among the enemy aliens interviewed by the tribunals, 55,460 (75 per cent) were classed as refugees from Nazi oppression.[26] On analysis of their occupations, more than one-third were found to be manufacturers, employers or businessmen, who had established some 250 enterprises and had revitalized the economy in the hitherto industrially depressed areas of Tyneside, South Wales, western Cumberland and Northern Ireland. In the process they had provided employment for as many as 25,000 persons.[27] Also revealed in the analysis was the fact that some 27 per cent of the men and 17 per cent of the women were doctors, dentists, pharmacists, opticians, psychologists, teachers, architects or consulting engineers. Another revelation was that women who had entered Britain as domestic workers represented one-quarter of all women who came before the tribunals.[28] Most of them were, in fact, refugees, who had agreed to the appellation and concomitant employment in Britain in order to escape the Nazis.

During the early months of the war, a diversity of employment opportunities in skilled and other occupations began to open for refugees as members of the British labour force were called into the armed forces and into war-related industries. Government employment exchanges were more ready at this time to issue them with work permits, providing as always that British labour was not available. As refugees were integrated into the labour force, pressures on the JRC began to lift and once more the Council began to conceive a plan for the gradual termination of its activity, confident that the assimilation of refugees would continue.[29]

The Council was guided by an address to the House of Lords on 24 October 1939, made by Viscount Cobham, the Under-Secretary of State for War, when he told his peers that the government had decided not to indulge in mass internment of enemy aliens, having learned of its injustice from the experience of the First World War when 'spy fever' had gripped the country. He proceeded optimistically, 'it is not likely to happen, as there are far fewer enemy aliens, especially of military age, in this country now than there were at the commencement of the last war, in spite of all the refugees'. The newly appointed Home Secretary, Sir John Anderson, articulated similar sentiments in the House of Commons.[30]

Internment

But these statements were made before Germany invaded the Low Countries, and before the fear of a German invasion gripped Britain. Once again the refugees were to be humiliated and uprooted. On 12 May 1940 the British government decided to intern all male refugees between 16 and 60 years of age who were located in the north and east of Scotland and the coastal areas in the east and south of England. Without prior notice, many were snatched from a semblance of normal life into internment. Before the end of May, all German and Austrian males and females between 16 and 70 years of age who had been placed in category B by the tribunals were also interned. Their number included mothers of children who had been evacuated. Following the intervention of the JRC, the children were permitted to join their mothers on the Isle of Man.[31]

Belgium and the Netherlands fell to the Germans a month after they were invaded. British government promises to enemy aliens were forgotten, and the Home Office issued a General Internment Order. All male German and Austrian nationals between 16 and 70 years of age were rounded up and interned, often in hastily erected facilities and in primitive conditions. Refugee scientists and humanists, many of whom had already submitted applications for British citizenship, and were vouched for by Britain's most eminent scholars, were not spared, and they too found themselves behind barbed wire. The Archbishop of Canterbury and other persons of note protested at this gross internment, but to no avail.[32] The refugees' lot was to worsen. During the summer of 1940, fearing that Britain would be invaded, the government decided that internment of enemy aliens was to include their mass deportation to Dominion countries. Refugees from the Nazis were not to be spared. Winston Churchill made this clear when he informed the House of Commons that he was aware that many of those who would be affected by the deportation orders were passionate enemies of Nazi Germany, but that the government could not 'draw all the distinctions which we should like to do'.[33] Thus, beginning early in July, some of the teenaged boys brought to England on children's transports, and refugee scientists working on projects vital to the war effort, were included among 8,000 male refugees deported to Australia and to Canada, some of whom the Council had helped rescue from German concentration camps.[34] Panic and despair gripped them and their families. Family members left behind were not informed of the men's destination or of their fate. Numbers of elderly and sick men, many of whom were Italians resident in Britain since childhood, were aboard the vessels transporting the refugees. Others aboard were Nazi sympathizers.

The *Arandora Star* and its human cargo set sail for Canada on 1 July 1940. The ship was torpedoed by a German U-boat off the west coast of

Ireland, and went down. Half of the ship's passengers were lost.[35] It was not long before other refugees and men from the Richborough Camp were put aboard another ship, the *Dunera*. Many of the 2,400 aliens were refugees. Survivors of the *Arandora Star* were also among the passengers, who were being transported to Australia. The refugees were grossly maltreated by the British soldiers who accompanied them. They were robbed of the few items they had salvaged from their homes before fleeing the Nazis. The British soldiers also stole their watches and prised wedding rings from their fingers.[36]

The imprudence of deporting refugees from the Nazis, and men who had lived almost a lifetime in Britain, was ultimately recognized by the government, and in July, August, October and December 1940, the Home Office issued White Papers in which it listed 22 categories under which aliens might be released from internment.[37] Julian Layton, the former liaison officer between the War Office and the Kitchener Camp at Richborough, where he had come to know many of the refugees, had been assigned to command the move from Richborough to the Isle of Man of those who were interned.[38] Now an army major, Layton was delegated to serve as the Home Office liaison officer in Australia. There, he participated in securing the release of refugees who had been transported aboard the *Dunera*. The army also authorized Major Layton to launch an official inquiry into the accusations made against the British soldiers reported to have maltreated and robbed the refugees aboard ship. Layton's inquiry was thorough and damning. It resulted in courts martial for the soldiers' commanding officer and two non-commissioned officers, and they were rigorously disciplined. The British government paid compensation to their victims, some of whom decided to remain in Australia rather than return to Britain.[39]

This was not the sole episode in which British army personnel abused refugees. When 1,714 aliens, including numbers of refugees aboard the *Ettrick* arrived in Canada in July 1940, they were searched by British and Canadian soldiers, who robbed them of most of their personal possessions and baggage. Added to this humiliation, refugees and other aliens who had been classified by the Aliens Tribunals in the B and C categories were housed together with those in category A – Nazis. Sir Alexander Paterson, a British government Commissioner of Prisons, and Chaim Raphael, a member of the JRC's Overseas Settlement Department (formerly the Emigration Department) and its liaison officer at the Lingfield Internment Camp, were sent by the Home Office to Canada, their mission similar to Julian Layton's.[40] Paterson issued a scathing report on the camp commandant's treatment of the refugees, all of whom were released from internment. A number of them decided to remain in Canada, others to return to Britain, where some of them joined the armed forces. Eventually, refugees were permitted to join combat units of the army, and as the Allies fought their way east from the Normandy beaches, some men found themselves back in their home towns in Germany.[41]

Emigration

Among the refugees interned in 1940 were a large number who were in possession of, or were about to receive, visas for the United States. Many were thus prevented from keeping long-awaited appointments at American Consulates, or from utilizing ship tickets. Otto Schiff and staff at the JRC held urgent consultations with officials at the Home Office, who were quick to recognize the internees' problems. Further consultations were held with the several other government departments involved in overseeing the internment of enemy aliens.

As a result of the JRC's intervention, the Home Office created special emigration camps. One that housed men was located in Lingfield, Surrey; another for women was at the Royal Patriotic School in Wandsworth, South London.[42] The JRC and other refugee organizations were permitted to appoint liaison officers to work with government officials in these camps, and their activities were co-ordinated, as was the preparation of necessary paper work and liaison with the United States and other countries' consulates. These efforts required that government departments including the Home Office, the Passport and Permit Office, the Police, the War Office and the Commandants of Internment Camps, as well as the refugee organizations, work together in the interest of those interned in the emigration camps.

The government designated the Overseas Settlement Department of the JRC to act for all refugee agencies in the matter of emigration, including contact with shipping agencies, since its experience in this regard was far more extensive than that of other organizations. Internees who received invitations to attend consulates were escorted by refugee agency personnel to interviews, and when visas were received and the government security agency gave its approval for their departure, these refugees were released from internment. Government authorities co-operated to ensure that refugees were able to leave the country, and the JRC recorded that the American Consulate, while adhering strictly to the law, was both helpful and courteous.[43]

These co-ordinated efforts of government agencies and refugee organizations enabled the JRC to report that in 1940 it had aided 6,109 refugees, including families, single persons and unaccompanied children, to complete their emigration plans successfully: 5,796 had left for the United States and 313 for other countries. The ship tickets for those without funds, or relatives able to assist them, were underwritten by the JRC. In a single month (March 1940), 900 refugees were embarked for overseas destinations, which is a tremendous accomplishment when the obstacles, and the low priority for shipping accorded to civilians in war-time, are taken into account. The number of departures in 1940 represented the greatest flow of refugee emigration recorded by the JRC since the beginning of the German-Jewish crisis.[44] It was achieved despite the fact that ships were frequently cancelled or rescheduled due to enemy action, and that emigrants were often given only a few hours' notice of a ship's impending departure. None the less, more than 2,500 visa-holders were still awaiting overseas shipping at the end of the year.[45] They undoubtedly left in the years that followed, for in 1944 the JRC reported that towards the end of 1943 the shipping position had improved. A government ban on civilian travel was imposed on 16 April 1944, but it was lifted during the last quarter of the year. During the months that civilians were able to leave Britain, the JRC reported that 321 individuals had emigrated. From the beginning of the war until the end of 1944, the number of refugees whose emigration the JRC aided totalled 10,471.[46]

Sosua Settlement, San Domingo

In January 1940, James Rosenberg, chairman of Agro-Joint, the resettlement agency of the JDC, established the Dominican Republic Settlement

Association (DORSA), for the purpose of aiding refugees from Nazi oppression. The contract signed with the Dominican Republic guaranteed settlers full economic and civil rights, and gave the DORSA corporation exemption from taxation.[47]

In June, Rosenberg cabled Sir Herbert Emerson, at the office of the Inter-Governmental Committee on Refugees, to advise him that 200 settlers, 500 trainees and 500 children would be accepted from Britain. Rosenberg further indicated that financial contributions were not expected from voluntary organizations, but that the cost of transportation for those accepted under the scheme would have to be paid by their sponsors.

Those approved would be between 20 and 35, preferably young childless couples or unmarried persons, or trainees between 15 and 20 who were 'physically strong, mentally sound, of good character and reputation', and who, after a period in a training camp, would be suitable for settlement mainly in agriculture. Unaccompanied children to the age of 14 were also acceptable.[48]

It was at Evian, in 1938, that the Council had first heard of San Domingo as a possible area of resettlement. Now the Council Executive met in an emergency session to consider and approve of Rosenberg's proposal.[49] There was no shortage of young adults who were ready to emigrate. San Domingo was, after all, much closer to the United States than Britain, and many refugees hoped to join relatives there. No less important was the fact that neither the United States nor San Domingo was involved in the war. Apart from knowledge that the JDC was its sponsor, the project was also of interest to the Council because it would be required to pay only half the £40 cost of each ship ticket; the government would pay the balance.[50]

Within a short time the selection committee in London received 550 applications from refugees, 10 per cent of which were submitted by Christian agencies. The Movement submitted the names of several teenagers who had expressed an interest in the project and twenty were accepted.[51] The JRC was soon able to arrange transportation for the first 78 refugees who had been approved and who, it was hoped, would rebuild their lives in the Sosua Settlement 'under arduous but healthy conditions'.[52]

In 1943 the JDC issued a report on the three-year life of the colony, which had been built from scratch by the 500 immigrants who had joined the settlement. They had prepared and planted 6,000 acres, built 37 homesteads, 11 milking barns and other farm buildings, a 15-bed hospital, a school, a community centre and administration buildings, and laid 47 kilometres of roads, fences, power lines and water pipes. They had also raised animals, and produced crops and cheese and butter for sale in the urban community. A productive economy had been created on a co-operative basis by people with little or no prior agricultural experience. While the standard of living in the settlement was superior to that of the indigenous population, it was lower than that to which many had been accustomed. None the less, they were in a safe haven. Several were able to have their elderly parents join them, and special arrangements were made to accommodate the 85 individuals involved. Some of them were tailors, shoemakers or barbers, and contributed their skills, but they were not suited to life in the colony, and it was planned that when conditions permitted they would emigrate. However, when the war ended several of the younger settlers also left for mainland America, where many of them undoubtedly joined family members in an urban environment. In 1946, six boys who were still in the settlement asked Lola Hahn-Warburg and Dorothy Hardisty to help them to return to Britain, but the government reminded their petitioners that the boys had originally been admitted to Britain as transmigrants. Whether or not they regained entry is not recorded. Like many others, they had not adjusted to the sub-tropical milieu of the colony with its small Caucasian community; nor were they disposed to continue life in a relatively primitive economy and society as workers supporting an agricultural community.[53]

Vichy France

Leaders in the Anglo-Jewish community continued to seek ways of rescuing Jews, despite the war. Fearing that Generalissimo Franco would deliver refugees in Spain to the Germans, Anthony de Rothschild and the Rev. Henry Carter asked Sir Alexander Maxwell at the Home Office whether the 1,500 refugees in Portugal and 2,000 in Spain could be evacuated to Britain. 'It is hardly necessary', they wrote, 'to add that the organizations represented in this committee will give all the help which you may require from them.'[54] Fortunately, neither Portugal nor Spain entered the war, and their refugees were not delivered to the Germans.

When news reached London, in 1942, that the Germans had ordered the deportation of Jews from Vichy France, Anthony de Rothschild cabled the JDC to ask whether the United States, which still had diplomatic relations with the Vichy government, could be prevailed upon to protest such action.[55] But no protest at this stage was of avail. None the less, the CBF, the Chief Rabbi and Sir Herbert Emerson all hoped to rescue children trapped in the area. Otto Schiff asked the Home Secretary, Herbert Morrison, to permit 300–350 children and persons over 60, with close relatives in Britain, to enter the country. Noting that Otto Schiff had guaranteed that 'these people would not become a charge on public funds', Morrison recommended to the War Cabinet that they be admitted, with the stipulation that eligibility be limited to children who had one or more parents in Britain. Herbert Morrison was not keen on their entry, in view of the 'anti-foreign and anti-semitic feeling which was quite certainly latent in this country (and in some isolated cases not at all latent)'.[56] The War Cabinet was more generous than Morrison and increased the number to be admitted to 500, broadening his definition of eligible children to include orphans with an aunt, uncle or grandparent in Britain. With their admission authorized, the struggle began to obtain exit permits from an unco-operative Vichy government.[57] Unfortunately, these efforts came to nought when, following the Allied armies' invasion of North Africa on 11 November 1942, the Germans occupied Vichy France.[58] A small number of children were able to escape into Portugal. Some 6,500 other children and adults fled from France to Spain and to Switzerland.[59]

Relief for Jews in occupied territories

Throughout the war years, the Council made efforts to help Jews trapped in Nazi-occupied territories. Most attempts were clandestine and, for that reason, available detail is sparse. But in 1943 Anthony de Rothschild and Lord Bearsted reported to the CBF, in the strictest confidence, that they were holding discussions with the government on the sending of food parcels to Jews in concentration camps. At the suggestion of the

Ministry of Economic Warfare, they discussed with Sir Herbert Emerson the use of the Inter-Governmental Committee as the conduit for the remittance of funds for the purchase of food.[60] Money could be remitted overseas only with government permission. The Inter-Governmental Committee would purchase the food in Switzerland, and packages would be sent to inmates incarcerated in Birkenau and Theresienstadt. Sir Herbert Emerson agreed to the proposal and the CBF allocated £5,000 to the Inter-Governmental Committee for the purpose.[61] The CBF also co-operated with the JDC, which was sending parcels of food to Theresienstadt, and to areas in Europe as they were liberated, as well as to Jews in the Soviet Union. The ICA financed this CBF effort.[62]

Substantial aid to survivors of the Holocaust, however, had to await the liberation of Nazi-occupied territory by Allied armies. Only then was it possible to organize relief efforts on a meaningful scale.

15

The Jewish Committee for Relief Abroad

WITH PRESCIENCE AND an unflinching sense of responsibility, the Executive of the Council agreed, in 1943, to finance the activities of a new organization, the Jewish Committee for Relief Abroad (JCRA).

In an act of faith, positive that they would win the war, the Allied governments appointed an inter-governmental committee that was charged with the development of plans for the immediate relief of the suffering populations of Europe at the cessation of hostilities.[1] British voluntary organizations with international affiliations which were concerned for post-war relief in Europe met to consider the establishment of a Council of Voluntary Relief Organizations, which would assist the governmental and international organizations that might be created for relief and reconstruction when the war ended.[2] The question of the funding of the CBF's participation would be paramount, but it advised the government that it was ready to discuss the matter in a united approach with the Joint Foreign Committee of the Board of Deputies and the Anglo-Jewish Association.[3]

On 24 January 1943, Professor Selig Brodetsky, who had succeeded Neville Laski as president of the Board of Deputies, called a conference to discuss Anglo-Jewry's participation in the Council of Voluntary Agencies. It was at this meeting that the JCRA was established. The CBF agreed to finance the JCRA, and its initial contribution to the new organization was £5,000. Dr Redcliffe N. Salaman was named chairman; its members were Sir Max Bonn, Norman Bentwich, Selig Brodetsky, F. Lichtenstein, Marjorie Raphael, Lady Eva Reading, Marie Louise Rothschild (widow of Lionel de Rothschild), Miriam Sacher (wife of Harry Sacher), Hilda Schlesinger, Schlomo Adler-Rudel, Leonard Stein and Rabbi Dr E. Munk.[4] This was the first time that a majority of participants in a CBF committee were not members of the cousinhood – a reflection of changes that had begun in the leadership of Anglo-Jewry. Leonard Cohen, a businessman from Manchester, directed the JCRA's operation until it was disbanded in 1950.[5]

The JCRA's stated purpose was to recruit qualified persons, who would volunteer their services to travel overseas and care for Jewish concentration camp and other survivors liberated by Allied armies. The volunteers would operate wherever their services might be used, but it was hoped that they would be assigned to care for Jewish survivors.[6]

The Council of British Societies for Relief Abroad (COBSRA) was constituted as the central co-ordinating agency for British voluntary relief work abroad.[7] Throughout 1943, many Jewish refugees in Britain volunteered to serve the JCRA when Europe was liberated, and many of them attended training camps and lecture series organized in co-operation with governmental and other experts.[8] They were chagrined when the government decided that enemy aliens, albeit refugees from the Nazis, would not be permitted to accept overseas assignments until the war in Europe ended.

Morris Feinman, chairman of the Manchester Jewish Refugees Committee, was the first of the JCRA volunteers to be given an overseas assignment, when late in 1943 he was appointed welfare officer at the Fedhala camp which had been established in Morocco to house displaced persons from Italy, Spain, Greece and Yugoslavia.[9] The United Nations Relief and Rehabilitation Administration (UNRRA), formerly established in November 1942, administered the camp.[10]

Work of the Jewish Relief Units

The first Jewish Relief Unit (JRU), three women and four men, joined by three members of the Friends Ambulance Unit (Quakers), with whom the CBF and JRC had a close working relationship, left Liverpool in February 1944. The JRU's identity badge, a shield of David, which Jewish survivors would easily recognize, was worn on their berets and sleeves. They sailed in convoy, destination unknown, and disembarked in Port Said, Egypt, where the army assigned them to Yugoslav refugee camps.

Together with members of other voluntary organizations, they served as an auxiliary of the British army in the uniform of army officers.

A camp at El Shatt already had a large population of Yugoslav men, women and children, and they were well organized. After a short period of training, the JRU volunteers and others were assigned to a newly established camp at Khatatba, located in proximity to the Suez Canal. There they helped receive and care for several thousand more Yugoslavs, mostly women and children, who had suffered hunger and other deprivation before being evacuated from the coast of Dalmatia by the British army.

Soon the JCRA was permitted to add volunteers to their number in Egypt, all of whom awaited assignment to Balkan countries or other areas of Europe when they were liberated. In October 1944, following the liberation of Yugoslavia, several of them were sent to southern Italy, *en route* to Dalmatia. However, political events intervened and instead these volunteers were permitted by the British army to volunteer their services to the JDC, which had already established offices in Rome. The JDC was pleased to accept the volunteer workers and assigned them diverse responsibilities. Some delivered food and other necessities to Jewish survivors as areas north of Rome were liberated, and they supplied matzoth (unleavened bread) to Jews in Florence in time for the Passover of 1945. Other JRU volunteers worked in displaced persons camps in Cina Città, the former film studios in Rome, and in Santa Maria di Banji in southern Italy. They aided in the reorganization of the Jewish orphanage in Rome, and served as administrators for the developing JDC programme. In April 1945 a member of the JRU was assigned to the JDC operation in Greece, and helped to develop its programme of relief and rehabilitation for former concentration camp prisoners who returned from Germany and Austria, and for other Jews who had survived in hiding.[11]

Early in 1945, JRU volunteers were permitted to land in the Netherlands, even though Allied armies had not yet cleared the area of remnants of the German armies. These members of JRUs provided the population of Nooddorp, in Rotterdam, with its first medical care, food and other supplies. As Jewish survivors began to return from concentration camps and others dared at last to leave their places of hiding, the CBF provided funding for additional volunteers to be dispatched to the Netherlands and to Belgium, where they cared for them and helped them to adjust to their personal loss and that of once thriving Jewish communities.

When the concentration camp at Bergen Belsen was liberated by British army personnel on 15 April 1945, JRU personnel were reassigned from the Netherlands and, together with doctors, nurses, social workers, teachers, rabbis and other professionals sent out by the JCRA from England, they cared for survivors in the Bergen Belsen displaced persons camp, which was created to house them in former German army barracks. Many of these volunteers, whose number now included former German refugees, provided medical, nursing and rehabilitative care at the Glyn Hughes Hospital (named after Brigadier Glyn Hughes, British medical officer, who entered the concentration camp with the liberating forces) in Belsen, which was housed in a former German Panzer medical facility. The volunteers worked without respite, and helped save the lives of many who might have died without the care they provided. They cared for child survivors and helped create an atmosphere in which the healing of body and mind could flourish. Rabbis dispatched by the JCRA were issued with all manner of religious requisites, including teffilim, prayer books and sefer torah, enabling them to conduct religious services and bring spiritual solace to those who had suffered so much.[12]

JRU volunteers organized welfare services for as many as 10,000 camp residents, and schools for children who had been deprived of educational facilities.[13] The British army made the former Warburg family home, 'Koesterburg' in Hamburg, available to the JRU, and it was used as a convalescent home for children and young adults from the Belsen displaced persons camp, whose residents were mostly Jews from Poland.

This was a time of close co-operation between the CBF and the JDC. JRU volunteers in Belgium, Holland, Italy and Germany assisted the JDC in the distribution of supplementary food to enhance the rations issued to survivors by the Allied armies. Basic toilet and medical requirements were also dispensed.

JRU volunteers were also assigned to Jewish displaced persons camps in the British Zone of Austria, where they provided services similar to those in Germany. Additional JRU personnel were assigned to work with the JDC in the American Zone of Germany. Jewish communities in Australia, New Zealand and South Africa were generous in their contributions of otherwise unobtainable supplies. South Africa also provided several social workers for Jewish displaced persons camps in Austria and Germany. Occupational training in a variety of trades in the camps was provided by the ORT.

For many months after the war ended, normal postal communication was not available to the civilian populations of Germany and Austria, or to persons in displaced persons camps. An activity of great significance was the immediate establishment of tracing bureaux, manned by JRU and JDC personnel, which served to reunite survivors in Europe and helped in communication with relatives abroad.

In the immediate post-war years, almost a hundred JRU volunteers were working in Germany, in addition to those on assignment in Austria, Italy and Greece. All volunteers had undertaken to serve for a minimum of twelve months. Some of them stayed for two or three years, until their charges had recuperated and had been able to begin a new life in Palestine, the United States or other countries. When the state of Israel was recognized in May 1948, many thousands of Jews in displaced persons camps in Germany, Austria and Italy immigrated to the Jewish homeland. Some of the JRU volunteers joined them. In 1948 Rabbi Leo Baeck visited the camp at Belsen and attended High Holyday service in one of the few remaining synagogues in Lübeck. It was a time of rejoicing.[14]

The small number of German Jews who survived the concentration camps did not look to displaced persons camps for shelter. They returned to their former areas of residence, some of them now housing only a few Jews. There they attempted to take up a semblance of normal life. Even fewer Austrian Jews returned to Vienna. The JCRA made the service of rabbis available in Austria, and provided religious requisites in addition to supplementary food and clothing.

More than 200 JRU volunteers served in Jewish displaced persons camps and Jewish communities in Germany, Austria, Italy and Greece, and many remained in those areas until the JCRA operation ended in 1950, when the last Jewish displaced persons camps in the British Zone of Germany were closed following the emigration of their former occupants, who were now resettled in Israel, the United States and other countries.

In recognition of the contribution of JCRA and other voluntary agency personnel to the civilian rehabilitation effort, the British government awarded them service medals which were normally reserved for military personnel. Further acknowledgement of their efforts was made in the King's Birthday Honours List in 1947, when Phyllis J. Gerson, the leader of the first Jewish Relief Unit, was awarded an MBE 'for services under the Jewish Committee for Relief Abroad'.

16

Children from the Concentration Camps

BOMBING ASSAULTS ON Britain had taken their toll of lives and of property, but German armies had not succeeded in landing there. As a consequence, Anglo-Jewry was the only major community in Europe to survive the war intact. On the continent, only Sweden, Switzerland, Spain and Portugal had been spared German occupation. Like Britain, these countries had granted asylum to several thousand Jews. The only other Jews to elude the Holocaust were those who had fled into the Soviet Union when the Germans invaded Poland. They had suffered harsh living and working conditions, but they too had survived.

Even before the war in Europe ended, Leonard Cohen and Leonard Montefiore received the blessing of the Foreign Office to travel to Paris to meet Dr Joseph J. Schwartz, the JDC's director of European operations, with whom they discussed the contribution that the CBF could make to the relief of survivors of the Holocaust.[1] The CBF was especially concerned for the welfare of children, and anxious to arrange for some of them to move to England where they could be provided with the care that they desperately needed.[2]

Soon after the meeting in Paris, Dr Schwartz attended a meeting of the CBF Executive in London. The war in Europe had ended two days earlier. Dr Schwartz reported that some 6,000 children were thought to have survived, and that almost all of them were believed to be orphans. He had discussed their evacuation from Germany with United States military authorities, which had advised him that it was not yet possible to deal with this question, more especially since transportation was not available for civilian use.[3]

While in Paris, Leonard Montefiore had written to Anthony de Rothschild in London, suggesting that the CBF attempt to persuade the Supreme Headquarters Allied Expeditionary Forces (SHAEF) 'to fly a few hundred children from Bergen Belsen or Buchenwald to the United Kingdom', where the CBF would arrange for their care.[4] Montefiore knew that the Royal Air Force was beginning to fly Allied personnel to their home countries in Europe, and that the planes were returning without cargo. He hoped that the authorities might be persuaded to allow the pilots to carry human cargo on the home run.

At the CBF's request, Otto Schiff had already asked Sir Alexander Maxwell at the Home Office for permission to bring 1,000 youngsters to Britain for temporary residence. Schiff suggested that it might be helpful if Lord Reading and Anthony de Rothschild, and perhaps the Liberal MP Graham White, chairman of the Parliamentary Committee on Refugees, who had already visited the liberated concentration camp at Buchenwald, pressed the children's case with the Home Office.[5]

The Home Office responded positively to the CBF's request, and with Leonard Montefiore as its chairman, Elaine Blond (formerly Laski), Carmel Gilbert (wife of Joseph Gilbert), H. Oscar Joseph, Anna Schwab and Lola Hahn-Warburg were asked to serve as members of the Post-War Orphans' Committee. Sir Keith Joseph and Major Edmund de Rothschild (still on active military service), son of the late Lionel de Rothschild, soon joined them. Elaine Blond and Lola Hahn-Warburg, both of whom had continued to give unstinting service to the children brought to Britain by the Movement, provided sage counsel. The Rev. Swift was invited to join the committee as representative of the Jewish ecclesiastical authorities.[6]

The Post-War Orphans' Committee agreed that on arrival in Britain the children should be housed together until they were ready to be absorbed into private families. For this reason, and also because only short notice would be given of their imminent arrival, Elaine Blond and Leonard Montefiore undertook to locate suitable housing for several hundred youngsters. German bombing had created a shortage of all types of accommodation, but they were able to rent part of a Ministry of Aircraft works hostel, located at Troutbeck Bridge, Windermere, in the Lake District, which would provide shelter for at least 300 children. The hostel was part of a bungalow camp, and it was still accommodating government workers.[7] Hostels that had housed refugee children who were being absorbed into the community would also be used at an appropriate time. Oskar Friedman, who was a trained child psychologist and a pre-war refugee from Germany, was employed to take overall responsibility for the youngsters, and Rabbi Dr Weisz was appointed to attend to their religious needs.

The first flight arrives

It was not until the first week of August 1945 that the CBF was advised that planes of the Royal Air Force, which were repatriating Czech Air Force personnel to Prague, would return to England carrying children. Only 24 hours' notice could be given of their impending arrival, and their exact number was not yet known. The CBF knew that a number of youngsters who had been liberated in Theresienstadt and other concentration camps had been gathered in a special reception centre in Prague, where they were fed and clothed, and inoculated against typhoid and other diseases, in readiness for their evacuation. A number of them had come to Prague following their return to home towns or villages in Poland, Hungary and Romania, where they had hoped for news of family members. All too many of them had learned that they were lone survivors.[8]

There were several delays in the date of departure from Prague, but as expected the CBF was given one day's notice, on 13 August, that the first plane carrying 30 children accompanied by two adults would arrive on the following day.[9]

It was a fine summer's evening, on 14 August 1945, when the plane touched down at the Carlisle airstrip, and CBF volunteers and staff greeted the first contingent of young survivors. Instead of 30 children there were 31; a boy of fifteen had stowed away on the plane. The youngster, who had not gone through the inoculation process, was taken to the Carlisle isolation hospital before being allowed to join the others. Ten other planes touched down at Carlisle that evening. They carried a total of 305 children and 33 adults. The youngest children were aged three, and sixteen of them were less than eight years old. Thirty-six of the youngsters were girls.

It was evident that those who had selected the youngsters had a broad and benign concept of what constituted children or young people under the age of seventeen. A few young men had obviously long passed their sixteenth birthday. In fact, the oldest of them was 23. The Home Office had not asked for documentation before approving their admission and no questions were asked when they landed. Few of them had, or were prepared to show, documents that would prove their age, name and place of birth. Norman Bentwich, who was at the airstrip when the eleven planes flew in, said, 'it may well be that no group of immigrants has ever entered this country with a more sympathetic welcome or with fewer formalities. The Immigration authorities made everything easy – no questions asked.'[10] All 33 adults who accompanied the children had relatives in Britain, and they were permitted to join them immediately contact was made.

A team of medical officers and nurses, led by Dr Dow, the medical officer for Westmorland, awaited the children at Windermere, and attended them until the last one was seen in the early hours of the morning. This was the team's first experience of contact with survivors.

Dr Dow reported that the general state of cleanliness of the youngsters was excellent and that not a single case of vermin was found. Some 80 per cent of them were thought to have survived typhus, which had been prevalent in the concentration camps. The risk of infection from that disease was thus considerably reduced. Dr Dow was solicitous of the children's well-being, and arranged for all of them to have tuberculosis examinations, dental treatment and general medical care. Although they had been liberated several months earlier, all the youngsters still showed symptoms of acute malnutrition and most of them were in poor health. Many were suffering from scabies, impetigo or other skin diseases. Eleven of them were suffering from active tuberculosis, while 51 others required medical supervision for the same disease. Several needed hospital care; others a period of convalescence.[11]

The senior dental officer who attended them reported that, on the whole, they had naturally well-calcified teeth, and that had it not been for this they would have been in a much worse state. Few, he said, had seen or used a toothbrush in five years. Almost all of them had caries or sepsis as a result of neglect, bad feeding and absence of vitamins from their diet. The molars of many of them had been fractured by blows from

SS guards. The dental officer noted that many incisor teeth were missing for this reason.[12]

During the course of their examinations, Dr Dow and his team learned that the youngsters had seen their parents dragged away or shot, and that for six years or more almost all of them had made their way alone through indescribable dangers. Dr Dow and his staff worked until 3.30 in the morning of 15 August, carefully examining and assessing the children, before each was escorted to bed. It was altogether an emotionally gruelling experience for this British medical team. Dr Dow recorded that 'hardly were the children safely disposed in bed when a detachment of infantry marched by celebrating VJ Day. After seeing and hearing all we had that night our feeling at being expected to celebrate a moment of victory and rejoicing can be imagined.'[13]

Several more groups of children arrived in the months that followed. Some arrived by air, while others came by land and sea, and despite the care given them on the continent while awaiting transport to Britain they, like those who had preceded them, were in need of medical, hospital and sanatoria care as well as dental treatment. It was not until June 1946 that the last airforce plane carrying children touched down at Prestwich airport, bringing to 732 the number of youngsters who entered Britain under the scheme.

Caring for the children

Most of the children were born in Poland; some in Czechoslovakia, Hungary or Romania. Many had spent years of their childhood in hiding, and all were former inmates of Auschwitz, Belsen, Buchenwald, Dachau, Theresienstadt or other concentration camps. A majority of them were children of orthodox and ultra-orthodox families, while some were from non-religious backgrounds and resentful of any attempt to impose religious rules or restrictions upon them.[14] Leonard Montefiore noted that they represented 'all sorts and conditions, a musician, an artist, a promising student of pure mathematics, a would-be-actor ... Yeshiva Bachurim (talmudic students) who cannot have changed much from their grandfathers, the pious men of old, who studied at Lodz or Cracow or Wilno'.[15]

The Post-War Orphans' Committee agreed that children under seven needed special care and should be sheltered together in a separate establishment. A house for the purpose, Weir Courteney, in Lingfield, Surrey, was made available by Sir Sidney Drage. Alice Goldberger, who had trained in child-care in her native Germany, and had worked with Anna Freud in London, was engaged as matron to the children. She remained with them for as long as Weir Courteney was their home, and gave them the stability, care and affection of which all of them had been robbed. It was home to a number of the younger children until 1957.

Members of the West London Reform Synagogue held annual money-raising events to fund the care of children at Weir Courteney during the years they were in residence.[16] The American Foster Parents Plan for War Children also helped fund the programme, in addition to providing food, clothing and other items in short supply in post-war Britain.

The Post-War Orphans Committee agreed that the youngsters not housed at Lingfield should not be separated, but accommodated in smaller groups than was possible in Windermere, and cared for by individuals who had the background and training to minister to them. Thus, when it was decided to abandon Windermere because it was isolated and school facilities were too distant, groups were placed in a number of hostels that offered a semblance of family life, and were in close proximity to sizeable Jewish communities in London, Manchester, Glasgow and other urban areas. A small number of older boys were placed with families.[17]

Again, not wishing to separate the youngsters whose illnesses were prolonged, and who were ordered extended bed-rest by their doctors, a house was purchased at Quare Mead, Ugley, near Bishop's Stortford, in Essex, where they could recuperate in a Jewish social setting.[18]

The CBF was concerned that a greater number of youngsters, who were housed in rudimentary conditions in displaced persons camps in the British Zone of Germany, had not applied to join a transport leaving for England, and Schlomo Adler-Rudel was asked to investigate. Adler-Rudel visited several of the displaced persons camps, the largest of which was located at Bergen Belsen, the home of the Zionist-oriented Central Committee of Displaced Persons. It was soon obvious that Zionists in the camps were frustrated and resentful of the fact that, despite the Balfour Declaration and the British Labour Party's support of a Jewish national home in Palestine, the party (in power since July 1945) had had a change of heart and had not lifted the quota of 1,500 immigrants permitted to enter Palestine each month, as decreed in the White Paper of 1939. Britain's Foreign Minister, Ernest Bevin, who made the jocular remark that the Jew should not push to the head of the queue, had incensed them. In Belsen this statement had 'sounded like the mouthing of a sadistic anti-Semite', more especially since neither Britain nor the United States was ready to admit those languishing in the camps.[19] The Zionist Central Committee was determined that the children would immigrate only to Palestine. It was emphatic that it would not allow them to go to England.[20] Dayan Grunfeld (the Chief Rabbi's alternate on the CBF) was distressed by the Central Committee's intransigence, but it would not be dissuaded.[21] The Central Committee later wrote to Adler-Rudel, acknowledging that conditions in Belsen were not good for the children, and promised that they would receive special care at the former Warburg home in Hamburg. It was only following David Ben-Gurion's intervention that, in 1946, two plane loads of children were permitted to leave for England.[22]

The impediment to removing children from the camps in Germany was partially resolved when Colonel Robert Solomon, adviser on Jewish Affairs to the British Military Government, secured 200 immigration certificates which enabled a number in Bergen Belsen and other camps in the British Zone to leave for Palestine.[23]

Leonard Montefiore cared deeply for the young people who were in England, and gave much time to those who caused the staff concern. They have experienced perilous adventures, he said. 'They were the survivors of forced labour or of railway trucks in which many others were frozen to death. They need time to catch up and enjoy forgone pleasures.' It is no easy matter, he continued, to provide for youth with such a background and whose future is uncertain. 'They need the benefit of trained experienced staff which is in very short supply. So long as these orphans remain in this country, they are our children and children who have been deprived and robbed of their birth right of irresponsible happiness. In some ways, at least, nothing we can do for them is too much. Nothing we can do for them can make up for what they have lost.'[24] Providing for these young people was the most expensive of the CBF's programmes in the post-war period.[25]

The younger children had had no schooling, while others had been deprived of education for six years or more. None the less, all of them were quick to respond to the educational opportunities offered them. Within a comparatively short time, some of the older boys were ready to pursue higher education and several qualified for entrance to universities. One young man, Kurt Klappholz, gained a research fellowship in pure mathematics and was later a Reader in Economics at the London School of Economics; another, Hugo Gryn, became an internationally known and respected senior rabbi of the West London Synagogue; and yet another, Ben Helfgott, became a Commonwealth and Olympic Games weight-lifting champion.[26] Some of the young men sought industrial training, while others, as Leonard Montefiore noted laconically, displayed no desire for any kind of work at all.

The JRC helped youngsters locate members of their families in overseas countries, and some 230 were able to join relatives in the United States, Canada or Israel before the end of 1948. At that date, the Post-War Orphans' Committee was also pleased to report that 21 of the 'children' had married.[27]

In December 1950, Leonard Montefiore advised Anthony de Rothschild that fourteen of the young people were still receiving treatment for tuberculosis and four were mentally unstable and not infrequently in need of institutional care. Four other children had not yet reached their sixteenth birthday and fourteen were still being cared for by the West London Reform Synagogue. Six young men were now Yeshiva students and eleven were at university or receiving technical training at university-equivalent educational institutions. The CBF was still helping some of them financially, or maintaining those who dropped out of work.[28]

When the house in Lingfield was returned to its owner, the CBF was pleased to report that the children had grown up to be quite ordinary, quite normal young men and women, and that no more, but also emphatically no less, was its intention and purpose.

To enable the '45ers', as they became known, to maintain their close bonds, and to provide them with facilities in which they could continue to meet and enjoy social and educational activities, premises were provided for their use in Belsize Park, north-west London. The club, which they named the Primrose Club after the local telephone exchange, later moved to larger premises in the Finchley Road. Oscar Joseph was pleased to serve as the club's president. The facilities made available to the members enabled them to maintain contact, as families might under more normal conditions.[29]

These young men and women created the 45 Aid Committee, through which they helped members of their group in need of assistance. That committee still functions, providing aid to its own members when need arises, and donating funds to welfare agencies, such as the CBF.

In 1954 the government offered British nationality to all of the orphans still resident in the United Kingdom. They were pleased to accept and thus cast off their stateless personae.[30] The Post-War Orphans' Committee, and all who were in contact with the children, were admiring of their resilience and strength, and their ability to adjust to life in a country that they now called home.

17

German Reparations for Victims of the Nazis

LESS THAN A MONTH after the war began, few in Britain doubted its outcome. It was manifest, too, that like many in Britain, the Council expected the war to be of short duration. With this prospect in mind, the Council created a committee to prepare an agenda item entitled 'reparations for persons who have suffered the destruction of their homes, their property and their livelihood by the German Government', which they hoped would be included in the peace settlement. The Council noted that in August 1939, in relation to its Danzig-Polish and German minorities problems, the German government had accepted the principle that wrongs inflicted on individuals should be indemnified. This obligation was regarded as binding on all parties.[1]

The Council assumed that German Jews would have the same right of reparation as was demanded by the Germans for their minorities. It recommended, therefore, that German refugee jurists in Britain form a committee to compile a list of the anti-Jewish legislative and administrative decrees, the damage to Jews, and the moneys raised in the various countries to assist them, so that claims might be formulated on pension and insurance funds, and proposals drawn up for international protection of the rights of Jewish minorities.[2] The Allied governments were of similar mind, and during the war they declared that all victims of the Nazis would receive restitution of stolen and confiscated property, and compensation for loss of liberty, health, employment and any other form of injury.[3]

When German cities lay in ruins six years later, the prospect for reparations for those who had been despoiled appeared dim. German thoroughness, however, had ensured that lists of confiscated property, which victims had prepared, had been preserved, as were the lists of members of the Nazi Party. Fortunately these documents were seized by the American military authority in Berlin, which assumed custodial responsibility for their preservation.

At war's end the Allied Military Command divided Germany into four zones, each occupied by American, British, French or Soviet armed forces. Each military government was authorized to enact legislation relating to restitution, which would be binding on the German people. A Property Control Office was established in each zone and a joint proclamation was issued, requiring every person who had acquired and possessed immovable property that had belonged to Jews and to other victims of the Nazis to notify the appropriate authorities. All trading in the property was blocked. Conrad Adenauer, West Germany's post-war Chancellor, who himself had suffered at the hands of the Nazis, acknowledged that restitution was a responsibility that his government must accept.

Uniform action on reparations legislation for the four zones was frustrated by the onset of the Cold War. Thus, the American and French military governments enacted restitution laws in 1947, but only in 1949, after continued pressure from Jewish organizations, did the British military government enact a similar law.[4] The Soviet Union did not accept the principle of restitution to individuals, and it was only after the fall of the Berlin Wall in 1989 that it was possible for individuals to initiate claims for restitution of personal property, and for claims by appropriate legally constituted agencies to be submitted for communal and heirless property located in East Germany and the eastern sector of Berlin.

The United Restitution Office, in whose founding the CBF participated, provided legal aid to individuals unable to finance the filing of their claims for restitution. Although claims took many months to process before compensation was approved, when payments were made, many former refugees were able to enjoy financial independence for the first time since they had fled their homeland. While money alone would never compensate for the pain and trauma and spoliation they had suffered, they could now enjoy a sense of dignity that their dependent state had denied them.

The CBF, the JDC and the Jewish Agency for Israel provided the funds for the establishment, in 1950, of the Jewish Trust Corporation for Germany, which processed claims for the recovery of heirless and communal property in Germany. It was a vast task, which took its legal staff many years to complete. Dr Charles I. Kapralik was responsible for its London office, and the Association of Jewish Refugees and the Council for the Protection of the Rights of German Jews, both headquartered in London, supported the work of the organization. Teams of lawyers, many of them former refugees from Germany, worked unceasingly over a period of years to identify and reclaim real estate and other property, so that the principles for which the war had been fought were upheld. As property was identified, and financial compensation was received, the income was allocated to Israel and to other countries in which numbers of refugees had settled. Moneys allocated to Britain were used to fund projects as diverse as care for elderly refugees in purpose-built residential homes, synagogues, and day schools for the children of refugees. When the Berlin Wall was dismantled in 1989, the reparations organization was again in high gear, seeking to recover property in the former Soviet Zone of occupation.

The Claims Conference on Jewish Material Claims Against Germany, of which the CBF was a founding member, continues to negotiate with German industrial organizations for the payment of compensation to former Jewish slave labourers. The CBF was also involved in the negotiations leading to the Federal Compensation Law. It is a member of the Memorial Foundation for Jewish Culture, which finances Jewish scholarship and learning as Jews worldwide continue their endeavours to restore the heritage that was lost when Jewish communities were obliterated by the Holocaust.[5]

Epilogue

THE CBF WAS established as an ad hoc organization, to be dismantled when the German-Jewish crisis ended. In the aftermath of that cataclysm, the CBF's original intention was rendered impossible. Survivors of German concentration camps were in critical need of aid, while in Britain elderly and disabled former refugees, and large numbers of children, many now orphaned, were still in need of care. The final chapter in their story will be concluded only when the last ageing survivor among those who found refuge in Britain is no longer in need of the services provided by its Jewish social welfare agencies.

During the twelve years of the German-Jewish crisis, the CBF called upon Jews in the British Isles to play a role in the refugee saga as it unfolded. They were repeatedly asked to contribute financially to enable Jews to emigrate from Nazi Germany and from Austria; and to help provide a measure of social and economic viability for those who came to Britain. Following *Kristallnacht*, they were invited to offer housing, employment and support for adults and children who, for the most part, were total strangers, and many responded.

From inception of the CBF until the end of the first year of the war, some £3 million was raised for the benefit of German and Austrian Jews, the greater part of which was contributed by members of the Anglo-Jewish community. It has been estimated that a like amount, in money and in kind, was spent in the interest of refugees by individuals in the wider community throughout the British Isles.

German and Austrian Jews who made Britain their permanent home have amply repaid the Anglo-Jewish community and, indeed, the British people at large. They have made a prodigious contribution to the country's centres of learning and its cultural and artistic life. They have also greatly enriched the religious life of the Anglo-Jewish community. In appreciation of the refugees' support of Britain's war effort, the government granted them permanent residence and offered them British nationality.

The activity that was initiated through the efforts of the men who created the CBF, and the women who worked with them, was an example *par excellence* of constructive community endeavour. From the beginning of the crisis in 1933, throughout the difficult pre-war and war years and into the peace, individuals who worked to ensure the success of the CBF's mission gave generously not only of their purse, but also of their daily lives. It was due to the persistent efforts of these community leaders, and countless volunteers throughout the country who heeded their call for help, that many thousands of adults, some 10,000 unaccompanied children, and many men and boys rescued from concentration camps in the months before the war found sanctuary in Britain.

Until the government agreed to help support refugees financially during the war years, bank loans were often a lifeline, for without them the CBF could not have carried out its programmes of rescue. These loans were repaid in full and with interest. Similarly, the government was also reimbursed for moneys it loaned to the CBF during the war years. How much more humane the British government is today in permitting asylum-seekers to enter the country and in providing for those in need.

When the state of Israel came into being in 1948, it was a beneficiary of the CBF's initial decision to help refugees immigrate to Palestine. The thousands of immigrants and the CBF's substantial financial investment in land purchase, housing construction, agricultural and industrial training, grants to the Hebrew University and to the Technion in Haifa and other institutions in Palestine all served as catalysts for the development of the Jewish infrastructure in the new country.

Political upheaval in Aden, Chile, Czechoslovakia, Egypt, Ethiopia, Hungary, India, Iran, Iraq, Poland and North Africa, the disintegration of the Soviet Union and more recently the conflict in the territory of the former Yugoslavia have brought fresh waves of Jewish refugees to Britain in every decade since the end of the war. In responding to their needs, and those of communities attempting to rebuild their infrastructures following the demise of the Soviet Union's dominance in eastern Europe, the CBF, now known as World Jewish Relief, appears to have assumed permanent status.

There is a Jewish legend that in every generation there are 36 righteous men (*Iamed vovniks*) through whose virtue the world is maintained. The leaders in the Anglo-Jewish community who inaugurated the CBF and helped save the lives of many thousands of men, women and children were such men of honour.

Appendix A: A Call for Community Action, April 1933

On 24 April 1933, Neville Laski and Leonard Montefiore wrote the following letter to Lionel de Rothschild:

> We feel that the time has come when a Special Committee should be established to deal with the problems which have arisen, and will arise, in relation to the economic and social welfare of our German co-religionists during the continuance of the present policy of discrimination. Having regard to the exceptional nature of the problems involved, the personnel of this Committee should not, in our view, be limited to members of the Board of Deputies or the Anglo-Jewish Association. We have carefully considered the proper composition of this Committee, and we feel that it could best be constituted as follows: The Chief Rabbi, Mr Lionel Cohen KC, Sir Robert Waley Cohen KBE, Mr O.E. d'Avigdor-Goldsmid DL, JP, Mr Neville Laski KC, Mr Simon Marks, Major H.L. Nathan MP, Mr Otto Schiff OBE, Dr C. Weizmann.
>
> We hope that you and your brother will consent to act as joint chairmen of this Committee. It is impossible for us exactly to define the scope and functions of this Committee, but generally speaking it will deal with questions of constructive work for the assistance of our German co-religionists and the raising of any necessary funds.

Lionel de Rothschild replied on the same day:

> My brother and I have received the letter that you and Mr Montefiore have addressed to us and in reply we shall naturally be willing to accept

your suggestion and call a meeting at New Court, at an early date, of the gentlemen you mention, to discuss how best we can carry out the suggestions you have made. All efforts to ameliorate the conditions of our co-religionists in Germany must have the sympathy of every member of the Community.

(*Jewish Chronicle*, 28 April 1933.)

Appendix B: Some Lists of Contributions to the CBF, 1933–36

(1) The following appeared in the *Jewish Chronicle* on 26 May 1933:

You are failing in your duty as a Jew – and your feelings for mankind, if your name is not in next week's list in this paper

The first response to the appeal for the

CENTRAL BRITISH FUND FOR GERMAN JEWRY

Messrs. N.M. Rothschild and Sons	£10,000
Messrs. M. Samuel and Co., Ltd.	10,000
Baron Family Trust	10,000
Marks, Mr. and Mrs. Simon	£4,000
Sieff, Mr. and Mrs. I. M.	1,500
Laski, Mr. and Mrs. Norman	1,500
Sacher, Mr. and Mrs. Harry	1,500
Marks, Miss Mathilde	1,500
	10,000
"G.J. and S."	2,000
Stern, Sir Albert, K.B.E.,C.M.G.	1,050
Abrahams, Isidor	1,000
Albu, L.	1,000
Anonymous, "H.H."	1,000
Anonymous	1,000
Burton, Sir Montague	1,000
Cohen, Lieut.-Col. Stanley S.G.	1,000
Cohen, Sir Robert Waley, K.B.E	1,000
Japhet, S.	1,000
Leigh, Claude M.	1,000
Melchett, The Rt. Hon. Lord	1,000
Montefiore, Dr. Claude G.	1,000
Weizmann, Dr. and Mrs. Chaim	1,000
Belisha, Albert I.	500
D'Avigdor-Goldsmid, O.E., J.P., D.L.	500
Franklin, Ernest L., J.P.	500
Goodenday, John	500
Solomon, Mr. and Mrs. Robert B.	500
Tuck, Gustave	500
Van den Bergh, Albert	500
Van den Bergh, Henry	500
Flatau, H.	300
Holt, David	300
Beddington, Gerald E., C.B.E	250
Cohen, Mr. and Mrs. Lionel L.	250
"H.L."	250
Jervis, Lieut.-Col. E.C.S., D.S.O.	250
Kosky, Harry, J.P.	250
Montefiore, Mr. and Mrs. Leonard G.	250
Samuel, Col. and Mrs. F.D.	250
Jacobs, Joseph I.	200
Loewi, Paul	200
Behrens, E. Beddington	150

Fill in - NOW

before you forget it.

The need is URGENT

Post Now!

Contributions should be sent to:—
Messrs. N.M. Rothschild & Sons, New Court, E.C.4,
and envelopes should be marked "Appeal."

I enclose my cheque
value.....................KINDLY ACKNOWLEDGE RECEIPT

NAME ....
ADDRESS ....
....
....

(2) The following appeared in the *Jewish Chronicle* on 6 April 1934:

THE SECOND APPEAL
of the
CENTRAL BRITISH FUND FOR GERMAN JEWS

Follow the lead of your leaders and give *at least as much* as last year.
The need is greater

Contributions to date amount to £56,573:0:6

FIRST LIST

Rothschild, Messrs. N. M. & Sons		£10,000 0 0
Samuel, Messrs. M. & Co., Ltd.		10,000 0 0
Marks, Mr. & Mrs. Simon	£4,000 0 0	
Sieff, Mr. & Mrs. I. M.	1,500 0 0	
Laski, Mr. & Mrs. Norman	1,500 0 0	
Sacher, Mr. & Mrs. Harry	1,500 0 0	
Marks, Miss Mathilde	1,500 0 0	
		10,000 0 0
Wolfson, I.		5,000 0 0
Lord Melchett's Family		2,000 0 0
d'Avigdor-Goldsmid, Sir Osmond, Bart.		1,050 0 0
Baron, Edward S.		1,000 0 0
Cohen, Harold L., J.P.		1,000 0 0
Cohen, Lieut.-Col. Stanley S.G.		1,000 0 0
Dreyfus, Dr. Henri		1,000 0 0
Fitzgerald, Lady Lily		1,000 0 0
Montefiore, Dr. Claude G.		1,000 0 0
Weizmann, Dr. and Mrs. Chaim		1,000 0 0
Stern, Major Frederick C., O.B.E., M.C.		500 0 0
Seligman Bros., Ltd.		500 0 0
Van den Bergh, Albert		500 0 0
Tuck, Gustave		500 0 0
Montagu, Captain the Hon. Lionel, D.S.O.		500 0 0
Franklin, Ernest L., J.P.		500 0 0
Asher, Mr. and Mrs. S.G.		250 0 0
Japhet, Saemy		250 0 0
Samuel, Frank		250 0 0
Sykes, J.F.		250 0 0
Lindenberg, Paul		250 0 0
Montefiore, Mr. and Mrs. Leonard G.		250 0 0
Beddington, Gerald E., C.B.E		250 0 0
Cohen, Dennis M.		250 0 0

Van den Bergh, Henry	£250 0 0
Davis, Mrs Abraham	200 0 0
Lewisohn, J.	200 0 0
Loewe, Paul	200 0 0
Turk, E.	200 0 0
Mocatta, Owen. E.	200 0 0
Schiff, Otto M., O.B.E.	200 0 0
British and Colonial Furniture Co., Ltd.	200 0 0
Samuel, Colonel and Mrs. F.D.	200 0 0
Cohen, Major J. Brunel	200 0 0
Cohen, Ernest M.	150 0 0
Cohen, Sir Leonard and Lady	150 0 0
Gollin, George, O.B.E	105 0 0
Waley, Mr. and Mrs. Philip S.	105 0 0
Bertish, M.	105 0 0
Lucas, Mrs. Henry	105 0 0
Myers, M. S.	105 0 0
Leon, Bros.	105 0 0
Fuerst, Max and Mrs. H. Irwell	105 0 0
Philipp, Oscar	105 0 0
Bauer, G.M.	100 0 0
Haldin, Mr. and Mrs. Philip	100 0 0
Bentwich, Helen and Norman	100 0 0
Levy, Mr. and Mrs. Lawrence	100 0 0
Goldstein, W.	100 0 0
Jacob, George G.	100 0 0
Rothman, Sydney	100 0 0
Abrahams, Louis	100 0 0
Davis, B.D.	100 0 0
Polhill, C.H.	100 0 0
Wolfe, Jonas	100 0 0

JEWS OF BRITAIN – *DO YOUR DUTY!*

You are failing in your duty if your name is not on next week's list in this paper.

(3) The following appeared in the *Jewish Chronicle* on 15 March 1935:

British Jewry's prompt reply
to the NAZI MENACE!

You too should give generously to the
CENTRAL BRITISH FUND FOR GERMAN JEWRY

FIRST LIST - THIRD APPEAL

		£	s.	d.
Marks, Mr. and Mrs. Simon	4,000			
Sieff, Mr. and Mrs. I. M.	1,500			
Laski, Mr. and Mrs. Norman	1,500			
Sacher, Mr. and Mrs. Harry	1,500			
Marks, Miss Mathilde	1,500			
		10,000	0	0
Baron Family Trust, The		5,000	0	0
Rothschild, Messrs. N.M. and Sons		5,000	0	0
Samuel, Messrs. M. and Co., Ltd.		5,000	0	0
Wolfson, Mr. and Mrs. Isaac		2,500	0	0
Gollin, George, O.B.E		1,050	0	0
"G.J. and S."		1,000	0	0
Albu, Leopold		1,000	0	0
Burton, Sir Montague, J.P.		1,000	0	0
Cohen, Lieut.-Col. Stanley S.G.		1,000	0	0
Ezra, Mr. and Mrs. Alfred		1,000	0	0
Fitzgerald, Lady Lily		1,000	0	0
Montefiore, Dr. Claude G., M.A.		1,000	0	0
Anonymous		500	0	0
Anonymous		500	0	0
Goldsmid, Sir Osmond d'Avigdor, Bart.		500	0	0
Joseph, J.E.		500	0	0
Melchett Family, The				
Erleigh, Viscount and Viscountess	}	500	0	0
Melchett, Lord and Lady				
Van den Bergh, Albert		500	0	0
Sterling, Louis		315	0	0
Levy Bros., Messrs		300	0	0
Montefiore, Mr. and Mrs. Leonard G.		300	0	0
Joel, Jack B.		262	0	0
Davis, Mrs. Abraham		250	0	0
Ehrlich, Leopold		250	0	0
Franklin, Ernest L., J.P.		250	0	0
Goodenday, Mrs. John		250	0	0
Japhet, S.		250	0	0
Lindenberg, Paul		250	0	0
Montagu, Capt. the Hon. Lionel, D.S.O.		250	0	0
Reading, The Most Hon. The Marquess of P.C., G.C.B.		250	0	0
Samuel, Max L.		250	0	0
Schlesinger, Richard A., M.B.E.		250	0	0
Solomon, Capt. Robert B., M.C., L.L.B.		250	0	0
Stern, Lady		250	0	0
Tuck, Gustave		250	0	0
Turk, Eric		250	0	0
Anonymous		210	0	0
Cohen, Ernest M.		200	0	0
Cohen, Colonel		200	0	0
Cohen, Major J.B. Brunel J.P.		200	0	0

		£	s.	d.
Lebus, Mrs S. Harris		200	0	0
Leon, Sir George and Lady		200	0	0
Mocatta, Edgar L. de M.		200	0	0
Schiff, Otto M., O.B.E		200	0	0
Ullman, Messrs. and Co.	105 0 0			
Ullam, Max	52 10 0			
		157	10	0
Blunt, Lady		150	0	0
Sebag-Montefiore, Major Geoffrey E.		150	0	0
Seligman, Professor and Mrs. C.G.		150	0	0
Ross, Cyril J.		120	0	0
Cohen, Lionel L., K.C.		105	0	0
Cope, David		105	0	0
Drage, Sir Benjamin		105	0	0
Irwell, Mrs. Henrietta and Fuerst, Max		105	0	0
Marx, Mr. and Mrs. H		105	0	0
Stern, Major F.C., O.B.E., M.C.		105	0	0
Waley, Mr. and Mrs. Philip. S.		105	0	0
Davidson, Fred		102	0	0
Asher, Mr. and Mrs. S.G.		100	0	0
Beddington, Lieut.-Col. E.		100	0	0
Benjamin, Frank D.		100	0	0
Bentwich, Professor and Mrs. Norman		100	0	0
Cohen, Arthur M.		100	0	0
Cohen, Dennis M.		100	0	0
Cohen, Sir Leonard and Lady		100	0	0
Conway, F.J.		100	0	0
Eder, Dr. and Mrs. F.D.		100	0	0.
Gluckstein, Mrs. Franceca, M.B.E., J.P.		100	0	0
Goldstein, William		100	0	0
Halford, F.L.		100	0	0
Kisch, A. Maitland		100	0	0
Kisch, H.M., C.S.I.		100	0	0
Kohn-Speyer, Paul		100	0	0
Lazarus, Leopold		100	0	0
Levine, A.		100	0	0
Levy, Miss Bertha		100	0	0
Mond, Sir Robert		100	0	0
Montefiore Endowment of the Spanish and Portuguese Congregation		100	0	0
Myers, Lady Vera		100	0	0
Pass, Charles H. de		100	0	0
Phillips, M. David		100	0	0
Pinto, Captain and Mrs. Richard		100	0	0
Samuel, Colonel and Mrs. F.D.		100	0	0
Sebag-Montefiore, Charles E.		100	0	0
Spielman, Sir Meyer and Lady		100	0	0
Stern, Sir Albert, K.B.E., C.M.G.		100	0	0
Swaythling, The Rt. Hon. Lord		100	0	0

Contributions to date amount to £54,234:7:8
LAST YEAR'S FIRST LIST TOTALLED £56,573:0:6
THE NEED IS STILL GREATER – DO YOUR DUTY.
See that your name is in next week's list in this paper.

(4) The following appeared in the *Jewish Chronicle* on 3 April 1936:

COUNCIL FOR GERMAN JEWRY

(British Section)

Appeal for

£1,000,000

PRELIMINARY LIST

	£	s.	d.
The Rothschild Family, certain members living in England	90,320	0	0
The Rt. Hon. the Viscount and Viscountess Bearsted The Hon. Mrs. N. Ionides The Hon. Mrs. Ida Sebag-Montefiore	90,320	0	0
Mr. and Mrs. Simon Marks Mr. and Mrs. I.M. Sieff Mr. and Mrs. Norman Laski Mr. and Mrs. Harry Sacher Miss Mathilde Marks	90,320	0	0
St. John's Wood Synagogue Preliminary List, Total:	19,500	0	0
including: Mr. Isaac Wolfson 12,900 Anonymous 1,290 Mr. L. Teller 1,290 Mr. Gustave Tuck 1,290			
Manchester–Preliminary List, Total:	15,000	0	0
including: Messrs Noah & Nathan Laski 5,000 Messrs. Nahum 2,000 Mr. Ephraim Sieff 1,500 Messrs. M. & H. Steel 1,000 Mr. I. Swift 1,000 Mr. P. Quas-Cohen 1,000			
Leeds - Preliminary List, Total:	14,000	0	0
including: Messrs. J.H. Abrahams & Sons 1,935 Messrs. M.J. & G. Stross 1,290 Messrs. L. and L. Zossenheim 1,290			

	£	s.	d.
The Baron Family Trust	10,000	0	0
Lady Fitzgerald	9,030	0	0
Liverpool - Preliminary List, Total:	4,200	0	0
New Synagogue - Preliminary List, Total:	4,100	0	0
Sir Osmond E. d'Avigdor Goldsmid, Bart, J.P.	2,710	0	0
Mr. Moss Myers	2,580	0	0
Sir Max J. Bonn, K.B.E.	2,500	0	0
Mr. Charles E. Sebag-Montefiore	2,260	0	0
Mr. and Mrs. Dennis M. Cohen	1,350	0	0
Major Geoffrey E. Sebag-Montefiore	1,350	0	0
"In Memory of our father, Herbert D. Cohen"	1,290	0	0
The Rt. Hon. Lord and Lady Melchett	1,290	0	0
The Marquis and Marchioness of Reading	1,290	0	0
Hull – Preliminary List, Total:	1,000	0	0
"Temple Bar"	1,000	0	0
Anonymous	1,000	0	0
Dr. Claude G. Montefiore	1,000	0	0
Colonel & Mrs. F.D. Samuel	1,000	0	0

The day is short, and the work is great. It is not thy duty to complete the work, but neither art thou free to desist from it.

Contributions should be sent to Messrs. N.M. Rothschild & Sons, New Court, London, E.C. 4

(5) The following appeared in the *Jewish Chronicle* on 19 June 1936:

THE COUNCIL FOR GERMAN JEWRY

Appeal for

£1,000,000

NINTH LIST

Name	£	s	d
Mrs. Pearl Merrons (Glasgow)	£2,000	0	0
Messrs. Henry Ansbacher & Co.	1,000	0	0
Messrs. L. and A. Froomberg, Ltd.	500	0	0
Sir George Jessel, Bart, M.C.	450	0	0
Messrs. Smartwear, Ltd.	330	0	0
Dr. Chaim Weizmann	250	0	0
Messrs. Levy, Langner & Co.	210	0	0
Dr. Redcliffe N. Salaman, F.R.S.	200	0	0
Simon Deyong, Esq.	180	0	0
I. Mail, Esq. (Glasgow)	180	0	0
M. Ziff, Esq. (Leeds)	145	0	0
"J.D."	135	0	0
S.L. Bensusan, Esq.	135	0	0
Mrs. Jane A. Bernstein	135	0	0
M. Bick, Esq. and M. Frumkin, Esq.	135	0	0
Lionel L. Cohen, Esq.	135	0	0
P. Lawrence Cohen, Esq.	135	0	0
Reuben Cohen, Esq.	135	0	0
A.E. Gentilli, Esq.	135	0	0
S. Glicker, Esq. (Manchester)	135	0	0
Sir Cecil & Lady Kisch	135	0	0
A.L. Lazarus, Esq.	135	0	0
Benjamin Strump, Esq., J.P. (Glasgow)	£135	0	0
Messrs. Tankel Bros. (Glasgow)	135	0	0
A.M. Wartski, Esq.	135	0	0
A.H. Weinbaum, Esq.	135	0	0
Messrs. David Baker & Sons (Manchester)	130	0	0
Joseph Blaiberg, Esq.	130	0	0
Messrs. P. S. & J. Ellis, Ltd. (Leeds)	130	0	0
Gerald Finestone, Esq. (Liverpool)	130	0	0
Sampson Freedman, Esq.	130	0	0
Miss Alice Hardy	130	0	0
Woolf Karp, Esq. (Liverpool)	130	0	0
Paul C. Kohn-Speyer, Esq.	130	0	0
Benn Wolfe Levy, Esq.	130	0	0
I. Jackson Lipkin, Esq. (Liverpool)	130	0	0
W. Miller, Esq. (Hull)	130	0	0
Max Robinson, Esq. (Liverpool)	130	0	0
S. Samuels, Esq. (Liverpool)	130	0	0
Miss Hilda M. Schlesinger	130	0	0
L.A. & Dr. S. Silman (Bradford)	130	0	0
Harry Solomon, Esq. (Liverpool)	130	0	0
T. Stanton, Esq.	130	0	0
Frank R. Waley, Esq.	130	0	0

Total to date **£626,195**

The response of the Anglo-Jewish community has been remarkable in the extreme but nearly Four Hundred Thousand Pounds still remain to be found. The final success of the appeal cannot be achieved unless all contribute to the limit of their resources. Has your name appeared on the lists published in this paper?

Contributions should be sent now to:

N.M. ROTHSCHILD & SONS, NEW COURT, E.C.4.

Notes

1: Introduction

1 Lloyd P. Gartner, *The Jewish Immigrant in England, 1870–1914* (Detroit: Wayne State University Press, 1960), 85.

2 Gartner, *The Jewish Immigrant*, 170–2; Theodore Norman, *An Outstretched Arm: A History of the Jewish Colonization Association* (London: Routledge and Kegan Paul, 1985), 219.

3 Chaim Bermant, *The Cousinhood: The Anglo-Jewish Gentry* (London: Eyre and Spottiswoode, 1971), 1–4; Paul H. Emden, *Jews of Britain* (London: Sampson Low, Marston and Co., 1943), 174–8; Vivian D. Lipman, *Social History of the Jews in England, 1850–1950* (London: Watts and Co., 1954), 82.

4 The London Jewish Board of Guardians was founded to enable the community as a whole to provide relief to persons in need, instead of individual synagogue congregations carrying this burden. Vivian D. Lipman, *A Century of Social Service, 1859–1959* (London: Routledge and Kegan Paul, 1959), 22–6.

5 Eugene C. Black, *The Social Politics of Anglo-Jewry, 1880–1920* (Oxford: Basil Blackwell, 1988), 38–43.

6 Aliens Restriction Act 1914 (I Statutes 913); Ian A. MacDonald, *Immigration Law and Practice in the United Kingdom* (London: Butterworth, 1963), 8.

7 David Cesarani, 'Joynson-Hicks and the Radical Right in England after the First World War', in Tony Kushner and Kenneth Lunn (eds), *Traditions of Intolerance* (Manchester: Manchester University Press, 1989), 123.

8 Bernard Wasserstein, 'The British Government and the German Immigration 1933–1945', in Gerhard Hirschfeld (ed.), *Exiles in Great Britain: Refugees from Hitler's Germany* (New Jersey: Humanities Press, 1984), 64.

9 Vivian D. Lipman, *A History of the Jews in Britain Since 1858* (Leicester: Leicester University Press, 1990), 140.

10 The ORT was founded in St Petersburg in 1880. It is the world's largest non-governmental education and training organization. See Max Beloff, 'Anglo-Jewry Revisited', *Jewish Journal of Sociology* Vol. XXXIII, No. 1, June 1991, 36.

11 Sir John Hope Simpson, *The Refugee Problem: Report of a Survey* (Oxford: Oxford University Press, 1939), 344; Aliens Restriction (Amendment) Act 1919 (I Statutes 917).

12 European Economic Community Treaty, Title III, Rome, 25 March 1957, Article 48 B10; European Communities Act 1972 (Cmnd 5179–1).

13 Avraham Barkai, *From Boycott to Annihilation: The Economic Struggle of German Jews, 1933–1943* (Hanover: University Press of New England, 1989), 1–2; Sarah Gordon, *Hitler, Germans, and the 'Jewish Question'* (New Jersey: Princeton University Press, 1984), 8–15.

14 Jack Wertheimer, '"The Unwanted Element": East European Jews in Imperial Germany', *Leo Baeck Yearbook*, Vol. XXVI, 1951.

15 Norman Bentwich, *The Refugees from Germany, 1933–1935* (London: George Allen and Unwin, 1936), 31.

16 See Vicki Caron, 'The Politics of Frustration: French Jewry and the Refugee Crisis in the 1930s', *Modern History*, Vol. 65, No. 2, June 1993, 311–56; Bentwich, *The Refugees from Germany*, 107–21.

17 Non-Aryans will be included in all further references to German actions directed against Jews.

18 William D. Rubenstein, *A History of the Jews in the English Speaking World: Great Britain* (London: Macmillan, 1996), 281.

2: Otto Schiff and the Jewish Refugees Committee

1 Joan Stiebel, interview, 18 October 1994. Stiebel was Otto Schiff's secretary from May 1933 until he retired in 1949; Norman Bentwich, *They Found Refuge* (London: The Cresset Press, 1956), 51.

2 HO 144/619/B35860/169290.

3 Stephen Birmingham, *'Our Crowd': The Great Jewish Families of New York* (New York: Harper and Row, 1967), 172–80.

4 Otto Schiff was later awarded the Commander of the British Empire (CBE)

for his work with refugees from Germany. Obituary on Otto Schiff, *The Times*, 18 November 1952, 10.

5 Joan Stiebel, interview, 18 October 1994; Ernst G. Lowenthal, 'Bloomsbury House: Flüchtlingshilfsarbeit in London 1939 bis 1946 aus persönlichen Erinnerungen', *Das Unrechtsregime* (Hamburg: Hans Christians Verlag, 1986), 297; see Tony Kushner, *The Persistence of Prejudice* (Manchester: Manchester University Press, 1989).

6 Leo Baker, *Days of Sorrow and Pain: Leo Baeck and the Berlin Jews* (New York: Macmillan, 1978), 145.

7 After two years of operation, the Reichsvertretung and the Zentral Ausschuss were restructured. The Reichsvertretung assumed the role of the Central Organization of German Jewry and the Zentral Ausschuss acquired responsibility for its departments. Bentwich, *They Found Refuge*, 9–21. In 1919, Carl Melchior was the German government's financial expert at the Hague Conference on War Indemnities.

8 The Nathan and Adolphe Haendler Charity was established in 1931 by Adolphe Haendler, a Russian Jew who moved from Germany to England after the First World War.

9 The First Lodge of the B'nai Brith was inaugurated in London 1910, despite opposition from leaders of the Anglo-Jewish community. They believed that they were well served by the philanthropic, political, social and educational institutions in place. Walter M. Schwab, *B'nai Brith, the First Lodge of England: A Record of Fifty Years* (England: Oswald Wolff, 1960), 17; Jews' Temporary Shelter, Forty-Second Report for the 2 years ending October 31st, 1966, 5–6.

10 Cissie Laski was a daughter of Dr Rabbi Moses Gaster, the spiritual leader (Haham) of the Sephardi Jewish community. Alice Model was awarded an MBE in 1934 in recognition of her efforts to professionalize child-care facilities in the East End of London. Anna Schwab was born in Frankfurt, Germany. JC, 4 January 1935, 6; Linda Gordon Kuzmack, *Woman's Cause* (Columbus: Ohio State University Press, 1990), 46–7, 87; Bentwich, *They Found Refuge*, 14–16, 50–1; Julia Neuberger, *On Being Jewish* (London: Mandarin, 1996), 29–32.

11 On 9 March 1933, a 24-year-old stateless Jew from Dresden, probably of Polish origin, was the first refugee to register (JRC Registration Index).

12 Lawrence Barton, *An Account of the Work of the Friends Committee for Refugees and Aliens, First Known as the German Emergency Committee of the Society of*

Friends 1933–1950 (London: Friends House, 1954); Ronald C.D. Jasper, *George Bell of Chichester* (Oxford: Oxford University Press, 1967), 135–63.

13 Schwab, *B'nai B'rith*, 86.

14 CBF Archives 34/217–217, First Annual Report, 2; Jewish Telegraphic Agency press release, 6 April 1933; *The Times*, 10 April 1933, 7.

15 Gesetz zur Wiederherstellung des Berufsbeamtentums. Vom 7 April 1933 (Reichsgesetzblatt Teil I, Seite 175; ibid., Seite 188).

16 Bentwich, *Refugees from Germany*, 174–97.

17 See Bruno Blau, *Das ausnahmerecht für die Juden in den europäischen Ländern, 1933–1945*; Herbert A. Strauss, 'Jewish Emigration from Germany' *Leo Baeck Yearbook*, No. XXV, 1980, 334–5.

18 In 1933 Max Warburg moved the Warburg Art Institute from Hamburg to London. Its director Dr F. Saxl (later a Fellow of the Royal Society) and other scholars and technicians also made the move. Max Warburg undertook to keep the Institute's home in Hamburg available for three years and to facilitate its return to Germany if conditions there allowed for the resumption of research activities. Lord Melchett and then Samuel Courtauld housed the holdings, and together with the Warburg family financed the maintenance. The Institute remained in London and is today an integral unit of the University of London. Norman Bentwich, *The Rescue and Achievement of Refugee Scholars: The Story of Displaced Scholars and Scientists, 1933–1952* (The Hague: Martinus Nijhoff, 1953), 42–3.

19 Sir John Gilmour, Home Secretary, Cabinet Committee on Alien Restrictions, 6 April 1933, CAB 27/549 AR (33).

20 Sir Ernest Holderness to Under-Secretary of State 31 March 1933, FO 371/16740, C2979/1621/18.

21 An agreement with Germany in 1928 had concluded with the mutual abolition of visas. A.J. Sherman, *Island Refuge: Britain and Refugees from the Third Reich 1933–1939* (London: Paul Elek, 1973), 89.

22 F.E. Foley to Chancery, 29 March 1933, PRO. FO 371/16721.

23 The Board of Deputies was founded in 1760 to protect the civil and political rights of Jews. It is the legal representative body of the Jewish community, and its members are drawn from synagogal constituencies.

24 HO 45/15882; Sherman, *Island Refuge*, 28; Andrew Scharf, *The British Press and Jews Under Nazi Rule* (London: Oxford University Press, 1964), 193.

25 HO 45/20528.

26 JC, 21 April 1933, 12; *The Times*, 10 April 1933, 7; ibid, 26 April 1933, 17;

Lucy S. Davidowicz, *The War Against the Jews, 1933–1945* (New York: Bantam, 1979), 72–3.

27 Committee on Alien Restrictions, report, 7 April 1933, 2, CAB 24/239.

28 Cabinet Meeting on Alien Restrictions, 7 April 1933, Appendix, CAB 24/239.

29 Severin Adam Hochberg, 'The Repatriation of Eastern European Jews from Great Britain: 1881–1914', *Jewish Social Studies*, Vol. 1, Nos 1–2, Winter–Spring 1988–92, 49–62.

30 'Negotiations are being conducted with the Government with a view to the refugees being given the right of asylum irrespective of whether they have funds or not, the fact being made clear that the Jewish community would be responsible for them.' JC, 14 April 1933, 21.

31 Raul Hilberg, *The Destruction of European Jews* (New York: Harper Colophon, 1961), 89–97.

32 See Kushner, *The Persistence of Prejudice.*

33 Letter, Otto Schiff to Secretary of State, 14 March 1938, BD ACC 3121 C11/12/1; see Geoffrey Alderman, 'Anglo-Jewry and Jewish Refugees', in *AJR Information*, June 1987, 3.

34 Cabinet Committee on Alien Restrictions, Appendix: Proposals of the Jewish Community as Regards Jewish Refugees from Germany, i, CAB 24/239.

35 Ibid. Neither Otto Schiff nor others could have foreseen the significance that registration with the JRC was to have for former refugees after the collapse of Nazi Germany in 1945. Now scattered in countries around the world, those who registered with the JRC and who require evidence in support of restitution and pension claims against Germany and Austria are able to secure proof of the date of their arrival in Britain from the archive of registrants which the JRC had maintained and which has been preserved.

36 Ibid.

37 Cabinet Committee on Alien Restrictions, memorandum by the Home Secretary, The Present Position in Regard to the Admission of Jewish Refugees from Germany to this Country, 7 April 1933, CAB 24/239.

38 BD, Joint Foreign Committee, 19 February 1933, 33.

39 Board of Guardians and Trustees for the Relief of the Jewish Poor, Seventy-Fifth Annual Report, 1 January 1933 to 31 December 1933, 13.

40 Cabinet Committee on Alien Restrictions, 7 April 1933, CAB 24/239.

41 Ibid.

42 Sherman, *Island Refuge*, 32–3.

43 Ibid.

44 RAL, XIV/35/19, memorandum of 26 October 1939; CBF, Report for 1933–43.

3: The Central British Fund for German Jewry is organized

1 Lord Reading (1889–1960), Viceroy of India, 1921–6; Foreign Secretary, 1931. Sir Herbert Samuel (1870–1963), first High Commissioner for Palestine, 1920–5. JC, 30 September 1960, 23; Lipman, *A History of the Jews in Britain Since 1858*, 251–5.

2 30 March, 6 April 1933, 134–5, 156, FO 371/16721.

3 Sharon Gewitz, 'Anglo-Jewish Responses to Nazi Germany, 1933–39: The Anti-Nazi Boycott and the Board of Deputies of British Jews', *Journal of Contemporary History*, Vol. 26, No. 2, April 1991, 255–76.

4 Bentwich, *They Found Refuge*, 21; Shimoni, 'From Anti-Zionism to Non-Zionism: Anglo-Jewry, 1917–1937', *Jewish Journal of Sociology*, Vol. XXVIII, No. 1, June 1986, 34.

5 CBF, minutes of Allocations Committee, 10 July 1933, 1; JC, 11 December 1964, 23.

6 Bentwich, *They Found Refuge*, 20.

7 CBF Archives, 109/7, extract of meeting of Keren Hayesod Committee, 16 May 1933; letter, Simon Marks to Lavi Bakstansky, CBF, 26 July 1933; CZA KHB/4821, letter, Lavi Bakstansky, Jewish Agency for Palestine, London, to Dr A. Hanke, Keren Hayesod, Jerusalem, 31 July 1934.

8 Robert Henriques, *Sir Robert Waley Cohen 1877–1952* (London: Secker and Warburg, 1966), 273–80.

9 CZA, A255/440, correspondence, Arthur E. Franklin and Otto Schiff, 25, 26 September 1933.

10 RAL, XIV/35/19, letter, Anthony de Rothschild to Simon Marks, 22 December 1939; ibid., letter, Sir Robert Waley Cohen to Anthony de Rothschild, 1 January 1940.

11 JC, 28 April 1933, 27, letter, Neville Laski and Leonard Montefiore, 24 April 1933.

12 Ibid., letter, Lionel de Rothschild to Laski and Montefiore, 27.

13 See Chaim Bermant, *The Cousinhood: The Anglo-Jewish Gentry* (London: Eyre and Spottiswoode, 1971).

14 Many of those who were later recruited to participate in the activities of the CBF and its auxiliary agencies as they evolved were also drawn from the cousinhood.

15 Frederic Morton, *The Rothschilds: A Family Portrait* (New York: Atheneum, 1962), 242.

16 *The Times*, 6 February 1961, 17; Evelyn de Rothschild, a third brother who held the rank of major in the army, was killed in Palestine in 1917 (RAL 000/313).

17 Lionel Leonard Cohen (1888–1973), vice-president of Board of Deputies of British Jews, 1934–8; president of Board of Guardians, 1940–7. See *The Times*, 10 May 1973, 20.

18 *The Times*, 29 November 1952, 8.

19 Sir Robert Waley Cohen (1877–1952), joined Shell Oil Company, 1901; represented Shell in negotiations on merger with Royal Dutch Petroleum Company; key role in ensuring oil supplies to Allies in First World War. Created KBE, 1920; later second-in-command of Shell Oil Group; United Synagogue vice-president, 1918–42, president, 1942–52; vice-president of Board of Deputies of British Jews, 1936–43; interview, June 1991, Kitty Stein, widow of Leonard Stein, KC, who in 1933 was involved in organizing the CBF. Henriques, *Sir Robert Waley Cohen*, 260–348; Bermant, *The Cousinhood*, 357; Lipman, *A History of Jews in Britain*, 248.

20 Sir Osmond E. d'Avigdor Goldsmid (1877–1940). The Jewish Colonization Association, a major philanthropic institution, was established by Baron Maurice de Hirsch to finance retraining and emigration of Jews from eastern Europe to countries in the Americas and to Palestine. President of Anglo-Jewish Association, 1921–6; president of Board of Deputies of British Jews, 1926–33; Paul H. Emden, *Jews of Britain* (London: Sampson Low, Marston and Co., 1943), 148–9; Bermant, *The Cousinhood*, 360.

21 Neville Jonas Laski (1890–1969), later successively recorder of Burnley, Judge of Appeal for the Isle of Man and recorder and judge at the Crown Court in Liverpool; served as officer in Lancashire Fusiliers in First World War; Lipman, *A History of the Jews*, 252; Norman Bentwich, *My Seventy-Seven Years: An Account of My Life and Times, 1883–1960* (London: Routledge and Kegan Paul, 1962), 124–5.

22 Simon Marks (1888–1964), chairman of the Board, Marks and Spencer, 1917–64; chairman of Keren Hayesod Committee; vice-president of Zionist Federation; member of Zionist Executive; president of Joint

Palestine Appeal; knighted, 1944; baronetcy, 1961, for 'public and charitable services'. JC, 4 July 1958; *The Sun*, 9 December 1964; Bentwich, *My Seventy-Seven Years*, 141–2; interview, Dame Simone Prendergast, niece of Simon Marks, 4 June 1991. Simone Prendergast was a long-time chairperson of the Jewish Refugee Committee, and treasurer of the CBF and World Jewish Relief.

23 Leonard Montefiore (1889–1961) served as an officer in the 9th (Territorial) Battalion of the Hampshire Regiment. He was second-in-command in India, and later in northern Russia until his demobilization in 1919. President of Anglo-Jewish Association, 1926–39; member of the Council, later chairman of the Jewish Colonization Association; see Leonard Stein and C.C. Aronsfeld (eds), *Leonard G. Montefiore in Memoriam* (London: Valentine, 1964).

24 Harry Louis Nathan (1888–1963). Liberal MP, 1929–34; Labour MP, 1937–40; elected member of the peerage, 1940; Parliamentary Under-Secretary of State for War, 1945–6; Minister of Civil Aviation, 1946–8; Privy Councillor, 1946; Bermant, *The Cousinhood*, 368; *Jewish Year Book 1947* (London: Jewish Chronicle, n.d.), 410.

25 Bentwich, *They Found Refuge*, 15; Stephen Birmingham, *Our Crowd*, 173; JC, 21 November 1952, 9.

26 Morton, *The Rothschilds*, 197–209; RAL, XIV/35/19, letter, Anthony de Rothschild to Simon Marks, 22 December 1939; see *The Memoirs of Israel Sieff* (London: Weidenfeld and Nicolson, 1970).

27 RAL, XIV 000/313, The League of British Jews, Minute Books; ibid., letter, Lionel de Rothschild to Secretary of State for the Colonies, 12 April 1923; Shimoni, 'From Anti-Zionism to Non-Zionism in Anglo-Jewry', 21–44; Wasserstein, *Britain and the Jews of Europe*, 2.

28 Bentwich, *They Found Refuge*, 10.

29 See David S. Wyman, *Paper Walls: America and the Refugee Crisis, 1938–1941* (New York: Pantheon, 1985); Amy Zahl Gottlieb, 'Refugee Immigration: The Truman Directive', *Prologue*, Journal of the National Archives, Washington, DC, Vol. 13, No. 1, Spring 1981, 5–17; Friedrich S. Brodnitz, 'Memories of the Reichsvertretung: A Personal Report', *Leo Baeck Yearbook*, Vol. XXXI, 1986, 270–1.

30 Wyman, *Paper Walls*, 1–37; CBF Archives, minutes of conference between delegates from European Refugee Committees and the Council for German Jewry, 23 April 1936, 2. See also Irving Abella and Harold Troper,

None Is Too Many (Toronto: Lester and Orpen Denny, 1982); Henry L. Feingold, *The Politics of Rescue* (New Jersey: Rutgers University Press, 1982); and Blakeney Michael, *Australia and the Jewish Refugees, 1933–1948* (Sydney: Croom Helm, 1985).

31 CBF Archives, 1A/9, 15 May 1933.

32 Leonard Stein and Leonard Montefiore met when both were students at Balliol College, Oxford. In 1910 Leonard Stein was the first Jew to be elected president of the Oxford Union. He was later president of the Anglo-Jewish Association. Stein was a cousin to Harry Nathan. (Interview, Kitty Stein, Leonard Stein's widow, 24 June 1991.)

33 CBF Archives, 1A/9, n.d.

34 CBF Archives, 1A/9, memorandum, n.d.

35 JC, 6 July 1962, 26; CBF Archives, 1/A1/A8; *The Times*, 19 May 1933, 9. Edward S. Baron was also a member of the Board of the Palestine Electric Corporation; Paul Emden, *Jews of Britain*, 314–15, 494. Philip S. Waley was a member of the cousinhood; Bermant, *The Cousinhood*, 272.

36 JC, 16 June 1933, 16.

37 The invitation was extended by Edward Baron, Philip Waley and Otto Schiff.

38 CBF Archives, 1A/4, minutes of Meeting of Organizing Committee, 16 May 1933. In 1934 the CBF was registered under the Companies Act, 4 October 1934. Names, addresses and descriptions of subscribers were: Anthony Gustav de Rothschild, New Court, St Swithin's Lane, EC4 (merchant banker); Osmond Elim d'Avigdor Goldsmid, Somerhill, Tonbridge (Baronet); Lionel Leonard Cohen, 3 Orme Square, W2 (KC); Otto Moritz Schiff, 25 Berkeley Square, W1 (member of London Stock Exchange); Chaim Weizmann, 16 Addison Crescent London W14; Leonard Nathaniel Goldsmid Montefiore, 37 Weymouth Street, W1 (merchant); Frederick Dudley Samuel, 8 Montague Square, W1 (banker); Selig Brodetsky, 3 Grosvenor Road, Leeds 6 (university professor); Harry Sacher, 5 Addison Road, London, W14 (barrister-at-law).

39 Jews' Temporary Shelter, Forty-Second Report for the 2 years ending October 31st, 1933, 6.

40 CBF Archives, 1/A4, meeting, 18 May 1933; JC, 24 April 1933, 27. Claude Montefiore was a founder, in 1910, of the Progressive Liberal Jewish Synagogue and president of the World Union for Progressive Judaism. Lord

Erleigh succeeded to his father's title, Lord Reading, on the latter's death in 1936.

41 CBF Archives, 1/A9; minutes of meeting of New Court Committee, 24 May 1933; copy of letter, 26 July 1933, Simon Marks, chairman, British Keren Hayesod to Lavi Bakstansky, CBF.

42 CBF Archives, 1/A9; minutes of meeting of New Court Committee, 24 May 1933.

43 JC, 26 May 1933, 17.

44 CBF Archives, 34/217; CBF First Annual Report, 1934.

45 JC, 26 May 1933, 19.

46 *The Times*, 2 June 1933, 9.

47 The Board of Guardians and Trustees for the Relief of the Jewish Poor, Seventy-Fifth Annual Report, 1 January 1933 to 31 December 1933, 13.

48 £1 in February 1933 was equivalent to £31 in February 1997. Thus, £7,750,000 would have had to be raised in 1997 to equal the £250,000 donated in 1933. (Data provided by the Bank of England.)

49 Bentwich, *They Found Refuge*, 21; Yehuda Bauer, *My Brother's Keeper* (Philadelphia: The Jewish Publication Society of America, 1974), 140.

50 Bentwich, *They Found Refuge*, 32.

4: CBF operations begin

1 'To deal with the allocation of funds a special committee shall be appointed by the New Court Committee and the Jewish Agency. Each body shall nominate three members and there shall in addition be a Chairman who shall be Mr O.E. d'Avigdor Goldsmid' (CBF Archives 1A/9).

2 Walter Cohen and Sir Robert Waley Cohen were first cousins. Walter was also Sir Robert's uncle by marriage. He was a co-founder with Sir Robert of the Palestine Corporation. Lionel M. Montague was a son of Lord Swaythling and a partner in Montagu Samuel and Co. (Henriques, *Sir Robert Waley Cohen*, 282; JC, 21 May 1954, 1; ibid., 2 September 1960, 26).

3 Barnet Litvinoff, General Editor, *The Letters and Papers of Chaim Weizmann* (Jerusalem: Israel Universities Press, 1978), Vol. XVI, Series A, June 1933–August 1935, Letter 24, 25–8; Henriques, *Sir Robert Waley Cohen*, 338.

4 CBF Archives, 1/A24, minutes of New Court Committee, 30 May 1933, 1; CBF communiqué, 10 July 1933.

5 CBF Archives, 1/A24, minutes of New Court Committee, 20 June 1933; Rosalie Gassman-Sherr, *The Story of the Federation of Women Zionists of Great Britain and Ireland, 1918–1968* (n.p., n.d.), 24–5.
6 Bentwich, *They Found Refuge*, 24–5; JC, 2 November 1934, 15.
7 JRC Report, March 1933 to January 1935.
8 JDC Archives, 404, meeting at Henry Street Settlement, 25 February 1934, 72–3; the CBF spent £42,692 (CBF, First Annual Report).
9 CBF, First Annual Report; Second Annual Report; Report of the Council of CBF, 1935; Naomi Shepherd, *Wilfred Israel: German Jewry's Secret Ambassador* (London: Weidenfeld and Nicolson, 1984), 47; Lilo Stone, 'German Zionists in Palestine before 1933', *Journal of Contemporary History*, Vol. 32, No. 2, April 1997, 181.
10 Stone, 'German Zionists in Palestine', 171–86.
11 CBF Archives, 34/217–27; CBF, Report of the Council, 26 June 1936; Adler Rudel, *Seven Years of Jewish Help*, Table VIII (n.d.).
12 CBF, minutes of Allocations Committee, 29 January 1934, 1.
13 CBF, minutes of Allocations Committee, 24 July 1933, 1; ibid., 31 July 1933, 1.
14 Felix Warburg was a brother of Max Warburg, Hamburg. See Birmingham, *Our Crowd*, 20.
15 CBF, First Annual Report.
16 AJA, Warburg Papers, 291/7, letter, Felix Warburg to Osmond d'Avigdor Goldsmid, 26 October 1933.
17 Bauer, *My Brother's Keeper*, 164–5.
18 CBF, minutes of Allocations Committee, 10 July 1933, 2.
19 Conference for the Relief of German Jewry, convened by Joint Foreign Committee, Board of Deputies of British Jews and Anglo-Jewish Association, Alliance Israelite Universelle, American Jewish Committee, American Jewish Congress and Comité des Délégations Juives, London, 29 October–1 November 1933.
20 CBF Allocations Committee, Joseph Cohen Report, 26 September 1933.
21 CBF Archives, 34/228, Second Annual Report of the Allocations Committee; minutes, 17 July 1933, 5. In Switzerland, refugee students were permitted to attend schools and universities, but were not allowed to accept employment. Report of J.L. Cohen on his visit to European countries, 18 August to 15 September 1933, 8.
22 CBF, Joseph Cohen Report, 26 September 1933, 8. Only in 1936 was the

effort first made to provide refugees with training in skilled trades (First Annual Report of the Council of German Jewry, 1936, 10).

23 Abraham Margaliot, 'The Problem of the Rescue of German Jewry During the Years 1933–1939: The Reasons for the Delay in their Emigration from the Third Reich', in Yisrael Gutman and Ephriam Zuroff (eds), *Rescue Attempts During the Holocaust*: Proceedings of the Second Yad Vashem International Historical Conference (Jerusalem, 1977), 262–3.

24 CZA KH4B/4821, letter, Chaim Weizmann to Dr A. Hanke, 14 August 1934.

25 CGJ, minutes of meeting, 4 April 1938, 2.

26 The Palestine Immigration Regulations and German Refugees, 30 June 1933; Proceedings Conference for the Relief of German Jewry: Jewish Agency for Palestine, Notes on Immigration into Palestine, London, 27 October 1933.

27 CBF, minutes of Council Meeting, 31 May 1935, 4.

28 CZA 247/18, letter, Chaim Weizmann to Simon Marks, 15 December 1935.

29 CBF, meeting of Allocations Committee, 7 May 1934, 2; CZA L13/149, letter, CBF to Chaim Weizmann, 8 May 1934, protesting the inadequate number of immigration certificates made available to German Jews; Bauer, *My Brother's Keeper*, 163–4.

30 Article IV of the League of Nations mandate for Palestine provided that a 'Jewish Agency' be formed to assume responsibility for Jewish immigration and settlement in Palestine, and to co-operate with the Mandatory power in all matters concerning the development of the Jewish national home; *The New Jewish Encyclopedia*, ed. David Bridger (New York: Behrman House, 1976), 238.

31 The agreement was reached in August 1933. See Edwin Black, *The Transfer Agreement* (New York: Macmillan, 1984), 246–50.

32 Bauer, *My Brother's Keeper*, 128.

33 Doron Niederland, 'Areas of Departure from Nazi Germany and the Social Structure of the Emigrants', in Werner E. Mosse, Co-ordinating Editor, *Second Chance: Two Centuries of German Speaking Jews in the United Kingdom* (Tubingen: J.C.B. Mohr (Paul Siebeck), 1991), 61. See also Barkai, *From Boycott to Annihilation*; Henry L. Feingold, 'Was There Communal Failure? Some Thoughts on the American Jewish Response to the Holocaust', *American Jewish History*, Vol. LXXXI, No. 1,

Autumn 1993, 60–80; and Edwin Black, *The Transfer Agreement.*

34 Conference for Relief of German Jewry, 29 October–1 November 1933, Doc. 2.

35 CBF Archives, 34/217, 34/227, First and Second Reports of the Allocations Committee; Bauer, *My Brother's Keeper*, 140.

36 CBF, First Annual Report; the figure for German (and Austrian) nationals in Britain is based on the Census of population and on the reports on 'Aliens Landed and Embarked' published by HMSO. Not all Germans (or Austrians) were refugees, but it was found necessary to provide the full number of these nationals. See Adler Rudel, *Seven Years*, legend, Table VII C; Joseph Cohen Report, 8.

37 CBF Archives, 34/227, Second Report of the Allocations Committee, 1934. It was at this time that the CBF was incorporated as a company limited by guarantee, and a CBF Executive was elected to assume financial decision making. A group of 243 German Jews, required by Brazilian regulation to travel first class, were aided in meeting this requirement by the JRC, ICA and JDC. See Mark Wischnitzer, *Visas to Freedom: The History of Hias* (New York: World Publishing Co., 1956), 141.

38 CBF, memorandum, Possibilities in the Colonies, Joseph L. Cohen, 24 July 1933; S.L. Besso, Ministry of Labour, to Otto Schiff, 27 July 1933.

39 Adler Rudel, *Seven Years of Jewish Help*, Table VII C; CBF, Report of the Council, 26 June 1936 (Third Report of the Allocations Committee).

40 JRC Report, March 1933 to January 1935, 1–4.

41 CBF Archives, 174/42, JRC, 20 February 1935; ibid., 174/58, JRC, 15 March 1935.

42 Academic Assistance Council, Annual Report, 1 May 1934. On the efforts of British colleagues to help refugee scholars through the AAC and later the Society for the Protection of Science and Learning, see R.M. Cooper (ed.), *Refugee Scholars: Conversations with Tess Simpson* (Leeds: Moorland, 1992); Gerhard Hirschfield, 'German Refugee Scholars in Great Britain, 1933–1945', in Anna C. Bramwell (ed.), *Refugees in the Age of Total War* (London: Unwin Hyman, 1988), 152–63.

43 Academic Assistance Council, Annual Report, 1 May 1934; CBF Archives, 1/A22.

44 CBF, First Annual Report. Nobel Laureate, Professor Albert Einstein, who had resigned from the faculty of the Kaiser Wilhelm Institute, visited London in 1933. During his stay in London he attended a CBF Allocations

Committee meeting (2 October 1933) and addressed a mass fund-raising rally in support of refugee scholars at the Royal Albert Hall; JC, 13 October 1933, 20; Ray Cooper, *Retrospective Sympathetic Affection: A Tribute to the Academic Community* (Leeds: Moorland, 1996), 63–81; Bentwich, *The Rescue and Achievement of Refugee Scholars*, 11.

45 CBF, minutes of Allocations Committee, 15 March 1934, 2–3.

46 Francis L. Carsten, 'German Refugees in Great Britain, 1933–1945', in Hirschfeld (ed.), *Exiles in Great Britain*, 11–28.

47 'Refugees and Industry', *Engineering Journal*, 10 July 1942.

48 See Cooper, *Retrospective Sympathetic Affection*; Bentwich, *The Rescue and Achievement of Refugee Scholars*, 99–102; Paul K. Hoch, 'Some Contributions to Physics by German-Jewish Emigrés in Britain and Elsewhere' in Mosse, *Second Chance*, 229–41; Cooper, *Refugee Scholars*, 100–3.

49 Lord Dawson of Penn, interview with Secretary of State on expatriated German doctors and students coming to the United Kingdom, 23 November 1933, HO 45/20428.

50 Viscount Templewood, *Nine Troubled Years* (London: Collins, 1954), 200.

51 CBF Archives, 174, letter, 30 October 1933, Medical Practioners' Union; Sherman, *Island Refuge*, 48.

52 Jews' Temporary Shelter, Annual Report for the year ending October 31st, 1939.

53 CBF Archives, 34/227, Second Report of the Allocations Committee 1934; JRC Report on the Work of the JRC from March 1933 to January 1935.

54 Doron Niederland, 'Areas of Departure from Nazi Germany', 57–68.

55 CBF Archives, 174/2/6, JRC, minutes of Executive Committee, 28 November 1934. See also Executive Committee Reports, JRC, 1934–7.

56 Philanthropists who had established the London Jewish Board of Guardians in 1859 had begun the practice of personal involvement in individual cases. See Vivian Lipman, *A Century of Social Service, 1859–1959: The Jewish Board of Guardians* (London: Routledge and Kegan Paul, 1959).

57 Stein and Aronsfeld, *Leonard G. Montefiore*; Toynbee Hall and the Jewish Community, n.p., n.d., 2.

58 CBF Archives, 174/42, JRC Executive Committee, 20 February 1935; ibid., March 1935; Doron Niederland, 'Areas of Departure from Nazi Germany', 68.

59 CBF Archives, 174/25, JRC Executive Committee, 16 January 1935; ibid., 174/116, 10 July 1935.
60 Ibid., 174/42, 20 February 1935.
61 Ibid., 174/58, 15 March 1935.
62 Ibid., 174/42, 174/58, 174/116, 20 February, 15 March, 10 July 1935.
63 CBF Archives, JRC 171/116, 10 July 1935; CGJ, minutes of Executive Committee, 21 April 1936, 2; ibid., 20 December 1937, 2.
64 CBF, minutes of Allocations Committee, 11 December 1934; CBF, Twentieth Annual Report, 1952, 4. (Jewish Resettlements Limited is not mentioned by Norman Bentwich in *They Found Refuge*).
65 In June 1934 the maximum amount of foreign currency in cash which could be taken out of Germany was cut from RM10,000 to RM2,000.
66 Home Office, memorandum, 8 September 1936, FO 371/20482, W11192/172/98.
67 Sherman, *Island Refuge*, 73; Herbert Loebl, 'Refugee Industries in the Special Areas of Britain' in Hirschfeld (ed.), *Exiles in Great Britain*, 219–49; Sir John Hope Simpson, *Refugees* (London: Royal Institute of International Affairs, 1938), 65.
68 Memorandum of Activities of HIAS-ICA Association (HICEM), 1942; Wischnitzer, *Visas to Freedom*, 141.

5: The calm before the storm

1 CBF, minutes of Executive Committee, 15 March 1934.
2 CBF, minutes of Allocations Committee, 11 December 1934.
3 CBF, minutes of Allocations Committee, 15 March 1934.
4 Ibid.
5 Ibid.
6 Reichsarbeitsblatt, Anordnung die Verteilung von Arbeitskraften von 28 August 1934, I 202.
7 CBF, letter, Otto Schiff to Sir Osmond d'Avigdor Goldsmid, 27 August 1934.
8 CBF, minutes of meeting at Office of Lionel L. Cohen, KC, 22 October 1944.
9 CBF, minutes of Allocations Committee, 3 September 1934, 3–4.
10 CBF, minutes of Allocations Committee, 3 October 1934.

11 Friedrich S. Brodnitz, 'Memories of the Reichsvertretung', *Leo Baeck Year Book*, Vol. XXXI, 1986, 268.
12 CBF, minutes of Executive Committee, 11 December 1934.
13 Ibid.
14 CBF, minutes of Allocations Committee, 3 October 1934; ibid., 30 October 1934; ibid., 4 December.
15 CBF, minutes of Allocation Committee, Dr Otto Hirsch's Report, 11 December 1934.
16 CZA KH4B/4821, letter, Lavi Bakstansky, joint secretary of CBF, writing from Jewish Agency for Palestine, Office of the Keren Hayesod, to Dr A. Hanke, Keren Hayesod, Jerusalem, 14 August 1934.
17 Lord Bearsted had been awarded the Military Cross while a colonel in the army in the First World War. See *Jewish Year Book 1949*, 324.
18 The appeal in 1935 raised £101,000 (CBF, Report of the Council, 26 June 1936).
19 CBF Archives, 1/A51, minutes of New Court Committee, 21 January 1935.
20 CBF, minutes of Council, 4 February 1935.
21 CBF Archives, 1/A51, minutes of New Court Committee, 21 January 1935.
22 CBF Archives, 1/A31, minutes of New Court Committee, 3 December 1934; ibid., 21 January 1935; ibid., minutes of Executive Committee, CGJ, 11 March 1936.
23 AJA, Warburg Papers, 336/2, letter, Neville Laski to Felix Warburg, 25 January 1937.
24 Beginning in February 1935, fund-raising meetings throughout the country were reported weekly in the pages of the *Jewish Chronicle*.
25 Chernow, *The Warburgs*, 432.
26 CBF, minutes of Council, 31 May 1935.
27 AJA, Warburg Papers, 325/II, letter, Norman Bentwich to Felix Warburg, 10 June 1936. Bentwich made his comment after visiting Emil Baerwald (brother of Paul Baerwald) and his wife, and a Mr Wasserman, in Berlin.
28 CBF, minutes of meeting, 1 May 1935, Dr Otto Hirsch, Berlin, and Sir Osmond d'Avigdor Goldsmid.
29 Reichsbuergergesetz vom 15 September 1935 (Reichsgesetzblatt Teil I, Seite 1146); *Manchester Guardian*, 17 September 1935, 8; *The Times*, 18 September 1935, 9.

6: The emigration programme and the Council for German Jewry

1 CBF Archives, minutes of meeting, 1 May 1935, Dr Otto Hirsch and Sir Osmond d'Avigdor Goldsmid; letter, Hans Mayer, business associate of Max Warburg, to d'Avigdor Goldsmid, 23 April 1935.

2 Abraham Margaliot, 'The Reaction of the Jewish Public in Germany to the Nuremberg Laws', *Yad Vashem Studies*, No. XII, January 1977, 82–3.

3 Ibid., 75–107.

4 Bauer, *My Brother's Keeper*, 151–2.

5 Columbia University Libraries, James McDonald Papers, letter, James McDonald to Felix M. Warburg, 7 November 1935.

6 Bauer, *My Brother's Keeper*, 142. The position of High Commissioner for Refugees (Jewish and Other) Coming from Germany was created by the Assembly of the League of Nations in September 1933; McDonald Papers, letter, McDonald to Felix M. Warburg, 7 November 1935; Bentwich, *My Seventy-Seven Years*, 141–2.

7 AJA, Warburg Papers, 291/7.

8 *The Letters and Papers of Chaim Weizmann*, Vol. XVI, letter, 21 November 1933, No. 136.

9 Bentwich, *My Seventy-Seven Years*, 142.

10 Bauer, *My Brother's Keeper*, 143–4; Bentwich, *They Found Refuge*, 25.

11 BD, minutes of Joint Foreign Committee, 6 September 1933.

12 Bentwich, *My Seventy-Seven Years*, 141–2; Zosa Szajkowski, 'Relief for German Jewry: Problems of American Involvement', *American Jewish Historical Quarterly*, Vol. LXII, December 1972, 136; Baker, *Days of Sorrow and Pain*, 218–20.

13 Wilfred Israel died in 1943 when his unarmed plane *en route* from Lisbon to England was shot down by the Germans. See Shepherd, *Wilfred Israel*.

14 CZA, A247/18, Simon Marks to Chaim Weizmann, 31 December 1935.

15 McDonald Papers, letters, 7 and 21 November 1935, McDonald to Felix Warburg. Lord Bearsted's father, a former Lord Mayor of London, was a founder of the Shell Oil Company; Bentwich, *They Found Refuge*, 31.

16 McDonald Papers, letters, 7 and 21 November 1935, McDonald to Felix M. Warburg. No extant record relating to Bearsted's contact with these men or financial contributions they may have made has been found.

17 Bentwich, *They Found Refuge*, 30–1; Bentwich, *My Seventy-Seven Years*, 131.

18 AJA, Warburg Papers, 327/5, CBF German Emigration Plan.

19 AJA, Warburg Papers, 327/5, CBF: Tentative Suggestions Towards A Four Year Plan of Emigration.

20 AJA, Warburg Papers, 327/5, CBF Emigration Plan.

21 Bauer, *My Brother's Keeper*, 153.

22 AJA, Warburg Papers, 320/16; Bentwich, *They Found Refuge*, 30–1.

23 AJA, Warburg Papers, 327/5, cable, Marks and Bearsted to Felix Warburg, 6 December 1935.

24 AJA, Warburg Papers, memorandum of visit, 7 February 1936, 5–6.

25 CBF Archives, minutes of New Court Committee, 13 February 1936.

26 AJA, Warburg Papers, 320/16, JDC Board meeting, 22 January 1936.

27 JDC Archives, 575, memorandum on conversations with Simon Marks, 17 February 1936; Bauer, *My Brother's Keeper*, 281.

28 CBF Archives, minutes of New Court Committee, 13 February 1936.

29 AJA, Warburg Papers, 320/16.

30 AJA, Warburg Papers, 327/5, CBF: Tentative Suggestions Towards A Four Year Plan of Emigration.

31 AJA, Warburg Papers, 320/50, meeting of the CGJ, New York, 4 December 1936; CGJ, report for 1936. The HICEM was funded by the ICA, the JDC and the CBF. From 1933 to 1939 the HICEM facilitated the emigration of approximately 50,000 persons at a cost of £542,855, 43 per cent of which was contributed by the ICA, 38 per cent by the JDC, 17 per cent by the CBF and 2 per cent by other organizations (CBF Archives, 101/2).

32 AJA, Warburg Papers, 320/16, minutes of meeting, 4 February 1936; ibid., 321/4, Lord Bearsted to Felix Warburg, 1 July 1936.

33 JDC Archives, 575, memorandum re conversation with Lord Samuel, 17 February 1939.

34 JDC Archives, 575, Morris C. Troper, memorandum on conversations with Simon Marks, 17 February 1939.

35 JDC Archives, 573, verbatim notes, meeting of the CGJ, New York, 4 December 1936, 8.

36 AJA, Warburg Papers, 320/10, memorandum on visit of Sir Herbert Samuel, Lord Bearsted and Mr Simon Marks, 21 January to 6 February 1936, 7–8.

37 Bauer, *My Brother's Keeper*, 140.

38 An attempt at joint fund raising in the United States had been made in 1934–5, but was rejected by the JDC. Only after the Nazis mounted their

Kristallnacht pogrom in November 1938 was such an effort instituted. Bauer, *My Brother's Keeper*, 254–5.

39 AJA, Warburg Papers, 321/4, letter, Lord Bearsted to Felix Warburg, 1 July 1936.

40 JDC Archives, 571, press release, 14 February 1936, 1.

41 JDC Archives, 571, meeting of Plan and Scope Committee for 1936, 23 February 1936; AJA, Warburg Papers, 327/5.

42 AJA, Warburg Papers, 325/7, letter, Rabbi Jonah Wise, national chairman of Fund-Raising Committee, JDC, to Frieda Warburg (wife of Felix), 10 March 1936.

43 CZA, A247/18, telegram, Simon Marks to Chaim Weizmann, Rehovot, 25 February 1936

44 12 September 1936, FO 371/20482. W11192. 6953. Archbishop Bell's appeal for £25,000, launched early in 1936, had raised only £8,250 by November of that year; Adrian Hastings, *A History of English Christianity, 1920–1990* (London: Collins, 3rd edn, 1991), 344.

45 AJA, Warburg Papers, 321/4, list of persons present at meeting at New Court, 13 February 1936; CBF Archives, 15/13, speeches delivered at Anglo-Jewish Conference convened by CGJ, Dorchester Hotel, 15 March 1936, 11.

46 Ibid., Bentwich, *My Seventy-Seven Years*, 142.

47 CZA, S7 243, cable signed Herbert Samuel Bearsted Simon Marks to VAAD LEUMI, Jerusalem, 31 March 1936.

48 CBF, speeches delivered at Anglo-Jewish Conference, 15 March 1936. The extended Bearsted, Marks and Rothschild families each contributed £90,320 (JC, 3 April 1936, 17).

49 AJA, Warburg Papers, 321/3, CGJ, Interim Report by the British Section, n.d.

50 CBF Archives, minutes of New Court Committee, 13 and 25 February 1936; AJA, Warburg Papers, 325/11, letter, Felix Warburg to Norman Bentwich, 6 April 1936.

51 AJA, Warburg Papers, 321/3, letter, Herbert Samuel to Felix Warburg, 28 April 1936.

52 British alternates were Capt. The Hon. Colonel S. Montagu, DSO, Lionel L. Cohen, KC, Professor S. Brodetsky, Ph.D., Professor L.B. Namier, MA. American alternates were: David Bressler, James Rosenberg, George S. Backer, Nathan Strauss, Rev. M.L. Perlzweig, MA, Dr Israel Goldstein,

James de Rothschild, MP, and Captain Robert B. Solomon. The last two names to the American team were Englishmen. CBF, Annual Report, 1936, 5.

53 Bentwich, *They Found Refuge*, 33.

54 CGJ, minutes of meeting of Executive, 21 April 1936.

55 CGJ, Report for 1936, 12. See also Sherman, *Island Refuge*, 74–8.

56 CGJ, Annual Report 1936, 7; Bentwich, *They Found Refuge*, 34.

57 CGJ, Report for 1936, 21.

58 Ibid., 21–3.

59 Ibid., 22.

60 Both banks provided the Council with overdraft facilities, at an interest rate of 2 per cent per annum, on security of payments expected under covenant and tax refunds to be claimed from the Office of Inland Revenue, CGJ, Report for 1937, 22.

61 AJA, Warburg Papers, 320/16, letter and telegram, Meyer Stephany, CBF, to Felix Warburg, 30 September 1936.

62 CGJ, Annual Report 1936, 4–8; AJA, Warburg Papers, 320/15, meeting of the Executive of the CGJ, 18 November 1936; CBF Archives, 20/1, minutes of meeting, 7 July 1937. See Chapter 9 for operation of the Exchange Rate Mechanism.

63 Following Arab unrest and a general strike in Palestine in April 1936, which led to open rebellion and attacks on Jewish settlers, the British government sent a Commission to Palestine headed by Lord Peel. The Commission's report, published in July 1937, recommended that Palestine be partitioned into sovereign Arab and Jewish states. Bernard Wasserstein, *Britain and the Jews of Europe, 1939–1945* (Oxford: Oxford University Press, 1988), 13–16.

64 CGJ, minutes of meeting, 4 April 1938.

65 Letter of resignation, James McDonald, High Commissioner for Refugees (Jewish and Other) Coming from Germany, to the Secretary General of the League of Nations, London, 27 December 1935. McDonald resigned his position after issuing a scathing report, condemning the ineffectiveness of the Commission created by the League and the apathy of the countries of the world to the plight of the refugees. Michael R. Marrus, *Unwanted European Refugees in the Twentieth Century* (New York: Oxford University Press, 1985), 158–64.

66 CGJ, Report for 1937, 19–20.

67 Bauer, *My Brother's Keeper*, 250. The JDC appointed Louis L. Strauss to fill Felix Warburg's seat on the CGJ.

7: German annexation of Austria

1 William L. Shirer, *The Rise and Fall of the Third Reich* (New York: Simon and Schuster, 1960), 351.

2 Drs Loewenherz and Rothenburg, leaders of the Kultusgemeinde and Palestine office in Vienna, were released by the Nazis, and were permitted to travel to London for the CGJ meeting on 7 June 1938.

3 CBF Archives, minutes of an emergency meeting of the Executive, CGJ, 29 March 1938; JDC Archives, 575, digest of minutes, meeting of the Executive of the CGJ, 25 July 1938.

4 Eichmann trial testimony, quoted in Gideon Hausner, *Justice in Jerusalem* (New York: Nelson & Sons, 1968), 38–40.

5 CGJ, report by Sir Wyndham Deedes on his visit to Vienna and Berlin, 2 May 1938.

6 CGJ, minutes of Executive Committee, 7 June 1938, 2–3.

7 JDC Archives, 575, report by Captain B.M. Woolf on his visit to Austria, 25 July 1938.

8 BD. ACC 3121 C11/12/1, letter, Otto Schiff to Secretary of State, 14 March 1938.

9 The loans and the overdraft were secured by outstanding covenants. CGJ, minutes of Executive Committee, 15 March 1938, 3–4.

10 CGJ, minutes of an emergency meeting of the Executive, CGJ, 29 March 1938, 1; ibid., 4 April 1938, 1.

11 C.D.C. Robinson, Home Office, to Sir Neville Bland, Foreign Office, 14 March 1938, FO 372/3182, T3398.

12 Ibid.

13 Ibid.

14 Sherman, *Island Refuge*, 91–3.

15 Ibid., 85–90. Louise London, 'Jewish Refugees and British Government Policy, 1930–1940', in David Cesarani (ed.), *The Making of Modern Anglo-Jewry* (Oxford: Basil Blackwell, 1990), 176–7.

16 Otto Schiff paid the penalty imposed (£571 10s). Case of Miss Ruth Fellner, September 1938, FO 371/22573.

17 From 2 May 1938, Austrian passport-holders were required to obtain

British visas. The ruling for German passport-holders came into effect on 21 May, FO 372 378/3398 T3272; Home Office memorandum, 14 March 1938, FO 372 3282, T3517/3272/378; JC, 29 April 1938, 13; see also Sherman, *Island Refuge*, 86–93.

18 Sherman, *Island Refuge*, 85–95.

19 Finegold, *The Politics of Rescue*, 21–2; Arthur D. Morse, *While Six Million Died* (New York: The Overlook Press, 1983), 202–14; Leonard Dinnerstein, *Anti-Semitism in America* (New York: Oxford University Press, 1994), 105.

20 Finegold, *The Politics of Rescue*, 20; Sherman, *Island Refuge*, 96.

21 Michael Blakeney, *Australia and the Jewish Refugees 1933–1948* (Sydney: Croom Helm, 1985), 124. Norman Bentwich noted that Australia was willing to admit 5,000 refugees annually. See Bentwich, *My Seventy-Seven Years*, 148.

22 See Abella and Troper, *None Is Too Many* (Toronto: Lester and Orpen Dennys, 1982).

23 Nicholas Gross, 'Sosua: A Colony of Hope', *American Jewish History*, Vol. 82, Nos 1–4, 237–42.

24 Sherman, *Island Refuge*, 119.

25 9 June 1938, FO 371/21749.

8: Germany tightens the screw

1 Hilberg, *The Destruction of the European Jews*, 84.

2 Ibid., 84–5.

3 *The Times*, Editorial, 1 October 1938, 12.

4 Prime Minister Chamberlain returned to London on 29 September; *The Times*, 1 October 1938, 13.

5 Bauer, *My Brother's Keeper*, 244.

6 Hilberg, *The Destruction of the European Jews*, 258–9; Bauer, *My Brother's Keeper*, 244–5.

7 Davidowicz, *The War Against the Jews*, 132–9; Morse, *While Six Million Died*, 222–3. A report in the Prime Minister's file at the PRO notes that 'as soon as the Pogroms had taken place [Goering] tendered his resignation to the Fuehrer who refused to accept it. The reason for this resignation was that the destruction of Jewish property brought an additional strain upon Goering's Four Year [self-sufficiency] Plan, as three million marks worth of glass had to be replaced by the purchase of Belgian glass, since Germany

was only capable of making a quarter of the amount destroyed. In addition, the majority of the goods destroyed in Jewish shops was the property of non-Jews and were on sale or return. Compensation, therefore, had to be paid to German citizens by the State. In addition, Goering realized how badly world opinion had been affected by the Pogroms (Prem 1/326 147635 21.11.38).

8 CCJR memorandum, 13 November 1938; CBF, minutes of Executive Committee, 14 November 1938.

9 Bentwich, *They Found Refuge*, 56; JDC Archives, 576, copies of telegrams between London and New York.

10 CBF Archives, 120/30; minutes of Executive Committee CGJ, 1 December 1938; CCJR, Report for 1939.

11 Anticipated annual receipt of contributions made under covenant and income tax refunds from the government, payable in each year until April 1945 inclusive, was used as the basis for the loan, which bore an interest rate of $4\frac{1}{2}$ per cent. See CGJ, minutes of Executive Committee, 10 August 1939, 4–5. However, at the CBF meeting held on 12 June 1944, it was recorded that the Prudential loan had been repaid early in 1943.

12 CCJR, Report for 1939, 5; JRC, Report for 1940, 5.

13 Rabbi Leo Baeck, 'In Memory of Two of Our Dead', *Leo Baeck Yearbook*, 1956, 51–6.

14 Dr Hirsch was arrested in the spring of 1941 and died in the Mauthausen concentration camp, 19 June 1941; Paul R. Mendes-Flohr and Jehuda Reinharz, *The Jew in the Modern World: A Documentary History* (Oxford: Oxford University Press, 1980), 504; Zdenek Lederer, *Ghetto Theresienstadt* (London: Edward Goldston, 1953), 150–1.

15 Norman Bentwich, memorandum: Officials of the Reichsvertretung, 4 January 1939; Baker, *Days of Sorrow and Pain*, 319.

16 The full story of the *St Louis* is told in Gordon Thomas and Max Morgan-Witts, *Voyage of the Damned* (London: Hodder and Stoughton, 1974) and Morse, *While Six Million Died*, 270–88.

17 Bauer, *My Brother's Keeper*, 277–80.

18 Ibid.

19 See US Department of the Interior, *Token Shipment: The Story of America's War Refugee Shelter* (Washington, DC: Government Printing Office, n.d.).

20 Rothschild Archives, letter and attached memorandum, Lionel de Roths-

child to The Rt Hon. Sir Horace Rumbold, 3 July 1939. See also Bauer, *My Brother's Keeper*, 273–8.

21 Sherman, *Island Refuge*, 252; Bauer, *My Brother's Keeper*, 280.

22 Sherman, *Island Refuge*, 252. The Inter-Governmental Committee for the Settlement of Refugees was created following the conference at Evian.

23 Thomas and Morgan-Witts, *Voyage of the Damned*, 279.

24 Bauer, *My Brother's Keeper*, 279–80; Morse, *While Six Million Died*, 271–88; Thomas and Morgan-Witts, *Voyage of the Damned*, 269–94.

25 Bauer, *My Brother's Keeper*, 289.

26 Jon and David Kimche, *The Secret Roads* (London: Secker and Warburg, 1956), 28–30.

27 Kimche, *The Secret Roads*, 20–44; Bauer, *My Brother's Keeper*, 286. Betar (Zionist Revisionists) and other political organizations also participated in arranging illegal immigration to Palestine. See William R. Perl, *Operation Action* (New York: Frederick Ungar, 1983).

28 In February 1939 the German government reconstituted the Reichsvertretung, which had been the representative organization of German Jews. It was replaced by the Reichsvereinigung (Alliance of German Jews), whose authority would come not from the Jewish community, but from the Interior Ministry: in other words, the Gestapo, which was empowered to assign it additional tasks. See Hilberg, *The Destruction of the European Jews*, 122–4.

29 JDC Archives, 575, letter, Paul Baerwald to Morris Troper, 11 February 1939; letter, Troper to Joseph Hyman, 2 February 1939; Troper memorandum re conversation with Lord Samuel, 17 February 1939.

30 Commissioner Sir Harold MacMichael to Secretary of State for Colonies, 2 December 1942, FO 371/32682 W16523.

31 CBF Archives, 174/163, minutes of German Jewish Aid Committee, 5 January 1938.

32 CBF Archives, minutes of Conference of Delegates from European Refugee Committee and Executive of CGJ, 23 April 1936; minutes, 26 September 1939 CGJ, 2; JDC Archives, 576, Joseph J. Schwartz to Rabbi Stephen Wise and Lewis L. Strauss, 27 September 1939.

9: The worsening situation of Jewish children in Germany

1 Nettie Adler, member of the Schools and Training Sub-Committee, and Alice Model and Anna Schwab of the Hospitality Committee, headed these efforts to place children. See Report of the Work of the JRC, 24 August 1936.

2 Law against Overcrowding Schools and Universities, 25 April 1933 (RGB1 I, 225).

3 CGJ, Joseph L. Cohen report on visit to Germany, January 1937.

4 As already noted, the CBF supported the Reichsvertretung's action and, in an exception to its funding policy for activities in Germany, allocated £10,000 for Jewish elementary and secondary school facilities. See minutes of Allocations Committee, 3 August 1933, 1; ibid., 11 December 1934, 4; ibid., 15 March 1934, 3–4; Baker, *Days of Sorrow and Pain*, 148.

5 CGJ, minutes of meeting, 27 March 1939.

6 Anna Essinger, born Ulm, Germany, 15 September 1879, lived in the United States. In 1914 she received an MA degree from the University of Wisconsin, where she taught German and served as head of the university's German House. Anna Essinger returned to Germany after the First World War (Anna Essinger, *Bunce School 1933–1943*, n.d.; Association of Jewish Refugees, Newsletter, September 1959, 7).

7 Movement for the Care of Children from Germany, Statistical Analysis, July 1939.

8 SCF, 146th Council meeting, 28 November 1935, C2114.

9 SCF, 149th Council meeting, 20 February 1936.

10 CGJ, minutes of Executive Committee, 21 April 1936; ibid., minutes, 4 May 1937; ibid., minutes, 10 May 1938.

11 SCF, 170th Council meeting, 20 January 1938, C2467; 173rd Council meeting, 21 July 1938, C2527; 174th Council meeting, 20 October 1938, C2541.

12 CBF Archives, 174/222, JRC, minutes of Executive Committee, 29 July 1936.

13 CBF Archives, 174/222, CJG, meeting, 15 April 1936; 174/222, JRC, minutes of Executive Committee, 29 July 1936.

14 Examples are the Claysmore and Bryanston schools in Dorset, which admitted the brothers Thomas and Richard Tietz, nephews of Ludwig Tietz and other boys, at half the regular fees; interview, Thomas Tait (Tietz), 23 September 1993. The Kingsmore School, Derbyshire, admitted

Eva Mitchell (née Rose) without cost. Adult refugees were also employed by the school; interview, Eva Mitchell, 17 September 1997.

15 Movement for the Care of Children from Germany, First Annual Report, 1938–9, 3.

16 J.E. Bailey, *A Quaker Couple in Nazi Germany* (York: William Sessions, 1994), 95.

17 Ibid.

18 CGJ, minutes of Executive Committee, 17 November 1938; *The Times*, 10 April 1971, 14.

19 CGJ, memorandum on a proposal to bring 5,000 refugee children from Germany to England immediately, 16 November 1938.

20 CGJ, minutes of Executive Committee, 17 November 1938; SCF, 175th Council meeting, 19 January 1939, C2556.

21 CGJ, minutes of Executive Committee, 17 November 1938.

22 Letter, Lord Samuel to Prime Minister, 15 November 1938, PREM 1/326 147635; CGJ, minutes of emergency meeting, 14 November 1938; CGJ, minutes of Executive Committee, 17 November 1938; Movement for the Care of Children from Germany, First Annual Report, 1938–9.

23 Letter, Lord Samuel to Prime Minister, 15 November 1938, PREM 1/326 147635.

24 Ibid.

25 Chamberlain was disdainful of Jews. 'No doubt Jews aren't a lovable people, I don't care about them myself', he wrote on 30 July 1939; quoted in Martin Gilbert, *The Holocaust: The Jewish Tragedy* (London: Fontana Collins, 1987), 81.

26 A precedent had been established in 1937 during the Spanish Civil War, when the British government had authorized the entry of 4,000 unaccompanied children from Spain (*The Times*, 20 May 1937, 15); SCF, 163rd Council meeting, 20 May 1937, C2395.

27 At the same meeting, Lord Bearsted and Anthony de Rothschild told the Prime Minister of the tremendous financial burden borne by the Anglo-Jewish community in aiding the emigration of children and adults at risk, and asked whether the government would help raise an international loan so that those in peril might be removed from Germany. The Prime Minister considered a loan as 'premature and hardly worth discussing' before a 'clearly defined plan' of use of a loan's proceeds were presented. Letter, 15 November 1938, Lord Samuel to Prime Minister, PREM 1/326 147635;

record of meeting by Prime Minister's Private Secretary, 16 November 1938, FO 371/22536, 15037/104/98, 16 November 1938; CGJ minutes of meeting, 17 November 1938.

28 See PRO. CAB 23/96 6953, Cabinet Conclusions 33 (38), 16 November 1938.

29 CJG, Norman Bentwich, memorandum: Admission of Refugees into England, 8 December 1938; CGJ memorandum: Placement of Old People from Germany, 16 December 1938.

30 The meeting took place on 21 November 1938. See FO 371/24085 XC/146099. Ben Greene was one of five Quakers sent from London to Berlin, at the request of Wilfred Israel, to work alongside Jewish welfare workers. See Bailey, *A Quaker Couple in Nazi Germany*, 95.

31 Hansard, 341, HC Deb., 1427–83, 21 November 1938. In contrast, Bills to permit the entry of 20,000 refugee children to the age of fourteen, introduced in the House and Senate of the United States Congress by Senator Robert F. Wagner (Democrat) and Representative Edith Nourse Rogers (Republican), failed to pass in either Chamber. See Wyman, *Paper Walls*, 75, and Morse, *While Six Million Died*, 252–69.

32 FO 371/24085 XC/146099.

33 Lord Gorell, 'Adventure and Opportunity', in Bentwich (ed.), *They Found Refuge*, 78.

34 CBF Archives, 156/1, L.H. Gluckstein served until the war as the Council's representative on the Movement's Executive, when military service compelled his resignation; John Presland, *A Great Adventure: Movement for the Care of Children from Germany Limited 1944*, July 1944; Bentwich, *They Found Refuge*, 67, 81–2. The Movement for the Care of Children from Germany was incorporated as a limited company, 5 April 1939, renamed the Refugee Children's Movement, 6 July 1940.

35 The organization was first known as the World Movement for the Rescue of Children from Germany: British Inter-Aid Committee. Helen Bentwich's position was later assumed by Major Geoffrey H. Langdon, a member of the Jewish Refugees Committee's Emigration Department. The SCF made temporary premises available and the Movement began operations on 22 November 1938, one day after the meeting with the Home Secretary. See Presland, *A Great Adventure*, 10.

36 The rumour may have arisen following a cable from Professor Cohen and Gertrude Van Tijn, Amsterdam, to Paul Baerwald in New York, advising

him that 'Lots of homeless children separated from parents straying in woods or put on trains alone by desperate mothers whose husbands arrested ...' (JDC Archives, 575, cable, Professors Cohen and Van Tijn to Paul Baerwald, 19 November 1938).

37 In 1918 Norman Bentwich had chaired the Palestine Orphans Committee; Herbert Agar, *The Saving Remnant: An Account of Jewish Survival* (New York: Viking, 1960), 58; Norman Bentwich, report on visit to Amsterdam, 25–6 November 1938; Movement for the Care of Children from Germany, First Annual Report, 1938–9.

38 Norman Bentwich, report on visit to Amsterdam, 25–6 November 1938; E. Rosenbaum, A.J. Sherman, *M.M. Warburg & Co., 1798–1938* (London: C. Hurst, 1976), 177.

10: The movement of children from Germany begins

1 CBF Archives, microfilm reels 36–7; *The Times*, 3 December 1938; JC, 9 December 1938, 17; JDC, 653, letter, Dr Bernard Kahn to Paul Baerwald, 2 December 1938.

2 *The Times*, 3 December 1938; Movement, First Annual Report, 1938–9.

3 CBF Archives, letter, 2 December 1938, Dr Joseph Herz to Lord Samuel.

4 Norman Bentwich attended the meeting. CGJ, minutes of Executive Committee, 1 December 1938.

5 AJH Archives, Solomon Schonfeld Papers 52/3/2, letter, Leo Baeck to Dr J. Herz, 2 December 1938; CBF Archives, letter, 2 December 1939, Dr Herz to Lord Samuel. According to Jewish law (*Pikku'ah Nefesh* – regard for human life), travel on the Sabbath would not be an act of blasphemy if lives would otherwise be endangered.

6 Bentwich, report on visit to Amsterdam, 25 and 26 November 1938.

7 Truus Wijsmuller-Meijer, *Geen Tijd Voor Tranen* (Amsterdam: P.N. Van Kampen and Zoon NV, n.d.), 62–75.

8 See Lore Segal, *Other People's Houses* (London: Victor Gollancz, 1965), 29–45; *New York Times*, 12 December 1938. Rabbi Leo Baeck attended a meeting of the Council for German Jewry on the day the children from Vienna arrived in Britain. He thanked the Council, and through the Council, British Jewry, for the help they were extending to his co-religionists (minutes of Executive Committee, CGJ, 12 December 1938).

9 CBF, Norman Bentwich, report on visit to Amsterdam; Darton, *An Account of the Work of the Friends Committee for Refugees*, 51–2.
10 Eva Reading, *For the Record* (London: Hutchinson, 1973), 167.
11 *Observer*, 10 July 1988, 33; *Sunday Mirror*, 28 February 1988, 19–21; Movement, First Annual Report, 1938–9; an account of Trevor Chadwick's efforts are contained in Gershon, *We Came As Children* (London: Victor Gollancz, 1965), 22–5.
12 See Lucy V. Davidson, ed. John S. Ross, *For a Future and a Hope: The Story of the Houses of Refuge in Chislehurst* (Kent: Christian Witness to Israel, 1989); Barbican Mission to the Jews, *Emanuel's Witness*, Vol. XV, No. 10, January 1939, 184–5.
13 *The Times*, 12 January 1939; Movement, First Annual Report, 1938–9.
14 Children's responses to their stay at Dovercourt and life in Britain are poignantly recorded in Gershon, *We Came As Children.*
15 Movement, First Annual Report, 1938–9.
16 CBF Archives, Movement, Statistical Analysis, July 1939; JC, 10 February 1939, 16; Reading, *For the Record*, 166.
17 Reading, *For the Record*, 116.
18 CBF Archives, RCM, 161/16; 161/37.
19 CBF Archives, 166/117, Movement, Statistical Analysis, July 1939; memorandum on the Movement's policy with regard to religious instruction of children; Reading, *For the Record*, 166–7; JC, 12 May 1939, 35.
20 Movement, Statistical Analysis, Second Issue, July 1939.
21 CGJ, Note on the Present Condition of the Movement for the Care of Children from Germany, 16 January 1939.
22 CGJ, minutes of meeting, 18 January 1939.
23 *The Times*, 9 December 1938.
24 Ibid., 16.
25 Ibid., 12 January 1939.
26 Ibid., 28 September 1939, 10.
27 CGJ, minutes of Executive Committee, 28 January 1939. Lord Victor Rothschild donated his portrait, *The Braddyll Family* by Joshua Reynolds, which was auctioned at Christie's, and donated the proceeds to the Baldwin Fund; Virginia Cowles, *A Family of Fortune* (London: Weidenfeld and Nicolson, 1973), 304.
28 CCJR, minutes of Executive Committee, 10 August 1939; CCJR, Report for 1939, 12.

29 The government also provided some 75 per cent of the Movement's administration costs; Third Annual Report, 1941–2, 1.

30 CCJR, minutes of Executive Committee, 6 February 1939; ibid., 14 March 1939; CBF Archives, 175/38, GJAC, minutes of Executive Committee, 1 March 1939.

31 Elaine Blond with Barry Turner, *The Memoirs of Elaine Blond* (London: Valentine Mitchell, 1988), 72; *Harwich and Dovercourt Newsman*, 24 December 1938.

32 CGJ, minutes of Executive Committee, 6 February 1939.

33 CBF Archives, 164/2–18, Memorandum of Association of the Movement for the Care of Children from Germany Limited, Company Limited by Guarantee and Not Having a Share Capital (Companies Act 1929). On 3 July 1940 the name was changed to Refugee Children's Movement Limited.

34 See Pressland, *A Great Adventure.*

35 CGJ, minutes of Executive Committee, 1 May 1939; ibid., 18 May 1939.

36 Kisch, Report, 4.

37 The eventual cost to the Council, following expiration of limited guarantees, was estimated at £16,000. CGJ, minutes of Executive Committee, 20 February 1939.

38 CGJ, minutes of Executive Committee, 18 January 1939.

39 Movement, First Annual Report, 1938–9, 14.

40 Pine Trees, Kent; Hale Nurseries, Hampshire; Gwrych Castle, North Wales; Whittingham House, Scotland; Great Egeham Farm, Kent; Tingrith House and Tythrop House and at an old fort on Alderney in the Channel Islands. Whittingham House, the home of the later Lord Balfour, was provided by his nephew Lord Traprail; Great Egeham Farm near Ashford was donated by Messrs Lesser and Stanley; Tingrith House in Bedfordshire by Messrs Beloff, Anker, Rubin and Oks. The CGJ provided financial assistance to these enterprises. Tythrop House, Oxfordshire, was run by a special committee in combination with the Oxford Co-operative Society, CCJR, Report for 1939, 12–13. Twenty-four young men were reported to be receiving training in Alderney; JC, 1 September 1939, 20.

41 CCJR, minutes, 17 June 1939, 2; Elaine Blond, *Marks of Distinction*, 66; CZA, S15/909, Youth Aliyah Training Centres in England (n.d.).

42 Movement, Third Annual Report, 1941–2, 4–5.

43 Erwin Lichtenstein, *Die Juden der Freienstadt* (Tubingen: Mohr Siebeck, 1973), 102–3.

44 Letter, Ruth Fallman (née Danziger) to CBF, 6 February 1995: 'I was one of about ten children... escorted by Dr Felix Reich'. These children arrived in Britain on 19 July 1939.

45 CGJ, minutes of Executive Committee, 27 March 1939; JC, 17 February 1939, 32; ibid., 1 September 1939, 20; CZA, S75/909, Youth Aliyah Training Centres in England (n.d.).

46 CBF Archives, Movement, Statistical Analysis, July 1939; Schwab, *B'nai B'rith*, 87–91.

47 CCJR, Report for 1939, 13.

48 See Lord Gorell, 'Adventure and Opportunity' in Bentwich (ed.), *They Found Refuge*, 78–85.

49 E.N. Cooper, Home Office, to D.P. Reilly, Foreign Office, 30 August 1939, FO 371/24085 XC/146099; 30 August 1939, telegram 3.15 p.m., Foreign Office to Sir N. Bland, the Hague, FO 371/24085 XC/146099. It is possible that Sir Charles Stead communicated by telephone, since no copy of a written message exists in the FO, RCM or CBF Archives.

50 The castle had been made available to the Youth Aliyah, rent free, by Lord Dundonald. CZA, S75 909. Youth Aliyah Training Centres in England. (The undated report appears to have been written within days of the children's arrival in Britain); Norman Bentwich, *Jewish Youth Comes Home: The Story of the Youth Aliyah 1933–1943* (London: Victor Gollancz, 1944), 75.

51 Movement, Second Annual Report, 1939–40.

52 Bentwich, *They Found Refuge*, 81.

53 CZA, 575/769, M. Schattner to M. Mitzman, Women's Appeal Committee, London, 8 September 1939; Bentwich, *Jewish Youth Comes Home*, 94–9.

54 Jacob Presser, *Ashes in the Wind: The Destruction of Dutch Jewry* (London: Souvenir, 1965), 8–9; Movement, Second Annual Report, 1939–40.

55 Movement, Second Annual Report, 1939–40; CCJR, minutes of Executive Committee, 27 July 1942.

56 CCJR, minutes of Executive Committee, 31 December 1940.

57 CBF, JRC, Statistical Report for 1944, 20 February 1945, 2.

11: Children in Britain during the war

1 Ben Wicks, *No Time to Wave Good-bye* (London: Bloomsbury, 1988), 12–15.

2 Ibid., 31–9.

3 Movement, First Annual Report, 1938–9.
4 Bentwich, *They Found Refuge*, 70.
5 Arnold Harris Archives, Report on Work with Refugee Children, 17 December 1964, Courtesy Ansell Harris (son of Arnold Harris).
6 Archives, Rugby Christadelphian Refugee Committee, letter, Movement for the Care of Children from Germany Ltd, 30 August 1939 (courtesy Paula Hill); Zoe Josephs, *Jewish Refugees in Birmingham, 1933–1935* (Birmingham: Meridian, 1988), 77–81.
7 CGJ, minutes, 17 November; ibid., 5 January 1939.
8 JC, 8 September 1939, 16.
9 CGJ, minutes of Executive Committee, 5 January 1939.
10 CGJ, minutes of Executive Committee, 11 March 1936; ibid., 9 July 1936; ibid., 15 July 1936; CZA, S7243, letter, Dr Martin Rosenbluth to Dr George Landauer, 16 July 1936.
11 CBF Archive, 161/39. Joint Committee for the Religious Education and Welfare of Jewish Children, established in 1942.
12 CBF Archives, RCM, 166/68; JC, 30 May 1941. At a meeting of the Board of Deputies, 27 May 1941, Harry Goodman launched a scathing attack on the Movement. RCM, 161/37, 6 August 1942; Pamphlet: 'Child-Estranging Movement,' Union of Orthodox Hebrew Congregations, London, January 1944.
13 CBF Archives, 167/7, resumé of Lord Gorell's speech, 11 January 1944. Rabbi Schonfeld married a daughter of Chief Rabbi Herz in 1940.
14 CBF Archives, RCM, 167/1/2, copy of letter, G. Berger, president of Union of Hebrew Congregations, to the Editor, *Jewish Chronicle*, 7 January 1944.
15 CBF Archives, RCM, 167/6–9, resumé of Lord Gorell's speech, 11 January 1944.
16 CBF Archives, 161/3. When a boy housed by the Barbican Mission was to be baptized against his father's wishes, Bishop Bell of Chichester was asked to remove him from the home; Dorothy Hardisty, Redraft of Report, 19 January 1944.
17 7 & 8 Geo. 6. The Guardianship (Refugee Children) Act, Ch. 8, March 1944.
18 CBF Archives, 169/54–62, Report on Jewish Children brought to England, May 1950.
19 CBF Archives, 159/1–6, Refugee Children's Movement.

20 Bentwich, *They Found Refuge*, 72–3; JC, 3 January 1947, 1; ibid., 10 January 1947, 10.

21 Letter, Kurt Fuchel to Harry Kleeman, chairman of CBF, 7 May 1995.

12: Kitchener Camp at Richborough

1 House of Lords, Samuel Papers, (X) A155, letter (delivered by courier), Wilfred Israel to Lord Herbert Samuel, 28 June 1938.

2 Ogilvie-Forbes to Halifax, 17 November 1938 (FO 371/21637, C14083), quoted in Sherman, *Island Refuge*, footnote 31, 183.

3 CGJ, minutes of Executive Committee, 12 December 1938. Rabbi Leo Baeck had accompanied a transport of children from Berlin, which had arrived in England that morning.

4 CGJ, minutes of Executive Committee, 1 December 1938.

5 7 December 1938, FO 371/22539, 286–9.

6 CGJ, minutes of Executive Committee, 1 December 1938; Sir Robert Waley Cohen is incorrectly identified as Robert Cohen. FO 371/22539 W146099, 286–90, 7 December 1938.

7 FO 371/22539, 286–90, 7 December 1938; Reading, *For the Record*, 186.

8 FO 371/22539, 286–90, 7 December 1938.

9 FO 371/22539 W16410 104/98.

10 FO 371/22539, 286–90.

11 CBF Archive, 1/3, CGJ, note of interview with Sir Alexander Maxwell, 3 January 1939; letter, H. Maxwell, Home Office, to Norman Bentwich, CGJ, 3 January 1939.

12 CBF Archives, 1/3, letter, H. Maxwell, Home Office, to Norman Bentwich, CGJ, 3 January 1939.

13 CGJ, Report for 1938, 22; JDC Archives, 575, letter, Norman Bentwich to Paul Baerwald, 11 January 1939; ibid., letter, Paul Baerwald to Norman Bentwich, 3 February 1939; ibid., 592, memorandum re Kitchener Camp, 17 February 1939.

14 CGJ, minutes of Executive Committee, 5 January 1939; Bentwich, *My Seventy-Seven Years*, 160.

15 CGJ, minutes of Executive Committee, 5 January 1939; JDC, 592, memorandum re Kitchener Camp, 17 February 1939. Sir Robert Waley Cohen reported that the rent would be £100 per annum but, as reported by

Troper, the owners of the property probably demanded the larger sum of £350.

16 Bentwich, *They Found Refuge*, 102–6; Bentwich, *Wanderer Between the Wars*, 288–9.

17 Walter H. Marmorek, who later served as a major in the army, had a distinguished military career. Norman Bentwich, *I Understand the Risks*, (London: Victor Gollancz, 1950), 19.

18 Helen C. Bentwich, *History of Sandwich, Kent* (private printing, 1971), 153.

19 CBF Archives, 91/10.

20 Bentwich, *They Found Refuge*, 102–4.

21 Bentwich, *History of Sandwich, Kent*, 153; CGJ, Robert Waley Cohen, Report on the Kitchener Camp, 2 August 1939, 1.

22 In fact, only 50 of the Czechs took up residence, and most were rehoused before the end of August. Henriques, *Sir Robert Waley Cohen*, 273–4.

23 JC, 8 September 1939, 24.

24 Peter and Loni Gillman, *Collar the Lot* (London: Quartet Books, 1980), 255–6.

25 JDC Archives, 592, Report by Messrs Layton, Gentilli and Baron on the Selection of Refugees for the Richborough Camp; CGJ, minutes of Executive Committee, 14 March 1939.

26 CGJ, minutes of Executive Meeting, 1 June 1939.

27 Ibid.

28 CCJR, memorandum, Norman Bentwich, notes on the Kitchener Camp, 21 November 1939; JRC Report, March 1940.

29 CBF Archives, 91/17; domestic workers were permitted to bring their children. Bentwich, *They Found Refuge*, 102–4.

30 CGJ, Report on the Kitchener Camp, 26 April 1939; ibid., 2 August 1939.

31 CGJ, minutes of Executive Committee, 27 March 1939; ibid., 13 April 1939. The Chief Rabbi's Emergency Council claimed that 1,300 individuals were rescued before the war. See Chief Rabbi's Religious Emergency Council, Report on 10 Years of Activities on Behalf of our Jewish Brethren Covering a Period from 21 June 1938 till June 1938. No mention is made in the report on the ongoing contributions from the CBF to the Chief Rabbi's Emergency Council.

32 CGJ, Robert Waley Cohen, Report on the Kitchener Camp, 2 August 1939, 1; Bentwich, *They Found Refuge*, 102–5.

33 Bentwich, *They Found Refuge*, 104–7.

34 CCJR, memorandum, Norman Bentwich, notes on the Kitchener Camp, 21 December 1939.

35 One of the two was later found to be reliable; Bentwich, *They Found Refuge*, 107.

36 Reading, *Memoirs*, 173.

37 CCJR, undated memorandum on the subject of military service of refugees; see John P. Fox, 'German and Austrian Jews in Britain's Armed Forces and British and German Citizenship Policies 1939–1945', in *Leo Baeck Institute Year Book*, Vol. XXXVII, 1992, 415–59.

38 Bentwich, *They Found Refuge*, 109–10.

39 See Cooper, *Refugee Scholars*, 154–228; Bentwich, *They Found Refuge*, 110.

13: Financial crisis, 1939–40

1 CCJR, Report for 1939.

2 RAL, XIV/35/109, Memorandum for Presentation to His Majesty's Government, 13 May 1940.

3 CCJR, minutes of Executive Committee, 10 October 1939.

4 Ibid.

5 Czech nationals were aided by the Czech Trust Fund, created by the British government with a capital of £4 million. It was stimulated 'by a sort of guilt consciousness for the dismemberment of the Czech State'; Bentwich, *They Found Refuge*, 35.

6 CCJR, minutes of Executive Committee, 10 October 1939.

7 Anthony de Rothschild offered a loan of £25,000 from his brother Lionel and himself to enable the Council to continue to function until government funding was provided. See CCJR, minutes of Executive Committee, 14 December 1939.

8 CCJR, minutes of Executive Committee, 14 December 1939, 4; ibid., 21 December 1939, 4–5.

9 CCJR, minutes of Executive Committee, 4 January 1940.

10 Ibid., 4 January 1940; ibid., 22 February 1940.

11 Ibid., 10 October 1939.

12 Ibid.

13 Ibid., 17 October 1939.

14 The Rothschild and Bearsted families and Simon Marks had each pledged £25,000 at the fund-raising campaign in June 1939; CBF Archives, 120/30,

letter, Meyer Stephany to Colonel F.D. Samuel; CCJR, minutes of Executive Committee, 14 November 1939.

15 See Birmingham, *Our Crowd.*

16 RAL, XIV/35/19, letter, Lewis Strauss to Lionel de Rothschild, 19 October 1939; CGJ, Report for 1938; Richard Pfau, *No Sacrifice Too Great: The Life of Lewis L. Strauss* (Virginia: University of Virginia, 1984), 59.

17 AJHS, Lewis Strauss Archives, cable, Lord Bearsted and Anthony de Rothschild to Lewis Strauss, 18 October 1939.

18 RAL, XIV/35/19, letter, Anthony de Rothschild to d'Avigdor Goldsmid, 20 October 1939; JDC Archives, 576, copies of telegrams between London and New York, 18 October–11 November 1939; AJHS, Lewis Strauss Archives, letter, Lewis Strauss to Alfred Jaretski, 20 October 1939.

19 RAL, XIV/35/19, cable, Lewis Strauss to Bearsted and Rothschild, 4 November 1939.

20 Ibid., letter, Lewis L. Strauss to Dear Friends, 3 November 1939.

21 Ibid., Walter (Lord Bearsted) to Anthony de Rothschild, 21 November 1939.

22 JDC Archives, 576, memoranda, Meeting of Budget and Scope Committee, 20 November 1939.

23 RAL, XIV/35/19, cable, Lewis Strauss to Bearsted and Rothschild, 4 November 1939.

24 Ibid., letter, Lewis L. Strauss to Dear Friends, 3 November 1939.

25 JDC Archives, 576, Memorandum 227, Dorothy L. Speiser to Paul W. Lew, 21 November 1939.

26 RAL, XIV/35/19, letter, Anthony de Rothschild to Walter (Lord Bearsted), 22 November 1939.

27 CBF, minutes of Executive Committee, 21 November 1939.

28 CCJR, minutes of Executive Committee, 28 December 1939.

29 AJHS, Lewis Strauss Archives, letter, Anthony de Rothschild to Lewis Strauss, 18 January 1940.

30 Ibid., letter, Lewis Strauss to Anthony de Rothschild, 7 February 1940.

31 Ibid., letter, Anthony de Rothschild to Lewis Strauss, 12 February 1940.

32 CCJR, minutes of Executive Committee, 14 November 1939, 3; CBF Archives, 6/19–20; Bentwich, *They Found Refuge*, 40. The Christian Council for Refugees from Germany and Central Europe was established in October 1938. Presidents: the Archbishop of Canterbury, the Cardinal Archbishop of Westminster and Moderators of the Church of Scotland and

the Free Church Federal Council. (E.C. Urwin, *Henry C. Carter, CBE: A Memoir* (London: Epworth, 1955), 89–90.)

33 Eleanor F. Rathbone, MP, had established the Parliamentary Committee on Refugees several years earlier. See CBF Archives, 113/6–9.

34 CBF, minutes of Executive Committee, 14 November 1939.

35 CCJR, minutes of Executive Committee, 21 November 1939.

36 RAL, XIV/35/19, memorandum, 26 October 1939.

37 Ibid., note, Robert Waley Cohen, 28 November 1939.

38 In 1937 the Reverend Henry Carter and his friend George Lansbury, MP, were on a visit to Bled, Yugoslavia, when they learned that the German-Jewish specialist attending their interpreter's mother had been warned that the Gestapo were looking for him and that he had to flee. The doctor had headed a Cancer Research Institute in Berlin. He had sought safety in Austria and escaped again at the *Anschluss*. 'In a flash the meaning of the Hitler persecution of the Jews stood revealed in its stark horror.' See Urwin, *Henry Carter*.

39 RAL, XIV/35/19, memorandum; letter, Anthony de Rothschild to Osbert Peake, 1 December 1939; CCJR, Report for 1940, 11.

40 CCJR, minutes of emergency meeting of Executive, 1 December 1939.

41 Ibid.

42 CCJR, minutes of Executive Committee, 12 December 1939.

43 RAL, XIV/35/19, letter, Anthony de Rothschild to Osbert Peake, 1 December 1939.

44 Ibid., letter, Anthony de Rothschild to Sir Robert Waley Cohen, 5 December 1939.

45 Conclusions of the Seventh Meeting of the Committee, 8 December 1939, CAB 98/1 145956.

46 Ibid.

47 Ibid.

48 RAL, XIV/35/19, letter, Anthony de Rothschild to Osbert Peake, 12 December 1939.

49 CCJR, minutes of Executive Committee, 14 December 1939.

50 CBF, minutes of proceedings, meeting of Anglo-Jewry, 6 February 1940, 6–7.

51 356, HC Deb., 1301–3, 1 February 1940.

52 357 HC Deb., 1636–9, 22 February 1940.

53 The Central Office for Refugees, *Bloomsbury House*, 1942.

54 JDC Archives, 591, memorandum, Refugees in England, 2.

14: War-time activities of the Council and the Jewish Refugees Council

1 Lord Reading, chairman of the CCJR, had joined the army; CCJR, minutes of proceedings, meeting of Anglo-Jewry, 6 February 1940.

2 See the Central Office for Refugees, Bloomsbury House.

3 CCJR, minutes of proceedings, meeting of Anglo-Jewry, 6 February 1940, 4. In September 1942 Anthony de Rothschild and an unnamed member of the Council attended the reception given for the Reverend Henry Carter on his retirement: 'That distinguished leaders of the Jewish community in Britain should thus come to do honour to a minister of Christ for his services to their people was a mark of high distinction'. See Urwin, *Henry Carter*, 86.

4 Address by Anthony de Rothschild, CCJR, minutes of proceedings, meeting of Anglo-Jewry, 6 February 1940, 3.

5 Only in 1954 was the CBF's 1940 financial commitment to the Keren Hayesod concluded. See CBF Archives, 51, letter, A. Scheinwald, Keren Hayesod Committee, to Meyer Stephany, CBF.

6 RAL, XIV/35/19, letter, Anthony de Rothschild to Walter Bearsted, 19 January 1940.

7 Ibid., XIV/35/33.

8 CCGR, minutes Executive Committee, 7 March 1940.

9 CCJR, Report for 1940.

10 Ibid.; Norman, *An Outstretched Arm*, 294.

11 CCJR, Report for 1940, 14–15.

12 Ibid., 4.

13 RAL, XIV/35/78, CGJ, 15 June 1939. Not all covenants were binding upon donors' heirs.

14 CCJR, minutes of Executive Committee, 15 October 1940.

15 RAL, XIV/35/109, Memorandum for Presentation to His Majesty's Government, 13 May 1940.

16 Ibid., letter, secretary of Central Committee for Refugees to Sir Alexander Maxwell, 13 May 1940; ibid., memorandum re meeting of representatives of Christian and Jewish Councils with Sir Alexander Maxwell and E.N. Cooper, Home Office, 20 May 1940.

17 CCJR, Report for 1940, 15.
18 Conclusions of the Seventh Meeting of the Committee, 8 December 1939, CAB 98/1 145956.
19 Sir Alexander Maxwell to the Secretary of State, 11 July 1941, HO 213/298.
20 CBF, minutes of Council meeting, 24 June 1941; agreement, the Secretary of State for the Home Department and the Central Committee for Refugees and Others, 12 July 1941, HO 213/298. Herbert Morrison, the Home Secretary, signed the agreement for the government; Sir Herbert Emerson and Clare Martin were signatories for the Central Committee for Refugees; Anthony de Rothschild and Colonel Frederick Samuel appended their signatures for the Council; and again Anthony de Rothschild, Otto Schiff and Meyer Stephany signed for the CBF.
21 CCJR minutes of Executive, 24 June 1941; copies of the agreement are in the CBF Archives and in the Home Office file at the PRO in Kew (HO 213/298, Aliens Department, Government Financial Assistance to the Jewish Council).
22 Government Financial Agreement with the Jewish Council, 3/11/44. The original document is in the file with a copy of the Secretary of State's letter determining the agreement. Alexander Maxwell's notation is dated 3/11/44, HO 213/298.
23 Davidowitz, *The War Against the Jews*, 173–4.
24 CBF, Annual Report, 1948, 15.
25 Gillman, *Collar the Lot*, 42–6.
26 Ibid.
27 H. Loebl, 'Refugee Industries in the Special Areas of Britain', in Hirschfeld (ed.), *Exiles in Britain*, 219–49.
28 François Lafitte, *The Internment of Aliens* (London: Penguin, 1940), 38–9.
29 CCJR, Report for 1940.
30 Gillman, *Collar the Lot*, 7–8.
31 Joan Stiebel escorted children taken to the Isle of Man. Joan Stiebel, 'Travelling Hopefully' (unpublished manuscript), September 1991.
32 Laffitte, *The Internment of Aliens*, 70–91; Cooper, *Refugee Scholars*, 137–43; see also Wasserstein, *Britain and the Jews of Europe*, 81–113.
33 HC Deb., 361, 794, 4 June 1940.
34 Bentwich, *They Found Refuge*, 71; Bentwich, *I Understand the Risks*, 24–34;

CBF Archives, 159/1/2/3, Memorandum for the Consideration of the Home Secretary; Cooper, *Refugee Scholars*, 134–91.

35 Gillman, *Collar the Lot*, 190–201.

36 Ibid., 255–6; CCJR, Report for 1940, 9.

37 JRC, Report for 1940.

38 Gillman, *Collar the Lot*, 255–6.

39 Bentwich, *They Found Refuge*, 129.

40 CCJR, Report for 1940, 8.

41 Gillman, *Collar the Lot*, 267–8.

42 JRC, Report for 1940, 10.

43 Ibid., 10–11.

44 RAL, XIV/35/109, Memorandum for Presentation to His Majesty's Government, 13 May 1940; JRC, Report for 1940.

45 JRC, Report for 1940; CCJR, Report for 1940.

46 Destinations of emigrants during 1944 were: USA 9,031; Australia and New Zealand 241; Canada 379; British Empire 53; Palestine 305; South and Central America 387; other countries 75 (CBF, JRC, Statistical Report for 1944).

47 Finegold, *Politics of Rescue*, 111–12.

48 CCJR, San Domingo file, memorandum, Emigration to San Domingo, 20 June 1940.

49 Ibid.

50 Ibid.

51 CCJR, San Domingo file, Statement of Progress, 11 November 1940.

52 JRC, Report for 1940, 10.

53 CCJR, Report on San Domingo Settlement (JDC, New York), December 1943; Re-Admission from San Domingo, HO 213/739.

54 FO 271/32682 W17093.

55 Cable, Anthony de Rothschild, CCJR, to JDC, 7 August 1942, FO 371/32680 W11053. The JDC, working with American Quakers, was able to rescue a small number of children before regular United States immigration channels were blocked in the summer of that year. Michael R. Marrus and Robert O. Paxton, *Vichy France and the Jews* (Stanford: Stanford University Press, 1981), 266.

56 FO 371 32680 W12687.

57 BD C2/1/1–7, Aliens Committee, Otto Schiff report, 8/12/1942.

58 FO 271/32680/W13107 W13371; CCJR, Report for 1942, 3; JRC, Report for 1942, 16.
59 CCJR, Report for 1942, 3; JDC, 924, press release, 29 October 1942.
60 CBF, minutes of joint meeting, Council and Executive of CCJR, 12 June 1944.
61 Ibid.; CBF Archives, 88:69/70; FO 371/42731, 147896.
62 CBF, Annual Report, 1944, 6–7.

15: The Jewish Committee for Relief Abroad

1 The committee was appointed in September 1941. See CCJR, minutes of Executive Committee, 3 March 1942.
2 CCJR, minutes of Executive Committee, 15 December 1942. The meeting was called by the Allied Post-War Requirements Bureau and the Ministry of Economic Warfare.
3 CCJR, minutes of Executive Committee, 15 December 1942.
4 See JCRA Minute Book, February 1943 to November 1944; Morton, *The Rothschilds*, 298.
5 Bentwich, *They Found Refuge*, 127–63.
6 JCRA, 9 March 1944, 1.
7 COBSRA, Report for 1947 (First Annual Report), 7.
8 CCJR, minutes of Executive Committee, 27 July, 1942; ibid., 15 December 1942, 2.
9 The first camp residents arrived in Morocco in June 1944. Morris Feinman suffered a heart attack, and died on 2 August 1944.
10 JCRA, minutes of Executive Committee, 22 June 1944.
11 The author was a member of the first Jewish Relief Unit assigned to the Middle East in 1944, and to the JDC in Greece in April 1945.
12 See n.a., *Belsen* (Israel: Irgun Sheerit Hapleita Me'Haezor Habriti, 1947).
13 See Hagit Lavsky, 'British Jewry and the Jews in Post-Holocaust Germany: The Jewish Relief Unit, 1945–50', in *The Journal of Holocaust Education* (London: Frank Cass), Vol. 4, No. 1, Summer 1995, 29–40.
14 Baker, *Days of Sorrow and Pain*, 323–4.

16: Children from the concentration camps

1 CBF, minutes of Executive Committee, 13 March 1945.
2 CBF, minutes of Council meeting, 28 May 1945.

3 Ibid., 10 May 1945.
4 CBF, letter, Leonard Montefiore to Anthony de Rothschild, 6 May 1945.
5 CBF, minutes of Council meeting, 10 May 1945. Graham White, who had succeeded Eleanor Rathbone (known as the 'Member for Refugees') as chairman, visited Buchenwald when it was liberated. Eleanor Rathbone died on 2 January 1946 (*The Times*, 3 January 1946, 13).
6 CBF, minutes of Executive Committee, 12 June 1945; CBF, minutes of Council meeting, 26 August 1947.
7 CBF, minutes of Council meeting, 22 August 1945.
8 The early lives of these young people, their suffering under the Germans, and their post-war rehabilitation is related in Martin Gilbert, *The Boys: Triumph Over Adversity* (London: Weidenfeld and Nicolson, 1996).
9 CBF, minutes of Council meeting, 22 August 1945; J.F. Dow and Marjorie A. Brown, *Evacuation to Westmorland: From Home and Europe, 1939–1945*, (Kendal: Westmorland Gazette, 1946), 53–4.
10 Bentwich, *They Found Refuge*, 75.
11 CBF, minutes of Executive Committee, 29 July 1946.
12 Dow and Brown, *Evacuation to Westmorland*, 59.
13 Ibid., 54–5.
14 CBF, minutes of Executive Committee, 10 May 1945; CBF, 198/4, memorandum, 12 November 1945.
15 Leonard Montefiore, address to CBF conference, Woburn House, 5 January 1947, 5.
16 Jessica Wyman, *The First 150 Years of the West London Synagogue* (issued by West London Synagogue in commemoration of 150th anniversary), 10.
17 CBF, minutes of Executive Committee, 2 October 1945.
18 CBF, notes for meeting of the Council, 24 February 1953, 3; CBF, minutes of Council meeting, 16 April 1953.
19 Richard Crossman, MP, *Palestine Mission* (London: Hamish Hamilton, 1947), 85.
20 S. Adler Rudel, 'The Surviving Children', in *Belsen*, 124–8. Richard Crossman noted that the Displaced Persons Committee had successfully blocked an UNRRA plan for the adoption in Great Britain and care in Switzerland of a number of orphans and unaccompanied Jewish children. See Crossman, *Palestine Mission*, 87.
21 CBF, minutes of Executive Committee, 14 January 1946.
22 Sadie Rurka, a member of the Jewish Relief Unit working in the camp at

Belsen, participated in the negotiations, and in arranging this transport; Interview, Sadie Hofstein (née Rurka), 17 March 1997.

23 CBF, minutes of Executive Committee, 13 November 1945; ibid., 3 December 1945; ibid., 14 January 1946. Adler Rudel visited Belsen on 5 December 1945. See Adler Rudel, 'The Surviving Children', in *Belsen*, 124–8.

24 CBF Archives, Committee for the Care of Children from the Camps, Report for 1948.

25 CBF Archives, 178. In the first year alone some £120,000 was needed to provide for their care. L.G. Montefiore, Committee for the Care of Children from Concentration Camps, 18 May 1946.

26 Gilbert, *The Boys*, 381–2, 411.

27 CBF Archives, Committee for the Care of Children from the Camps, Report for 1948.

28 RAL, XIV/35/126, letter, Leonard Montefiore to Anthony de Rothschild, 13 December 1950.

29 See Erica Wagner, 'The Liberty Fraternity' in *The Times Magazine*, 11 January 1997, 13–21.

30 CBF, minutes, 12 June 1945.

17: German reparations for victims of the Nazis

1 'The Reich Government are convinced that it is essential that economic and physical damage done since 1918 should be exposed and repaired in its entirety.' See CCJR, Note on a Committee to Examine the Question of Reparation for the Jews in Germany, 10 November 1939.

2 Ibid.

3 Bentwich, *They Found Refuge*, 183.

4 The British sector of Berlin was embraced by the reparations law in July 1949. See Norman Bentwich, 'Nazi Spoliation and German Restitution: The Work of the United Restitution Office', in *Leo Baeck Year Book*, Vol. X, 1965, 204–24.

5 See C.I. Kapralik, *Reclaiming the Nazi Loot: A Report on the Work of the Jewish Trust Corporation for Germany* (London: n.p., 1962) and C.I. Kapralik, *The History of the Work of the Jewish Trust Corporation for Germany* (London: n.p., 1970); n.a., *Five Years Later: Activities of the Conference on Jewish Material Claims*

Against Germany 1954–1958 (New York: Conference on Jewish Material Claims Against Germany, Inc., n.d.); and Nehemiah Robinson, *Ten Years of German Indemnification* (New York: Conference on Jewish Material Claims Against Germany, 1964).

Index